Meteor Cookbook

Over 65 hands-on recipes that cover every aspect
of building and deploying elegant, full-stack web
applications with Meteor

Isaac Strack

PACKT PUBLISHING

open source
community experience distilled

BIRMINGHAM - MUMBAI

Meteor Cookbook

First published: May 2015

Production reference: 1220515

Published by Packt Publishing Ltd.
Livery Place
35 Livery Street
Birmingham B3 2PB, UK.

ISBN 978-1-78328-029-2

www.packtpub.com

Credits

Author
Isaac Strack

Reviewers
Jebin B V
Ryan Wilcox

Commissioning Editor
Pramila Balan

Acquisition Editors
Vinay Argekar
Llewellyn Rozario

Content Development Editor
Shubhangi Dhamgaye

Technical Editor
Shivani Kiran Mistry

Copy Editors
Brandt D'Mello
Ulka Manjrekar
Gladson Monteiro
Stuti Srivastava

Project Coordinator
Harshal Ved

Proofreaders
Stephen Copestake
Safis Editing

Indexer
Monica Ajmera
Hemangini Bari

Graphics
Abhinash Sahu

Production Coordinator
Arvindkumar Gupta

Cover Work
Arvindkumar Gupta

About the Author

Isaac Strack is a speaker, author, inventor, technologist, and a strong advocate of STEM education. With over 15 years of experience in Management Information Systems (MIS) and web/mobile technologies, he enjoys discovering and applying new technologies to make our lives more enjoyable and productive.

An early adopter of Meteor, Isaac is the author of *Getting Started With Meteor.js JavaScript Framework, Packt Publishing*, and the recently released video series *Learning Meteor Application Development, Packt Publishing*.

He currently serves on the board of directors for the Wasatch Institute of Technology (`http://wasatchinstitute.net`), one of Utah's newest and most innovative high schools, employing a project-based, agile teaching methodology known as Next Generation Education.

When he isn't poking around new JavaScript frameworks, advocating more and better STEM education in the state of Utah, or playing a mean game of mediocre middle-aged soccer, Isaac is at home with his amazing wife, Kirsten, and his four daughters, one of whom will most certainly rule the world (our money is on the youngest).

I'd like to thank all of the folks at Packt Publishing (especially Shubhangi Dhamgaye) for their patience, diligence, and kindness. I'd also like to thank my most excellent managers, Tim Plumer and Lynn Grillo at Adobe Systems, for never being anything but my personal champions. I'd like to thank Reza Jalili for sharing his enthusiasm and for turning what could have been a burden into a joyful experience. Thanks and love go out to my family. We've been through so much this last year. It's a miracle and a blessing to have each other and to need each other. I can't imagine life without all of you. Lastly, I'd like to thank my Heavenly Father and my Savior. Our hearts and minds are prone to wander. Grace, it seems, is the sweetest, most powerful call home.

About the Reviewers

Jebin B V is a young frontend developer by profession and a full-stack developer by experience. He has been into web development for the past 4 years and has a good command of the design and development of commercial web applications. He also has a very good sense of design, interaction, and UX when it comes to web development.

He has developed applications for real-time messaging, big data management, visualization, network shopping management, CMS, social networking, and so on. He has great interest in Javascript, so anything that is from a Javascript background excites him. He also has experience in PHP and Java.

He possesses a very good notion of application-level design when it comes to building frontend applications. He has a nonstop habit of learning on an everyday basis. He spends a great deal of time updating himself with new avenues coming up in frontend technologies. He loves to learn, teach, master, and lead in his field of expertise.

Ryan Wilcox has been programming desktop and web applications for the last 15 years using a wide variety of technologies, from C++ to Objective-C, and Python to Ruby and Javascript development, both server and client side. He's also spent the last 2 years working with Node on various-sized projects and is excited about how Meteor solves the client/server dichotomy present in other Javascript web application solutions.

www.PacktPub.com

Support files, eBooks, discount offers, and more

For support files and downloads related to your book, please visit www.PacktPub.com.

Did you know that Packt offers eBook versions of every book published, with PDF and ePub files available? You can upgrade to the eBook version at www.PacktPub.com and as a print book customer, you are entitled to a discount on the eBook copy. Get in touch with us at service@packtpub.com for more details.

At www.PacktPub.com, you can also read a collection of free technical articles, sign up for a range of free newsletters and receive exclusive discounts and offers on Packt books and eBooks.

https://www2.packtpub.com/books/subscription/packtlib

Do you need instant solutions to your IT questions? PacktLib is Packt's online digital book library. Here, you can search, access, and read Packt's entire library of books.

Why Subscribe?

- ▸ Fully searchable across every book published by Packt
- ▸ Copy and paste, print, and bookmark content
- ▸ On demand and accessible via a web browser

Free Access for Packt account holders

If you have an account with Packt at www.PacktPub.com, you can use this to access PacktLib today and view 9 entirely free books. Simply use your login credentials for immediate access.

Table of Contents

Preface

Stop and think for just a minute about the last time you were *delighted*.

I'd bet good money that whatever that delightful experience was, it had nothing to do with a new JavaScript framework. Well, that is about to change.

Meteor is not just another JavaScript framework that you'll forget the name of a few weeks from now. It was created—and is continuously improved upon—by legit *computer scientists* driven by a vision of how software development should be. Their mantra is that "programming should be fun" and as you go through this list of Meteor recipes, you will see exactly how much fun it really is to develop applications using Meteor.

Meteor is modular and declarative, supports data-on-the-wire, is well supported by a thriving development community, and implements full-stack reactivity. This sounds like a bunch of meaningless buzzwords, until you fully grasp their impact on your day-to-day development efforts.

Because Meteor is modular and well supported, it works easily with all of your favorite JavaScript frameworks. You can use the entire Meteor stack, or you can mix and match it with community packages to complement your existing infrastructure / skill set.

Meteor supports data-on-the-wire through the Distributed Data Protocol (DDP). This innovation is significant in that it allows you to create elegant, powerful client applications responsible for their own rendering. You no longer have to rely on complex, outdated server technology rife with state and rendering problems that (frankly) should have been solved years ago. DDP is not unique to Meteor or even to JavaScript. DDP clients are available in nearly every major programming language! This opens up many elegant, powerful integration possibilities, allowing you to build upon existing platforms and infrastructures.

Combining DDP with full-stack reactivity opens up an entirely new way of developing frontend applications. Templates, database transactions, and view/controller logic are vastly simplified, allowing you to write clean, concise, declarative code. Your frontend development efforts will go from *weeks* to *hours* as you stop worrying about tedious state and CRUD operations and focus on rapid, elegant prototyping.

The more acquainted you become with Meteor, the more effective and prolific you will become as a developer. Programming with the Meteor framework is truly an enjoyable experience. The recipes found in this book will get you well on your way to being *delighted* by each project you complete and will serve as an indispensable reference for many projects to come.

What this book covers

Chapter 1, *Optimizing Your Workflow*, walks you through all the aspects of the Meteor development workflow. It includes best practices for repeatable, consistent project templates; for customizing your Meteor development environment; and for deploying your completed projects.

Chapter 2, *Customizing with Packages*, covers every aspect of the modular Meteor packaging system. Recipes that cover searching, installing, removing, modifying, creating, and deploying packages of all kinds are included. Information on how to use some of the more useful and popular packages, including npm modules and Iron Router, is also included.

Chapter 3, *Building Great User Interfaces*, contains essential recipes to develop front-end applications using Blaze, Meteor's reactive template engine. Everything from basic templates to custom components and animations is covered.

Chapter 4, *Creating Models*, provides clear, concise examples of the reactive data/model capabilities Meteor provides. From implementing a simple data collection to advanced filtering and upserts, this chapter will be your go-to reference for all of your reactive data needs.

Chapter 5, *Implementing DDP*, covers the major uses of the Distributed Data Protocol. Everything from reading the raw DDP stream to using the protocol with other programming languages is covered, with examples for easy implementation.

Chapter 6, *Mastering Reactivity*, takes you through the more advanced aspects of Meteor reactivity on the frontend. These recipes take you "under the hood" and show you how to customize and create reactive components as well as how to integrate nonreactive components (such as JQuery UI) into smooth, effective user interfaces.

Chapter 7, *Using Client Methods*, contains advanced UI recipes designed to take advantage of some of the more useful HTML5 components. Information and examples to create dynamic SVG graphs, implementing touch-based Canvas components, or uploading and serving images with the FileReader are all found in this chapter.

Chapter 8, *Integrating Third-party Libraries*, walks you through the use of standalone third-party libraries. Instructions and explanations on directly using npm modules, implementing sophisticated D3.js graphs, and building complete UIs with Polymer are included. This chapter uses these examples as guidelines, which you can extend to implement any third-party library in Meteor.

Chapter 9, Securing Your Application, goes through all of the fundamental security features of Meteor. When your application is ready to be deployed to production, the recipes in this chapter will ensure that your app is secure and performant.

Chapter 10, Working with Accounts, dives into the robust and flexible Meteor Accounts packages. You will learn how to customize the Accounts UI, use external OAuth providers such as Twitter, and even perform two-factor authentication.

Chapter 11, Leveraging Advanced Features, provides "graduate-level" methods and examples of how to take advantage of Meteor's full capabilities. Primarily focused on server-side functionality, this chapter covers extending/marshaling objects with EJSON, server methods, and the use of Fibers to elegantly handle asynchronous functions and callbacks.

Chapter 12, Creating Useful Projects, is the culmination of the other chapters in the form of a useful, complete application. The recipes walk you through creating REST services, adding social sharing to an existing app, building a complete application with Iron Router, and deploying to mobile devices.

What you need for this book

This book assumes that you have a working knowledge of JavaScript and HTML. Being familiar with Node, npm, GitHub and the command line/terminal will be very helpful (but not critical) to getting the most out of the recipes in this book.

You will find recipes to install Meteor on Mac OS X or Linux, with links to using Meteor on Windows and Google Chromebooks. In every instance, you will need access to the Internet to download Meteor and community packages, and you will need installation privileges for your developer machine regardless of the operating system.

For deployment to production environments or to mobile devices, the requirements will vary from recipe to recipe. To complete all of the recipes successfully, you will need your own hosted server and DNS domain as well as iOS, Android, or Windows mobile devices and SDKs.

Who this book is for

This book is meant for developers of all experience levels looking to create mobile and full-stack web applications in JavaScript. Many of the simple recipes can easily be followed by less-experienced developers, while some of the advanced recipes will require extensive knowledge of existing web, mobile, and server technologies. Any application or enterprise web developer looking to create full-stack JavaScript-based apps will benefit from the recipes and concepts covered in this book.

Sections

In this book, you will find several headings that appear frequently (Getting ready, How to do it, How it works, There's more, and See also).

To give clear instructions on how to complete a recipe, we use these sections as follows:

Getting ready

This section tells you what to expect in the recipe, and describes how to set up any software or any preliminary settings required for the recipe.

How to do it...

This section contains the steps required to follow the recipe.

How it works...

This section usually consists of a detailed explanation of what happened in the previous section.

There's more...

This section consists of additional information about the recipe in order to make the reader more knowledgeable about the recipe.

See also

This section provides helpful links to other useful information for the recipe.

Conventions

In this book, you will find a number of text styles that distinguish between different kinds of information. Here are some examples of these styles and an explanation of their meaning.

Code words in text, database table names, folder names, filenames, file extensions, pathnames, dummy URLs, user input, and Twitter handles are shown as follows: "You must have curl installed in order to install Meteor."

A block of code is set as follows:

```
<head>
<title>FileTemplate</title>
</head>
<body>
<h1>Welcome to Meteor!</h1>
{{> hello}}
</body>
```

When we wish to draw your attention to a particular part of a code block, the relevant lines or items are set in bold:

```
Package.onUse(function(api) {
api.versionsFrom('1.0.3.2');
api.addFiles('testpack.js', 'client');
api.addFiles('servertestpack.js', 'server');
});
```

Any command-line input or output is written as follows:

```
$ sudo apt-get install curl
```

New terms and **important words** are shown in bold. Words that you see on the screen, for example, in menus or dialog boxes, appear in the text like this: "Click on the button labeled **NEW ORGANIZATION** at the bottom of the screen."

Warnings or important notes appear in a box like this.

Tips and tricks appear like this.

Reader feedback

Feedback from our readers is always welcome. Let us know what you think about this book—what you liked or disliked. Reader feedback is important for us as it helps us develop titles that you will really get the most out of.

To send us general feedback, simply e-mail feedback@packtpub.com, and mention the book's title in the subject of your message.

If there is a topic that you have expertise in and you are interested in either writing or contributing to a book, see our author guide at www.packtpub.com/authors.

Customer support

Now that you are the proud owner of a Packt book, we have a number of things to help you to get the most from your purchase.

Downloading the example code

You can download the example code files from your account at `http://www.packtpub.com` for all the Packt Publishing books you have purchased. If you purchased this book elsewhere, you can visit `http://www.packtpub.com/support` and register to have the files e-mailed directly to you. Optionally, the code samples can also be downloaded from `https://github.com/strack/PacktMeteorRecipes`.

Downloading the color images of this book

We also provide you with a PDF file that has color images of the screenshots/diagrams used in this book. The color images will help you better understand the changes in the output. You can download this file from `https://www.packtpub.com/sites/default/files/downloads/MeteorCookbook_ColorImages.pdf`.

Errata

Although we have taken every care to ensure the accuracy of our content, mistakes do happen. If you find a mistake in one of our books—maybe a mistake in the text or the code—we would be grateful if you could report this to us. By doing so, you can save other readers from frustration and help us improve subsequent versions of this book. If you find any errata, please report them by visiting `http://www.packtpub.com/submit-errata`, selecting your book, clicking on the **Errata Submission Form** link, and entering the details of your errata. Once your errata are verified, your submission will be accepted and the errata will be uploaded to our website or added to any list of existing errata under the Errata section of that title.

To view the previously submitted errata, go to `https://www.packtpub.com/books/content/support` and enter the name of the book in the search field. The required information will appear under the **Errata** section.

Piracy

Piracy of copyrighted material on the Internet is an ongoing problem across all media. At Packt, we take the protection of our copyright and licenses very seriously. If you come across any illegal copies of our works in any form on the Internet, please provide us with the location address or website name immediately so that we can pursue a remedy.

Please contact us at copyright@packtpub.com with a link to the suspected pirated material.

We appreciate your help in protecting our authors and our ability to bring you valuable content.

Questions

If you have a problem with any aspect of this book, you can contact us at questions@packtpub.com, and we will do our best to address the problem.

1
Optimizing Your Workflow

In this chapter, we will cover the following topics:

- ▶ Installing Meteor
- ▶ Finding documentation for Meteor
- ▶ Getting help with questions
- ▶ Setting up your project file structure
- ▶ Setting up your development environment
- ▶ Using the web console
- ▶ Deploying a test app to Meteor
- ▶ Deploying to Meteor using a CNAME redirect
- ▶ Deploying to a custom hosted environment
- ▶ Deploying with Meteor Up (MUP)
- ▶ Using CoffeeScript
- ▶ Using CSS compilers

Introduction

Welcome to the wonderful world of Meteor! This chapter will walk you through some of the best practices for optimizing your Meteor workflow. From installing Meteor to deploying your finished application on your own custom server, the recipes found here will get you up and running and provide a great reference as you start working with Meteor on a daily basis.

Installing Meteor

The folks at Meteor have made installation a breeze. As long as the system you're working on (Linux or Mac OS X) is reasonably up to date, installing Meteor should be very simple. We have included it as a recipe so that when you're installing Meteor on a new machine, you have it handy. We will also include installation instructions directly from GitHub, just in case you want to use a development branch.

Getting ready

You must have `curl` installed in order to install Meteor. If you are on Mac OS X, `curl` is already installed. If you are on Linux, `curl` is usually installed. To check for `curl`, open a terminal window and execute the following command:

```
$ curl
```

If `curl` is installed, you will receive the following message:

```
curl: try 'curl --help' or 'curl --manual' for more information
```

If `curl` isn't installed, you will receive a message similar to the following:

```
-bash: /usr/bin/curl: No such file or directory
```

To install `curl`, use `apt-get` or `yum` (depending on your Linux version). The following is the command to install `curl` on Ubuntu. Simply replace `apt-get` with `yum` in the command to install it on Fedora, Debian, or CentOS:

```
$ sudo apt-get install curl
```

You should see an installation message, with perhaps a prompt to install. Complete the installation process; you will then be ready to install Meteor.

How to do it...

Open a terminal window and execute the following command:

```
$ curl https://install.meteor.com/ | sh
```

How it works...

The `curl https://install.meteor.com/` command is used to retrieve an installation script directly from Meteor. Once the script is downloaded, the `| sh` argument tells your system to execute the script, which installs Meteor at `/usr/local/bin/meteor` (which should be in your path). Once the entire script is executed, you will be able to run the `meteor` command from any location.

There's more...

The preceding recipe covers the default/stable Meteor installation. If you'd like to install Meteor directly from the source code or if you'd like to install a development branch (for example, the current nightly), you can do so using `git`.

The Meteor repository is located at `https://github.com/meteor/meteor`. You can find various development branches at this location, in addition to the main Meteor repository.

Assuming you have `git` installed and would like to install the main Meteor build, open a terminal window and execute the following command:

```
$ git clone git://github.com/meteor/meteor.git
```

This will clone the latest Meteor build into a subfolder named `meteor`. Note that this does not install Meteor globally on your machine. This means that in order to run the `meteor` command, you will need to navigate to (or reference) the `meteor` folder where you just cloned the Meteor repository.

 Various other installation arguments and customizations can be used, depending on your situation. To see more comprehensive instructions, visit the Meteor GitHub main `README.md` page at `https://github.com/meteor/meteor`.

Finding documentation for Meteor

Meteor has finally reached version 1.0, and as such, it's various libraries and features are beginning to stabilize. However, there are still some parts of Meteor that are in flux. It is therefore important to have the latest documentation handy. This recipe will show you where you can find the official Meteor documentation when you need it.

How to do it...

Simply navigate to `http://docs.meteor.com/` in a browser and bookmark the page.

How it works...

That's all there is to it. The Meteor folks keep the documentation up to date, and you can be sure to find all production-ready features, along with a lot of great advice, at that location.

There's more...

If you would like to have an offline copy of the documentation and still make sure you have the latest and greatest version of documentation, you can use Meteor's GitHub repository to serve up a local copy of the latest documentation.

To get the initial copy of the documentation, navigate to where you would like to store the documentation (for example, your Documents directory) and clone the latest Meteor repository with the following command:

```
$ git clone git://github.com/meteor/meteor.git
```

If you've already done this, and would like to make sure you have the latest and greatest, navigate to the meteor subfolder (created when you did the initial Git clone) and run the following command:

```
$ git pull origin master
```

This will update the Meteor repository with the latest and greatest.

Once you've got the latest documentation, you can access it via a web browser by navigating to the docs directory:

```
$ cd docs/
```

Then, run the meteor command:

```
$ meteor
```

Once the packages are updated, the Meteor documentation project will start and you will see the following in the command line:

```
=> Meteor server running on: http://localhost:3000/
```

You can now use a browser to navigate to http://localhost:3000/ and read the latest documentation.

Getting help with questions

The more you use Meteor, the more familiar the major packages will become. However, you may also want to start branching out and doing more advanced things with some of the lesser-known packages. You may also come up with an idea for a new application of Meteor. In any case, you will eventually run into a situation where you need more information than what is contained in the documentation. Here are some quick tips on where to go when you need your questions answered.

How to do it...

There are three major sources for getting your questions answered:

1. For specific technical questions or problems, head over to `http://stackoverflow.com/questions/tagged/meteor`. Search for questions others have already asked; if you can't find an answer, go ahead and submit a question of your own.

2. For general questions and comments, visit the Meteor forums at `https://forums.meteor.com/`.

3. To work in real time with multiple Meteor developers (including members of the core team), you can visit the IRC #meteor chat room on `irc.freenode.net`.

How it works...

Let's look at some tips on using each of the previously mentioned resources.

Stack Overflow

Stack Overflow is a very active community of developers, many of whom are eager to help others with their technical questions. For Meteor-specific help, once you've navigated to `http://stackoverflow.com/questions/tagged/meteor`, you can perform a search using the keywords that best describe your question, for example, if you are interested in getting Meteor to work inside a PhoneGap application, you may want to search all the tagged **[meteor]** questions for `cordova`, as follows:

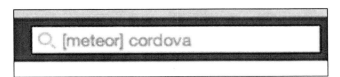

This will search all the previously submitted questions tagged with the keyword **[meteor]**, which also contain the word `cordova` somewhere in the question. You will want to look through the results to see whether your question has already been asked. If one of the questions (and the answer to that question) satisfies your needs, great! If your question hasn't been answered already, you can ask your own question.

Click on the button labeled **Ask Question**:

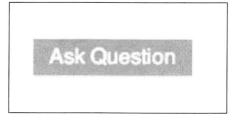

Fill out the details of your question. Don't forget to include tags to more easily identify and categorize your question. Submit your question and the Stack Overflow community will most likely have an answer for you very quickly.

Meteor forums

Meteor forums are also very active, with lots of enthusiastic Meteor developers visiting the site daily. You can ask questions, view discussions, and leave comments on a lot of different Meteor-related topics. Most of the time, if you have a technical question or problem, it's best to use Stack Overflow. However, forums are also a great resource for more abstract or specific questions about Meteor.

The #meteor on IRC

The #meteor IRC channel is a great channel to join in and listen to. You'll be able to interact with all kinds of brilliant developers, many of whom are willing to answer your questions immediately. Do keep in mind that most questions or problems you're having (especially when you're new to Meteor) have already been addressed on Stack Overflow or the Meteor forums, and it is courteous to first check and make sure your question hasn't been answered there before asking in the IRC chat.

There's more...

Keep in mind that since Meteor is still new, there are many who are struggling with questions that you may be able to answer. Also, when you find the answer to your own question, it may be worth putting it up on Stack Overflow. This will help you save time for other people who may run into the same problem.

Answering other people's questions on Stack Overflow, the Meteor forums, and even on #meteor IRC is a great way to contribute to the community.

 Don't forget to answer your own questions on Stack Overflow, if you happen to find the answers yourself!

Setting up your project file structure

When you spin up a new project in Meteor, the default file configuration is built to get you up and running immediately. That's great, but if you're looking to keep your code optimized and easily understood, you'll need to tweak the file structure a bit. The following recipe maps out the file structure that you can use for the majority of your projects.

Getting ready

You'll want to create a new base Meteor project, which we will then modify to suit our needs. In a terminal window, navigate to the folder where you would like to create the project and enter the following command to create a project called `FileTemplate`:

```
$ meteor create FileTemplate
```

Downloading the example code

You can download the example code files from your account at `http://www.packtpub.com` for all the Packt Publishing books you have purchased. If you purchased this book elsewhere, you can visit `http://www.packtpub.com/support` and register to have the files e-mailed directly to you. Optionally, the code samples can also be downloaded from `https://github.com/strack/PacktMeteorRecipes`.

This will create the base file structure. Now, navigate to the folder in the File Explorer window of your choice. For this exercise, we'll use a Mac OS X Finder window so that we can visualize the folder structure:

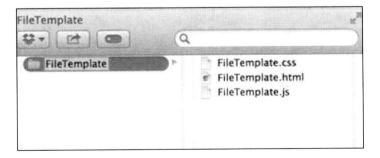

Always start with a fresh Meteor project (don't try to create your folder structure manually). Even though the file structure looks simple, there are hidden files and folders created by the `meteor create` command that you can't live without!

How to do it...

To set up your project file structure, proceed with the following steps:

1. In your root folder, delete the default `.css`, `.js`, and `.html` files. **FileTemplate** should now appear empty, similar to the following screenshot:

 Instead of deleting the base `.html`, `.css`, and `.js` files, you could break them apart using the code/file entries discussed in the following steps.

2. Create the following subfolders in your root folder:
    - `client`
    - `server`
    - `both`
    - `private`
    - `public`

3. Navigate to the `client` subfolder. Create a new file named `main.html`. Edit this file and add the following code (taken from `FileTemplate.html`):

```html
<head>
  <title>FileTemplate</title>
</head>

<body>
  <h1>Welcome to Meteor!</h1>

  {{> hello}}
</body>

<template name="hello">
  <button>Click Me</button>
  <p>You've pressed the button {{counter}} times.</p>
</template>
```

4. Create a new subfolder in the `client` folder named `scripts`.

5. Inside `scripts`, create a new file called `main.js`. Edit this file, adding the following code (taken from the `Meteor.isClient` section of `FileTemplate.js`):

```
// counter starts at 0
Session.setDefault('counter', 0);

Template.hello.helpers({
  counter: function () {
    return Session.get('counter');
  }
});

Template.hello.events({
  'click button': function () {
    // increment the counter when button is clicked
    Session.set('counter', Session.get('counter') + 1);
  }
});
```

6. Create a new subfolder in the `client` folder named `lib`. Create two subfolders named `scripts` and `styles`.

7. Inside `styles`, create a new file called `style.css`.

8. Navigate to the `server` subfolder. Create a new file named `server.js`. Add the following code to the `server.js` file and save the changes:

```
Meteor.startup(function () {
  // code to run on server at startup
});
```

Your completed file structure should now look like the following screenshot:

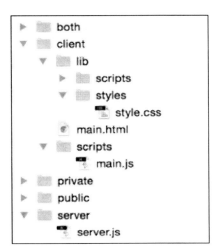

How it works...

We'll break down this file structure in pairs for the most part. This is because for almost every folder, there is another folder that serves the opposite purpose.

client/server

The `client` folder is interpreted by Meteor as code that belongs exclusively to the client. The `server` folder is the exact opposite and tells Meteor that any files contained inside should only apply to server-side processing.

Having separate `client` and `server` folders logically separates your code (making it easier to visualize), saves unnecessary processing, and prevents errors (client templates and rendering code will throw errors if processed by the server).

Inside of the `client` folder, we've placed a `scripts` subfolder and two files, both with the main prefix (`main.html` and `main.js`). The `scripts` subfolder is for our benefit, separating out HTML and JavaScript so that when we go back and review our code, it will be easy to read and segment.

main/lib

The `main` prefix is used to tell Meteor: *run this code last*. When Meteor goes about processing and compiling files, it waits to process anything named `main` until the very end. This helps in situations where libraries or scripts need to be initialized before you can take advantage of them.

Conversely, the `lib` folder tells Meteor: *run this code first*. Anything placed inside, or as a child of, the `lib` folder will be run first by Meteor at runtime. This is a great place to put global variables, common libraries not already included as packages (see *Chapter 2, Customizing with Packages*), and of course any style sheets. This is why we've included a `scripts` and `styles` subfolder and have created an initial generic `style.css` file.

Using the `main` prefix and the `lib` folder together helps us maintain proper sequences and ensures that our styles load as quickly as possible.

public/private

The `public` folder is a repository for assets that need to be accessed globally. It's a very good place to store non-sensitive information, such as images and text files. It's also easy to remember. If you need something to be shown publicly, put it in the `public` folder.

The `private` folder is the opposite. It's a place to store assets that can only be seen by the server. This is a good place to put moderately sensitive information (you'll want additional security, such as a database, for the information you want to keep more secure). Any files placed in the `private` folder can be referenced by the server with no special path or navigation arguments.

both

The `both` folder stands all by itself as the folder accessible by both the client and the server. When you are creating models and collections (see *Chapter 4, Creating Models*) you'll want to put the declarations in a file inside of the `both` folder. The main reason for doing this is so that you don't duplicate code, and you can ensure that both the client and the server are working from the same model declarations.

There's more...

Obviously, you don't need to create this file structure from scratch every time. You can use your favorite script engine (Grunt, Gulp, Shell Script, and so on) and create a script that can make the necessary changes with a single command. Alternatively, you can create the template once, copy the entire folder to a new location, and then use it as if it were a new project.

If you do decide to use this recipe rather than an automated script, make sure you update your base template to the latest Meteor build periodically and each time you make a copy. This can be done very easily in a terminal window. Navigate to the root folder (for example `~/Documents/Meteor/FileTemplate`) and run the following command:

```
$ meteor update
```

You will either receive a message letting you know that the folder is already up to date, or Meteor will update the project to the latest version.

See also

- ▶ *Chapter 2, Customizing with Packages*

Setting up your development environment

While you're developing your project, there are several default packages and settings that make your debugging and development work much easier. This recipe will give you suggestions to help create an ideal development environment.

Getting ready

You'll want to make sure you have Meteor installed (of course), and you will need a default project file structure set up. You can either use the *Setting up your project file structure* recipe from earlier in this chapter, or create a brand new Meteor project using the `meteor create [...]` command.

This recipe assumes that you have some Mongo collections and/or some kinds of user accounts set up. If you don't have a collection added, you may want to add one just for testing purposes. To do so, create a file named `[project root]/both/model.js` and enter the following line of code:

```
testCollection = new Mongo.Collection('testCollection');
```

With a project in place and at least one Mongo collection to monitor, we're ready to start developing and debugging!

How to do it...

First, we want to make sure that the `insecure` and `autopublish` packages are installed, which is usually the case with a default Meteor project.

1. In a terminal window, navigate to the root folder of your project and enter the following command:

   ```
   $ meteor list
   ```

   This will list all the packages used by your project. You should receive something similar to the following:

   ```
   autopublish       1.0.2
   insecure          1.0.2
   meteor-platform   1.2.1
   ...
   ```

2. If the `autopublish` or `insecure` packages are missing, you can add them manually by entering the following commands:

   ```
   $ meteor add autopublish
   $ meteor add insecure
   ```

3. Next, install the `msavin:mongol` smart package. In the terminal window, enter the following command:

   ```
   $ meteor add msavin:mongol
   ```

   After a short installation process, you should receive a message indicating that the `msavin:mongol` package was installed correctly.

4. Start your `meteor` project by entering the following command in your terminal window:

   ```
   $ meteor
   ```

5. Open your app in a browser by navigating to `http://localhost:3000`. Once there, press *Ctrl + M* and look towards the bottom-left of the screen. You will see a small expandable dashboard, similar to the following screenshot:

Clicking on any of the collection names or the **Account** tab will let you view, update, delete, and insert records, as shown in the following screenshot:

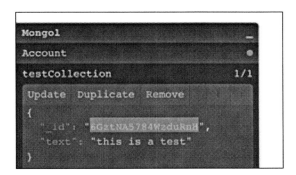

This comes in very handy when you're building your app, as you have instant access to your collections and user account profiles.

How it works...

The following line is all that's needed to install a package:

```
$ meteor add msavin:mongol
```

This tells Meteor to go and find the `msavin:mongol` package, with all of its dependencies, and add the package to your project. This is a third-party package, and more details on the package can be found at `https://atmospherejs.com/msavin/mongol`.

Once installed, you can access it on your browser page by the *Ctrl + M* shortcut. Under the hood, the `mongol` package is monitoring for any collections, specifically filtering user-account-related collections into the **Account** tab. Other than that, all collections are treated the same, and this interface just simplifies your debugging/development process when you need to see what's going on inside your collections.

There's more...

Mongol is very new but it is getting better all the time. You can read about all it's current features and preview upcoming features by visiting `https://github.com/msavin/Mongol`.

See also

▶ The *Adding Meteor packages, Removing Meteor packages*, and *Using npm modules* recipes in *Chapter 2, Customizing with Packages*

▶ The *Basic safety – turning off autopublish* and *Basic safety – removing insecure* recipes in *Chapter 9, Securing Your Application*

Using the web console

Sometimes modifying your code while debugging is just too slow. This recipe will introduce you to the web console and give you some pointers on using it.

Getting ready

We will need a sandbox to play in. For the purpose of this recipe, we'll use one of the default examples built into Meteor.

In a terminal window, enter the following command:

```
$ meteor create --example leaderboard
```

Once created, navigate to the `leaderboard` folder and start Meteor:

```
$ cd leaderboard
$ meteor
```

We can now navigate to our leaderboard example page (`http://localhost:3000`) using the web browser of our choice.

We need to enable the web console in various browsers. In no particular order, here's how to get to the web console on the browsers you're likely to be working with:

Safari

Enable the **Develop** menu by going to **Safari | Preferences | Advanced** (*CMD+*, shortcut if you prefer) and making sure the **Show Development Menu in menu bar** option is enabled:

Now, on any web page, click on **Show Error Console** under **Develop** (or use the *CMD + Alt + C* shortcut):

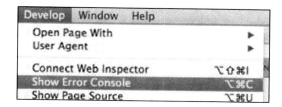

This will bring up the web console, as shown in the following screenshot:

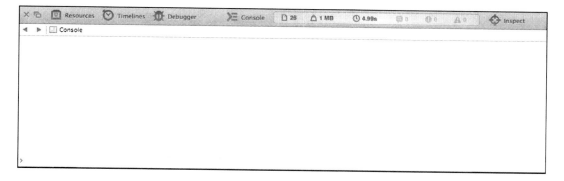

Firefox

On any web page, click on the **Web Console** menu option (*CMD + Alt + K* shortcut) under **Tools | Web Developer**:

The web console now appears as shown in the following screenshot:

Chrome

On any web page, click on the **Developer Tools** menu item (*CMD + Alt + I* shortcut) under **View | Developer**:

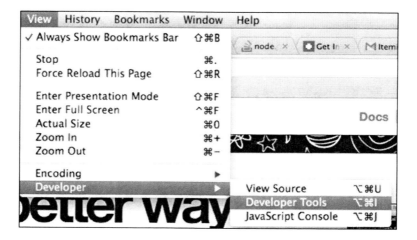

This will bring up the web console, as shown in the following screenshot:

How to do it...

To show what's possible with a web console, let's create a new scientist, and add some points to Tesla. Because, Imma let you finish, but Nikola Tesla was the greatest scientist of all time. Of. All. Time.

1. If you haven't done so already, navigate to `http://localhost:3000/`.

2. Now, open the web console if it's not already open.

3. In the console, run the following command:

   ```
   > Players.insert({name:"Stephen Hawking"})
   ```

4. The name **Stephen Hawking** will now be in the list. You can select his name and add some points:

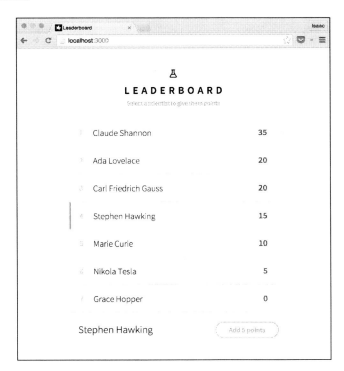

5. Now, let's give Tesla the love he deserves. First, let's find the `_id` value for the Tesla record. Run the following command in the console:

```
> Players.findOne({name:"Nikola Tesla"})
```

6. Harvest the `_id` valuefrom the result and modify the score, similar to the following:

```
> Players.update({_id:"bPDpqp7hgEx4d6Eui"},
{$set:{score:334823}})
```

Tesla will now be placed at the top of the leaderboard:

7. One last manipulation, let's deselect any of the scientists mentioned in the preceding screenshot. Enter the following command in the console:

```
> Session.set("selectedPlayer",null)
```

You will notice that, now no scientist is selected.

You can run through the previous commands in the web console by pressing the up or down arrow keys.

How it works...

The web console acts as an extension of your code. You are able to receive log messages, call exposed methods and events, or change and instantiate global variables. You are able to do this dynamically in real time, which can have a lot of advantages as you're testing or debugging.

With a few well-composed lines of code, we were able to replicate the behavior found in the event handlers and methods that belong to the app. In other words, we were able to manually test things, rather than having to modify, save, and retest the code. This kind of impromptu testing can really save us time.

There's more...

The web console and the associated development tools can perform all kinds of client-side debugging and testing tasks. You can run prewritten scripts, pause code during execution, monitor variables and the call stack, and even create your own methods and variables dynamically.

 The web console varies a little bit from browser to browser, but you can find instructions that apply to nearly every web console at `https://developers.google.com/chrome-developer-tools/docs/console`.

Deploying a test app to Meteor

As you've come to expect, Meteor makes just about everything easier to do. Testing your application on a server is no exception. This recipe will show you how to deploy your application to Meteor servers, where you can test (and show off!) your new application.

Getting ready

The only requirement for this recipe is that you have a working application.

Your app doesn't need to be fancy or complete, but it should at least render something on the screen so that you can verify it is running on Meteor servers.

For this recipe, we will use the default `leaderboard` example, which is created using the following command in a terminal window:

```
$ meteor create --example leaderboard
```

How to do it...

To deploy a test app to Meteor, proceed with the following steps:

1. First, you need to pick an application name.

   The application name will appear on Meteor servers as a subdomain of the URL where your app is being served, such as `http://myproject.meteor.com`.

   However, there are a lot of people testing applications on Meteor servers. Chances are pretty good that a generic name, such as "myproject" or "leaderboard", is already taken. So, we need to pick something unique.

   For this recipe, I will use this application name `packtrecipe`. You will obviously need to pick something else. I got here first!

    Your project and application name do *not* need to match. The application name is only an identifier so that Meteor servers know how to route to your application.

2. Now that we've selected an application name, we will open a terminal window and navigate to the root directory of our project:

   ```
   $ cd leaderboard
   ```

3. Once we're in the correct folder, we will issue the `deploy` command as follows:

   ```
   $ meteor deploy packtrecipe
   ```

4. Meteor will bundle and deploy your application. Upon completion, you should see something similar to the following in the terminal window:

   ```
   Deploying to packtrecipe.meteor.com.  Bundling...
   Uploading...
   Now serving at packtrecipe.meteor.com
   ```

5. Navigate to the URL Meteor gave you (in this case, `http://packtrecipe.meteor.com`) in a browser and you will see your newly deployed application, as follows:

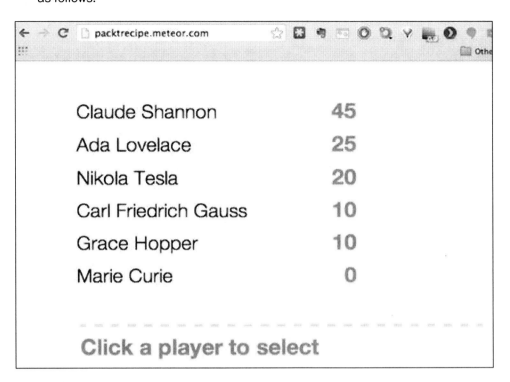

How it works...

It's magic! The folks at Meteor are sorcerers!

Actually, the core development team has worked very hard to make deployment as easy as possible. Under the hood, your local Meteor installation is packaging the correct files, compiling package lists and dependencies, and then sending a request to the Meteor servers. Once the Meteor servers receive the request, all the necessary error checking is done, and the packages, database, and application are created and initialized. A virtual host address is added, and voila! Your app is up and running.

There's a lot more detail (and code) involved, but this should give you a general idea of what goes into deploying to the Meteor test servers. Aren't you glad you didn't have to write all of that code?

There's more...

You probably noticed that you had to create a Meteor developer account in order to deploy. This is as it should be, because if there were no login/security details, someone could come along and override your deployment with one of their own.

This requirement, however, is quite flexible, allowing you to add other users or even organizations so that multiple people can deploy or update your app.

To set up an organization, navigate to `https://www.meteor.com/account-settings/organizations` and click on the button labeled **NEW ORGANIZATION** at the bottom of the screen. You can then add individual users to the organization, similar to the following screenshot:

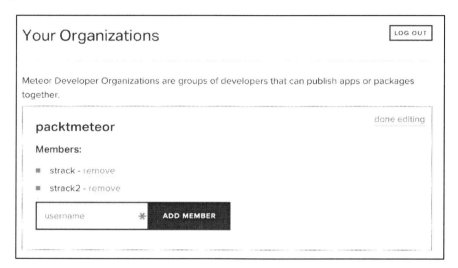

Once you've deployed your application, you can authorize the changes made by an individual or an organization through the `meteor authorized` command. Use the following syntax to add authorized accounts:

```
$ meteor authorized [your-url.meteor.com] --add [user/organization]
```

So, for example, we would use the following to add the `packtmeteor` organization to our deployed app:

```
$ meteor authorized packt.meteor.com --add packtmeteor
```

Likewise, if we wanted to remove authorization (for example, let's remove the `strack2` account), we would enter something like this:

```
$ meteor authorized packt.meteor.com --remove strack2
```

Meteor developer accounts have other useful functions as well. To explore what you can do with your account, please visit `https://www.meteor.com/account-settings`.

See also

▶ The *Building a custom package* recipe in *Chapter 2, Customizing with Packages*

Deploying to Meteor using a CNAME redirect

Deploying to Meteor test servers is all well and good, but what if you want to use your own custom domain name? The folks at Meteor have created a simple way for you to do just that. This recipe will show you how to take advantage of this simple, yet powerful feature.

Getting ready

You will need to create a **CNAME** redirect to `origin.meteor.com` on the hosting service where your domain is registered. How to do this varies pretty widely, so consult your hosting service's knowledge base on the exact steps. For this recipe, we'll use the cPanel interface of a hosting service for the `packtpub.com` domain.

Enter the subdomain you wish to use in your **CNAME** redirect (for example, `meteor.packtpub.com`) and set the redirect location to `origin.meteor.com`. Click on **Add CNAME Record** to submit the record:

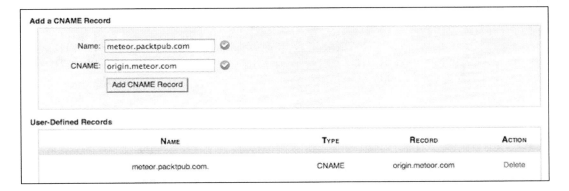

How to do it...

Let's assume the subdomain we're going to use is `meteor.packtpub.com`. In order to deploy to the Meteor environment, perform the following steps:

1. Once you have your **CNAME** redirect properly set, open a terminal window, navigate to the root directory of your project, and enter the following:

   ```
   $ meteor deploy meteor.packtpub.com
   ```

2. Meteor will deploy your app and provide feedback as the bundling, uploading, and serving steps are completed:

   ```
   Deploying to meteor.packtpub.com.  Bundling...

   Uploading...

   Now serving at meteor.packtpub.com
   ```

3. To verify the application, navigate to your application's URL (for example, `http://meteor.packtpub.com`) in a browser. If everything was deployed correctly, you will see your application up and running.

How it works...

This Meteor deployment feature is nearly identical to the default deployment, with just a little bit of extra code built in to interpret the origin of **CNAME** redirect.

When a request comes in to `origin.meteor.com` via a **CNAME** redirect, Meteor takes the **CNAME** redirect's original destination and uses it as the unique identifier for the application deployment. Meteor also uses future requests to `origin.meteor.com` from this **CNAME** redirect to serve the application.

In this particular case, the original **CNAME** destination was `meteor.packtpub.com`. When the request is redirected to `origin.meteor.com`, Meteor recognizes the **CNAME** redirect and uses it to direct traffic to the deployed application.

See also

▶ The *Deploying a test app to Meteor* recipe in this chapter

Deploying to a custom hosted environment

When you are ready to actually deploy your app to a production environment, you will need to convert your Meteor application to a straight up Node application. There are multiple methods to do this, all of which are (currently) manual processes and not for the beginner. A lot can go wrong. This recipe will show you how to manually deploy your Meteor application to a production server as a Node application.

Getting ready

As mentioned, there are multiple methods and server configurations that can successfully host a Node application. There are, however, some commonalities, all of which you will need for this recipe.

First, you will need a hosted **MongoDB** database.

Your MongoDB database can be hosted remotely or on the same machine from where you will deploy your Node application. For this recipe, we have deployed a default MongoDB database to the same machine where we will host the app. Our MONGO_URL value will therefore be:

```
MONGO_URL=mongodb://localhost:27017
```

 Installation instructions (and tutorials) for MongoDB can be found at http://docs.mongodb.org/manual/installation/.

Free or cheap but dedicated MongoDB service hosting also exists. Run a quick Internet search for *MongoDB hosting* or visit http://www.mongodb.com/partners/cloud for a list of providers.

Next, your hosting environment will need the latest stable Node and npm modules.

Installation instructions for each of these programs are beyond the scope of this book. For installation instructions and advice on how to get started, visit the following:

▶ Node (http://nodejs.org)

▶ npm (https://www.npmjs.com/)

The latest or nightly builds of these programs will likely cause you problems in a production environment. Be sure to use the stable versions, unless you have thoroughly tested a different version.

Lastly, you will need the `forever` npm module installed in your hosting environment. From a terminal window on your hosted environment, run the following command:

```
$ npm install -g forever
```

Note that you may need to use the `sudo` command to install the package globally. This will depend on how npm was installed on your server. The preceding command will install `forever` on your machine, and you are now ready to prepare and deploy your application to production.

How to do it...

To deploy to a custom hosted environment, proceed with the following steps:

1. Open a terminal window in your development environment and navigate to the root folder of your Meteor project. In this root folder, execute the following command:

   ```
   $ meteor build [your-build-location] --architecture [x]
   ```

   Replace the placeholders in the preceding line of code with your build location (for example: `~/Documents/builds/mybuild`) and an architecture (the options are `os.osx.x86_64`, `os.linux.x86_64`, and `os.linux.x86_32`). The `--architecture` option is optional if you are building this on the same server where you will deploy your app.

2. Meteor will bundle, extract, and repackage a clean production copy of your Meteor project, preparing it to be used in your hosting environment. While it is being built, Meteor will update you with the status in the terminal window.

3. Once the build is finished, navigate to the build folder you specified, for example, if you specified `~/Documents/builds/mybuild` as your build location, you would need to enter the following command:

   ```
   $ cd ~/Documents/builds/mybuild
   ```

4. In the build folder, you will see a `tarball` file with a name similar to `[your-project-name].tar.gz`.

   So, for example, if the name of my project was `leaderboard`, the name of the `tarball` file would be `leaderboard.tar.gz`.

5. Make a note of the name and location because you'll need it when you copy and extract the build to your server.

6. For this recipe, let's assume you're using a Linux server to host your production application. Let's create a `meteorapps` folder using the following terminal command:

```
$ mkdir /home/meteorapps
```

7. Next, copy the `tarball` file from your development environment to the `/home/meteorapps/` folder in your production-hosted environment.

   If you build your application on a different machine, you can transfer it via SCP, FTP, a common file server, a Git repository, and so on. It really doesn't matter how you copy it over, as long as a copy of the `tarball` file is now in your hosted environment.

8. Once it's copied over, run the following command on the `tarball` file:

```
$ tar -xf  [your-tarball-name].tar.gz
```

   This will extract the file to a folder named `bundle`. If you navigate to the `bundle` folder, you will find a `README` file. The next steps in this recipe are taken from this `README` file, so feel free to check them out for a more concise set of instructions. If you check the contents of the folder, you should see something similar to the following:

```
README    main.js    programs    server    star.json
```

9. We will now install the npm packages needed to run our application. Navigate to `bundle/programs/server` and execute the following command:

```
$ npm install
```

 Note that we did not use the `-g` argument, as we are only installing the local npm packages specified in the bundled folder.

10. Next, we will need to set the `PORT` and `MONGO_URL` export arguments so that Node knows how to host our application. Enter the following commands in the terminal window:

```
$ export PORT=8080
```

```
$ export MONGO_URL=mongodb://localhost:27017
```

   These two export commands tell your Node server what port to listen on, and where to find the `mongodb` hosted instance (we're using a local instance in this example).

   You will also want to configure the `ROOT_URL` and `MAIL_URL` environment variables. The syntax to enter them is similar to the following export commands:

```
$ export ROOT_URL='http://[your-hostname.com]'
```

```
$ export MAIL_URL='smtp://user:password@mailhost:port/'
```

Now, we can run our application. Instead of using the default `node` command, remember that we installed the npm `forever` package. The `forever` package allows us to run our Node application and will automatically restart it if we encounter an error. Run the following command in the terminal window:

```
$ forever start main.js
```

This command instructs Node to start `main.js` as a node application, and to restart it if there are any issues.

 You can stop the application later on by issuing the following command from the `bundle/` directory:

```
$ forever stop main.js
```

Now it's time to test whether your application is successfully running by opening a browser and pointing it to your host environment, on the port you specified, for example, if our production environment was hosting the `meteorapp.packtpub.com` subdomain, and we specify `port 8080`, as shown in the preceding example, we would navigate to `http://meteorapp.packtpub.com:8080` in a browser.

Your app should be up and serving pages.

How it works...

Node is built to run as quickly as possible. To do so, it will run a little differently on different hardware and software configurations. This means that the Node and npm packages you use in your development environment (for example, on MAC OS X) are slightly different than the corresponding Node and npm packages in your production environment (for example, Linux Ubuntu 12.4 LTS Precise). This is especially true for foundational packages, such as the npm fibers package.

Also, although Meteor is built on top of Node, it isn't a native Node application. There are some additional layers of abstraction and processing that make your life easier as a developer, but they don't make for the prettiest native Node production environment.

The `meteor build` command takes care of this for us and creates a build without the npm packages installed. Instead, it lists any of the npm packages as dependencies. Because the specific npm packages aren't included (Meteor listed them in a package manifest file instead), there are no compatibility issues. We simply tell Node to find and install the packages specific to the current environment, using the package manifest file as a sort of a laundry list. We did this when we issued the `npm install` command.

Once npm has read the manifest file, retrieved and installed all the needed packages, and informed us that the installation was completed correctly, we can run our new native Node application.

We then set some export variables (`PORT`, `MONGO_URL`, `ROOT_URL`, and `MAIL_URL`) and ran our application using the `forever` npm package, rather than the normal node command. Using `forever` helps us with not having to go back to the server every time it crashes. Ideally, we would never have an application crash, but we live in the real world, and `forever` is a huge time saver when an app restart is needed.

There's more...

If our application is truly production-ready, we also want it to start automatically whenever the server reboots. There are various ways to do this, depending on the operating system your production server is running on, and we won't cover all of them.

We will give an example script and instructions on how to do this on Ubuntu and let you modify the script as needed for other environments.

Whenever an Ubuntu server restarts, it runs any `*.conf scripts` script found in the `/etc/init/` folder. We'll assume that our application is located at `/home/meteorapps/prodapp/bundle/`, that we are going to listen on `port 8080`, and that we are using the local MongoDB service (feel free to adjust these settings as appropriate).

Using a terminal window with `sudo` privileges, add the following `meteorapp.conf` script to `/etc/init/` to your production server:

```
#  prodapp configuration file
#  /etc/init/meteorapp.conf

start on (local-filesystems)
stop on shutdown
script
    cd /home/meteorapps/prodapp/bundle/
    export MONGO_URL=mongodb://localhost:27107 PORT=8080
    export ROOT_URL='http://example.com'
    export MAIL_URL='smtp://user:password@mailhost:port/'
    exec forever start main.js
end script
```

Let's break down what this script does.

The first two lines (`start on` and `stop on`) tell the OS when to run this script. In this case, we run it as soon as the local file systems are ready, and we stop it as soon as a shutdown request comes in.

We then have our script that will be run. We navigate to our application folder using `cd /home/meteorapps/prodapp/bundle`.

Then, we declare the location of our MongoDB service and the port we would like the Node to listen on.

Finally, we execute the `forever` command, asking it to start `main.js` as a Node application.

The Meteor Group is currently working on a project called **Galaxy**, which will make deployment to custom servers as easy as deployment to their test servers. Once Galaxy is available, it will make this recipe obsolete, but that's a good thing! As mentioned, this recipe covers only one way of deploying to production. You may find another, easier method just by browsing `https://forums.meteor.com` or visiting other sources for Meteor information.

See also

▶ The *Getting help with questions* recipe in this chapter
▶ The *Deploying with Meteor Up (MUP)* recipe in this chapter
▶ The *Deploying apps to mobile devices* recipe in *Chapter 12, Creating Useful Projects*

Deploying with Meteor Up (MUP)

We would be remiss if we didn't add one final method of deploying Meteor apps to a production server. This method is called **Meteor Up** (**MUP**). Using a fairly simple configuration file, MUP vastly simplifies the server deployment process. And until we get to see what Galaxy (Meteor's deployment platform) looks like, MUP is the easiest way to deploy to a custom environment. This recipe will show you how to deploy your app to a custom server using Meteor Up.

Getting ready

To complete this recipe, you will need a working Meteor application. It doesn't need to be fancy, but it does need to be functional so you can see whether it was installed properly on your server at a glance.

How to do it...

MUP is installed via npm. It needs to be installed globally, so we will use the `-g` argument. To deploy your app to a custom server using MUP, perform the following steps:

1. To install MUP, open a terminal window and execute the following command:

   ```
   $ npm install -g mup
   ```

   This will take a bit to install, but once complete, you'll be ready to configure and use MUP to deploy your application.

2. To run `mup init`, navigate to the root folder of your project in a terminal window and enter the following command:

```
$ mup init
```

You will receive a message similar to the following:

Empty Project Initialized!

This process will create two files in your project's root folder. We don't need to worry about the first file (`settings.json`). We will configure our app using the second file, named `mup.json`.

3. Now, we'll configure `mup.json`. Open the `[project root]/mup.json` file in an editor. The top part of the file will have our remote server information. It should look similar to the following lines of code:

```
"servers": [
    {
        "host": "hostname",
        "username": "root",
        "password": "password"
        // or pem file (ssh based authentication)
        //"pem": "~/.ssh/id_rsa"
    }
],
```

The `host` property will be the name of the server you will be accessing via SSH/SCP. If our server name was `my-production-server.com`, the host property would look similar to the following:

```
"host": "my-production-server.com",
```

The `username` and `password` properties are the user/pass combination you would use if you were to `ssh` into the remote server.

The next four properties help us to configure our server. If we want MUP to install Mongo, Node, or PhantomJS (all necessary to deploy via MUP), we can specify the code as follows:

```
"setupMongo": true,
"setupNode": true,
"nodeVersion": "0.10.33",
"setupPhantom": true,
```

 As of the printing of this book, the latest stable Node version is `0.10.33`. You may want to check this and modify the `nodeVersion` property as appropriate.

If Mongo/Node/PhantomJS is already installed, you can change the preceding properties to `false` (which will speed up your deployment).

Next, we specify specify what we want our app to be called. This is done by modifying the `appName` property:

```
"appName": "[your-app-name-here]",
```

We need to specify the folder on our local machine where our to-be-deployed app is located. This is determined in the `app` property:

```
"app": "/path/to/the/app",
```

The last property we need to set is `env`. This instructs Node which `ROOT_URL` and `PORT` to run our Meteor application from. If, for example, we were redirecting incoming HTTP traffic to a localhost, on `port 1337` (which is done using a reverse-proxy, such as `nginx`, or a virtual host, such as `apache`), our `env` configuration would look like the following code:

```
"env": {
  "ROOT_URL": "http://localhost",
  "PORT": 1337
},
```

4. Now let's configure our remote server with `mup setup`. In the terminal window, navigate to your project's root folder and enter the following command:

```
$ mup setup
```

This will install MongoDB, Node, and PhantomJS on the remote server. It will also configure our remote server environment and install some helper npm packages, such as `upstart`.

5. Let's deploy our app with `mup deploy`. Once the `mup setup` command is complete, we'll be ready to deploy our app. Execute the following command in the terminal window:

```
$ mup deploy
```

MUP will bundle your app locally, upload the build, configure the requisite npm packages on the remote server, and then serve up your app. As it runs through this process, MUP will give you status updates in the terminal.

Once complete, your app should be up and running. Test it out by either visiting your external URL (for example, `http://my-custom-server.com`) or by logging in to a remote server via `SSH`, and testing the build with a `curl` command on the localhost (for example, `curl http://localhost:3000`).

You may have a bit of troubleshooting to do to make sure your virtual host or reverse-proxy is configured properly, but after some small adjustments, you'll find that, at present, MUP is definitely the best way to deploy to a custom server.

How it works...

MUP takes all the steps we would normally have to implement manually (as in the *Deploying to a custom hosted environment* recipe in this chapter) and implements them automatically. There are three main parts to pulling this off successfully.

First, MUP creates a default configuration file when we execute the `mup init` command. We edit the newly created file with all the settings to install the right software on the remote server, configure environment variables, and upload our production build.

Second, we use `mup install` to install all the needed software on the remote server, as specified in the `mup.json` configuration file.

Lastly, our application is bundled, uploaded, extracted, initialized with environment variables, and set to run on the remote server. This is all accomplished with the `mup deploy` command.

MUP performs these tasks based on the configuration file we edited.

> There are many additional settings we can configure and some great features of MUP that we can explore by visiting the MUP repo, which is found at `https://github.com/arunoda/meteor-up`.

See also

▸ The *Deploying to a custom hosted environment* recipe in this chapter

Using CoffeeScript

Many people prefer CoffeeScript to the standard JavaScript syntax. If you are one of those people with a preference, Meteor has you covered. This recipe will show you how to quickly enable CoffeeScript in your development environment.

Getting ready

Nothing is needed to prepare for this recipe, other than having Meteor installed, and a project created so that you can begin using CoffeeScript.

How to do it...

To use CoffeeScript, proceed with the following steps:

1. Open a terminal window and navigate to the root folder of your project.
2. Enter the following command:

   ```
   $ meteor add coffeescript
   ```

   You should see the following response in the terminal window:

   ```
   coffeescript  added, version 1.0.
   ```

   CoffeeScript is now installed and ready to go!

You can test the installation by creating a `.coffee` file and adding a script (for example, add `test.coffee` to your `client` folder). When you start your Meteor application with the `meteor` command, the script should execute as designed.

 You can uninstall CoffeeScript easily. Simply execute the following terminal command:

```
$ meteor remove coffeescript
```

How it works...

Behind the scenes, the CoffeeScript package you just installed looks for any and all `*.coffee` and `*.litcoffee` files, compiles them into native JavaScript, and then bundles them for use in your running Meteor application.

 As with all other files in a running Meteor application, changes to your CoffeeScript are immediately processed.

See also

▶ The *Adding Meteor packages* recipe in *Chapter 2, Customizing with Packages*

Using CSS compilers

As any CSS junkie already knows, using standard CSS to create style sheets can be tedious, redundant work. Many designers and developers prefer to use a dynamic style sheet language or preprocessors, such as Less, Stylus, and SCSS/SASS.

Meteor not only enables the use of preprocessors, but also treats them just like any other file so that changes are reflected immediately.

This recipe will show you how to enable some of the more popular CSS compilers in your Meteor application.

Getting ready

Nothing is needed to prepare for this recipe, other than having Meteor installed, and a project created so that you can begin using CSS compilers.

How to do it...

We're going to cover three different preprocessors, as they all work in a similar way.

Using Stylus

1. Open a terminal window and navigate to the root folder of your project.

2. Enter the following command:

```
$ meteor add stylus
```

You should see a response similar to the following in the terminal window:

```
stylus  added, version 1.0.7
```

Stylus is now installed and ready to be used. You can test this by creating a .styl file and adding a script (for example, add test.styl to your client/styles folder).

When you start your Meteor application with the meteor command, Stylus files will be processed and proper CSS will be rendered.

 You can use the nib code in Meteor as well. Just add @import 'nib' to your .styl files, and Meteor takes care of the rest.

Using Less

1. Open a terminal window and navigate to the root folder of your project.

2. Enter the following command:

```
$ meteor add less
```

You should see the following response in the terminal window:

```
less  added, version 1.0.14
```

Now the Less package is installed, and you can use the Less stylesheet syntax to create your CSS.

As with Stylus, you can test this by creating a `.less` file and adding some style declarations (for example, add `test.less` to your `client/styles` folder).

When you start your Meteor application with the `meteor` command, the Less files will be compiled by Meteor into standard CSS and rendered as usual.

 If you're fond of using `@import` statements in your Less stylesheets, make sure you use the `.lessimport` extension. Otherwise, Meteor will automatically import and compile any and all `.less` files it can find.

Using SCSS / SASS

1. Open a terminal window and navigate to the root folder of your project.

2. Enter the following command:

```
$ meteor add fourseven:scss
```

You should see a response similar to the following in the terminal window:

```
fourseven:scss  added, version 2.1.1
```

SCSS and SASS files can now be used to style your CSS. Just as before, you can test this by creating a `.scss` or `.sass` file and adding some style declarations (for example, add `test.sass` to your `client/styles` folder).

When you start your Meteor application with the `meteor` command, the SCSS or SASS files will be compiled by Meteor into standard CSS and rendered.

How it works...

When you installed any of the preprocessors with the `meteor add` command, it installed the corresponding npm packages tailored to work inside of Meteor.

As with other files, Meteor will monitor changes to any `*.styl`, `.less`, `.scss`, and `.sass` files, compile the changes into CSS, and render the changes immediately.

See also

▶   The *Adding Meteor packages* recipe in *Chapter 2, Customizing with Packages*

2
Customizing with Packages

In this chapter, we will cover the following topics:

- ▶ Adding Meteor packages
- ▶ Removing Meteor packages
- ▶ Discovering new packages with Atmosphere
- ▶ Creating a multipage application with Iron Router
- ▶ Building a custom package
- ▶ Using npm modules
- ▶ Publishing custom packages to Atmosphere

Introduction

The package system in Meteor makes your development life much easier. It also speaks to one of Meteor's core principles—modular development. If you want to use the entire default Meteor stack, great! If you don't like a particular part and want to swap it out with a third-party package, great! It's completely up to you. Meteor allows you to quickly add and remove functionality, use the latest code shared by others, and create your own reusable code segments. This chapter will provide you with the recipes needed to take full advantage of the Meteor packages system.

Adding Meteor packages

The core **Meteor Development Group** (**MDG**) have developed over 140 packages for you to use. These packages provide features and functionality ranging from simple display tweaks, to fully integrated account management. Not only are these packages useful, but they're extremely easy to add to your project. In addition to the core MDG packages, there are hundreds of third-party packages available, all of which are free and could be just as easily added. This recipe will show you how to add Meteor packages to your project.

Getting ready

You will need Meteor installed and have a project created. Any project will do. You should also have a terminal window open and navigate to the root folder of your project, for example, if the name of your project is `packagesTest`, located in the `~/Documents/MeteorProjects` folder, you would enter the following command in a terminal window:

```
$ cd ~/Documents/MeteorProjects/packagesTest
```

How to do it...

Let's install the `fastclick` package as an example. This package removes the 300 ms delay for mobile/touchscreens.

In your terminal window, in the root folder, enter the following command:

```
$ meteor add fastclick
```

This will install the bootstrap package into your project, with a message similar to the following:

How it works...

The `meteor add [package name]` command tells Meteor to find the named package in the Meteor packages registry and copy the appropriate files over to your project. In addition, the package name is added to the declaration files of your project so that when Meteor starts up your project, the appropriate files for the named project are added and executed.

There's more...

As mentioned, you can install third-party packages using the same `meteor add` command. The difference between a core MDG package and a third-party package is that third-party packages have the creator's account ID as a prefix, for example, to add the excellent HammerJS package to your app, you need to enter the following command:

```
$ meteor add chriswessels:hammer
```

Other recipes in this chapter will walk you through discovering and implementing third-party packages, so stay tuned!

See also

▸ The *Discovering new packages with Atmosphere* recipe in this chapter

Removing Meteor packages

Removing Meteor packages is just as easy as adding them. This recipe will show you how to quickly remove a Meteor package.

Getting ready

You will need Meteor installed and have a project created. You should also have a terminal window open and navigate to the root folder of your project. For example, if the name of your project is `packagesTest`, located in the `~/Documents/MeteorProjects` folder, enter the following command in a terminal window:

```
$ cd ~/Documents/MeteorProjects/packagesTest
```

How to do it...

Let's remove the `insecure` Meteor package. In your terminal window, enter the following command:

```
$ meteor remove insecure
```

This will remove the `insecure` package.

How it works...

The `meteor remove [package name]` command will direct Meteor to look for the named package in your project declaration files and remove the declaration and source files for the package from your project.

There's more...

It's sometimes very helpful to check and see which packages you have added to your project. To see this list, enter the following command in your terminal window:

```
$ meteor list
```

This will give you a quick list of all the packages contained in your project.

Discovering new packages with Atmosphere

Meteor is an emerging platform, growing in popularity every day. The Meteor community is coming up with new packages and integrations with existing JavaScript libraries on almost a daily basis. Because the core Meteor team doesn't have time to test and apply every new package made by the community, a package registry, with a streamlined installation process, has been created. This package registry is called Atmosphere. Atmosphere has a clean, simple UI, which allows you to search for, rate, and discover new packages by popularity. This recipe will show you how to use Atmosphere to find and implement both Meteor and third-party packages.

Getting ready

There's nothing really to do here, but you'll definitely want to have Meteor installed and a project created to start using the packages listed on Atmosphere right away!

How to do it...

To discover new packages with Atmosphere, proceed with the following steps:

1. In a browser, navigate to `https://atmospherejs.com`. You should see a very simple page with a centered search input box. Let's look for the official Twitter `bootstrap` package.

2. Type in the word `bootstrap` and watch the search results appear as you type. You should see something similar to the following screenshot:

You'll notice that each card in the search results has some statistics at the bottom. The down arrow statistic is the number of downloads, which (with the age of the package) is the primary statistic in the search results ranking. You will see a star, which represents the number of developers that have favorited/starred the package. Finally, you will see a gray line in the background, indicating popularity over time.

 The second result (`twbs:bootstrap`) is the official Twitter Bootstrap package.

3. Click on the `twbs:bootstrap` card and an overview of the package will appear. You will see additional information about the package. This includes usage instructions, a link to the GitHub repository (if available), an expanded history of the package, related packages, dependants, and dependencies. At the very top of the page will be the instructions to add the package to your project:

4. You can copy the text and execute it in a terminal window, in your root project folder, as shown in the following code:

```
$ meteor add twbs:bootstrap
```

After a brief download process, the official Bootstrap package will be installed in your project.

As mentioned in the previous example, Atmosphere has several additional discovery options. There are links to the package contributors' profiles (so you can see other packages they may have contributed to), as shown in the following screenshot:

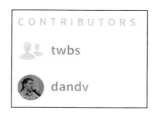

There are links to related packages, as shown in the following screenshot:

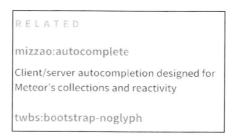

There are links to dependants and dependencies as well, as shown in the following screenshot:

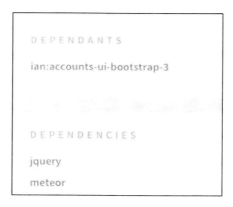

Any of these links will help you to discover other packages that will complement the original package and could be useful in your application.

Yet even more options exist for discovering packages in Atmosphere. If you navigate back to the home page at `https://atmospherejs.com/` and scroll down, you will see sections for **Trending**, **Most Used**, **Recent**, and **Top Searches**. All of these are worth perusing to discover some of the latest and greatest packages available for use:

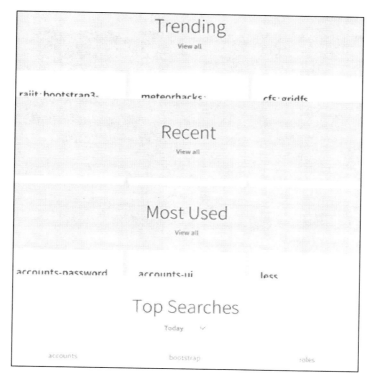

Feel free to explore and discover. You'll find some hidden gems in Atmosphere, and more than anything else, you'll come to realize that a Meteor package exists for almost everything. If it doesn't, create one yourself, with the *Building a custom package* recipe found later in this chapter.

How it works...

The Atmosphere site simply puts a user-friendly wrapper on top of the Meteor package repository. It does this very well, and the contributors/creators of the site are to be commended. Atmosphere is improving over time, and you can contribute to its success if you are so inclined. You can check out what's coming down the pipe by visiting the Atmosphere FAQ, found at `https://atmospherejs.com/i/faq`.

There's more...

If you're in a hurry or really really love the command line, you can perform searches in a terminal window, in the root folder of your project. Here's an example of a CLI-based search:

```
$ meteor search bootstrap
```

The results will be listed, with a brief explanation for each result, in alphabetical order:

Be sure to note that the results from this can be pretty hefty (there's no prioritization of results), so the effectiveness in using a CLI-based search will vary.

See also

  ▸ The *Building a custom package* and *Publishing custom packages to Atmosphere* recipes in this chapter

Creating a multipage application with Iron Router

Iron Router is an extremely useful Atmosphere package. It allows you to quickly and easily add multiple server pages to your Meteor project. This recipe will show you how to configure your project to use Iron Router.

Getting ready

You need to have Meteor installed. You will also need a blank Meteor project (see the *Setting up your project file structure* recipe in *Chapter 1, Optimizing Your Workflow*).

Finally, you will need to add the Iron Router package to your Meteor project. You can reference the *Adding Meteor packages* recipe found previously in this chapter, or enter the following command in your terminal window, in the root folder of your project:

```
$ meteor add iron:router
```

How to do it...

We are going to create a very simple example of multiple pages and we will use a fresh blank project to do so.

1. First, set up the route paths for the multiple pages. Create a subfolder called `router` in the `both` subfolder of your project. This can be done in a terminal window with the following command after navigating to the root folder of your project:

   ```
   $ mkdir both/router
   ```

2. Now, create a new file named `router.js` in the `router` folder. Open the `router.js` file in a text editor, add the following code, and save your changes:

   ```
   Router.configure({
      layout:'routeexample'
   });

   Router.map(function (){
       this.route('thing1', {
       path: '/'
       });
     this.route('thing2', {
       path: '/second'
       });
   });
   ```

3. Next, open your `main.html` file, located in the `client` subfolder, in an editor. Add the following template declarations to the bottom of the file and save your changes:

   ```
   <template name="routeexample">
   {{yield}}
   </template>

   <template name="thing1">
   <div> I am the FIRST page</div>
   </template>

   <template name="thing2">
   <div> I am the SECOND page</div>
   </template>
   ```

4. Now, open the `main.js` file found at `[project folder]/client/scripts/main.js` in an editor. Locate the `Template.hello.events` method and change the `'click button'` function body to the following:

```
Template.hello.events({
    'click button' : function () {
      Router.current().route.getName()=='thing1'?
Router.go('thing2'): Router.go('thing1');
    }
  });
```

5. Save your changes to all the files and run your application using the `meteor` command.

   When you navigate to your project's home page in a browser (`http://localhost:3000/`), you should see something similar to the following screenshot:

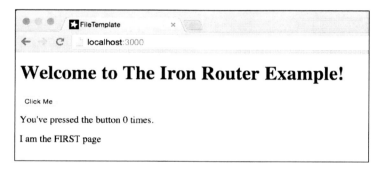

6. Click on the button marked **Click Me**, or navigate to `http://localhost:3000/second/` and the screen should change to the following:

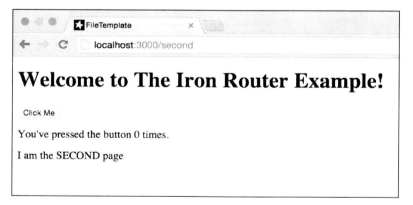

7. You can continue to toggle between the two pages by clicking on the onscreen button.

How it works...

Iron Router uses the path in your URL to invoke events in both the client and server. In most cases (unless you explicitly set the Iron Router path to render on the server, using the `where` parameter) the events and subsequent rendering happen in the client only.

In essence, Iron Router uses the path as an arguments list, invoking functions and rendering appropriate templates based on the information contained in the path.

Let's break down the code we just entered to get Iron Router up and running, starting with `router.js`:

```
Router.configure({
    layout:'routeexample'
});
```

This code snippet tells Iron Router to use the `<template>` tag named `routeexample` as the main/default template for the page.

We created the `routeexample` template in `main.html`, like so:

```
<template name="routeexample">
{{yield}}
</template>
```

The `yield` statement found in this template is known as the main yield. It is a placeholder for other templates that will be rendered once Iron Router completes its mapping process.

Continuing, in `router.js`, we have the `Router.map` function:

```
Router.map(function (){
  this.route('thing1', {
    path: '/'
  });
  this.route('thing2', {
    path: '/second'
  });
});
```

This creates two mapped routes, using the `this.route` function. In each function call, the first parameter specifies the name of the route, and because we didn't specify a specific template, it also implies the name of the template to use. In this case, we used the `thing1` and `thing2` templates, which we created in `main.html`:

```
<template name="thing1">
<div> I am the FIRST page</div>
```

```
</template>

<template name="thing2">
<div> I am the SECOND page</div>
</template>
```

These are very simple templates, and this is what makes them easy to understand for our example. Each template renders a simple `div` element with a message inside of it, indicating what page the user is on.

Going back to `router.js`, each `this.route` function call has a path argument inside of it. This path argument tells Iron Router what to look for in the URL to determine mapping. In the case of our first page (rendering the `thing1` template), the `path` element was set to "/", or the root path. In the case of our second page (rendering the `thing2` template), the `path` was set to "/second".

At this point, Iron Router was properly mapped, meaning this will have rendered the appropriate template based on the mapped routes. We wanted to make switching back and forth between the two routes easy, so we modified the `main.js` script as follows:

```
Template.hello.events({
    'click button' : function () {
       Router.current().route.getName()=='thing1'?
Router.go('thing2'): Router.go('thing1');
    }
  });
```

Now, when our button is clicked, we are checking to see whether the name of the currently mapped route (found using `Router.current().route.getName()`) is thing1. If it is, we tell Iron Router to change the currently rendered template (and the URL path) to our second template, named `thing2`, with a `path` value set to "/second". If the currently mapped route isn't `thing1`, then we toggle back to the original mapped route.

The `Router.go` statement changes the URL path, thereby setting events in motion to render the appropriate template and insert it into the main yield.

There's more...

Iron Router is a very sophisticated and powerful package, with many helpful features including pre-rendering events, setting data context, and access to server-side functions. If you are looking to build a multipage Meteor application, you will want to peruse the full documentation, found at `https://github.com/EventedMind/iron-router`.

See also

▶ The *Creating a complete app with Iron Router* recipe in *Chapter 12, Creating Useful Projects*

Building a custom package

As you become more familiar with Meteor, you will want to start creating your own custom package, which consolidates the code you may find useful in multiple projects. This recipe will walk you through the basics of creating your own personal Meteor package.

Getting ready

The only thing you need for this recipe is Meteor and a text editor.

How to do it...

We will create a package that will allow us to easily write to the console in not only the client web console, but also in the server terminal console.

1. To create a new baseline package, open a terminal window and navigate to where you would like your package to reside. Once there, execute the following command:

   ```
   $ meteor create --package [myMeteorID]:testpack
   ```

   Make sure you replace `[myMeteorID]` with your own Meteor Developer Account ID or with the ID of the Meteor organization you belong to, for example (and for the rest of this chapter), we will use the `packtmeteor` organization. So our command will look like the following:

   ```
   $ meteor create --package packtmeteor:testpack
   ```

2. We will now add the code for our package. Open the file named `testpack.js` and add the following code:

   ```
   TestPack = {
     log: function(msg){
       console.log(msg);
       Meteor.call('serverlog',msg);
     }
   };
   ```

Save your changes and create a new file in the same folder named
`servertestpack.js`. Open this file for editing and add the following code:

```
Meteor.methods({
  serverlog : function(msg){
    console.log(msg);
  }
});
```

3. We now need to make a few modifications to `package.js`, to make sure our
   package will work properly. Open `package.js` and modify the `Package.onUse()`
   method to look like the following:

```
Package.onUse(function(api) {
  api.versionsFrom('1.0.3.2');
  api.addFiles('testpack.js', 'client');
  api.addFiles('servertestpack.js', 'server');
});
```

Next, add the following code inside the `Package.onUse()` method, just after the
last `api.AddFiles()` call:

```
Package.onUse(function(api) {

  api.addFiles('servertestpack.js', 'server');

  if (api.export){
    api.export('TestPack');
  }
});
```

Finally, modify the `Package.onTest()` method by removing the prefix from the
test's filename, like so:

```
Package.onTest(function(api) {
  api.use('tinytest');
  api.use('packtmeteor:testpack');
  api.addFiles('testpack-tests.js');
});
```

4. Save all your changes, and your package will be ready to be used in an application. Select a project you have underway, or create a default Meteor project using the `meteor create` command, and add a subfolder named `[project root]/packages/`. Copy the `testpack/` folder and paste it into the `[project root]/packages/` folder. Then, in a terminal window, execute the following command:

```
$ meteor add packtmeteor:testpack
```

Your custom package will be registered for use in your project, and you can now start your application:

```
$ meteor
```

Open a browser, navigate to `http://localhost:3000` and open the web console. In the web console, enter the following command:

```
> TestPack.log('my package is worky!')
```

You should see the following screen in the browser console:

```
> TestPack.log('my package is worky!')
  my package is worky!
< undefined
>
```

You should see the following in the server terminal console:

```
=> App running at: http://localhost:3000/
I20150312-22:43:47.563(-6)? my package is worky!
```

Congratulations! You've just created your own personal package.

How it works...

Packages in Meteor are really just collections of organized files, with a configuration file that tells Meteor how to use those files.

In this case, we created a default package template using the `meteor create --package` command. Note that we followed the `[owner]:[package name]` naming convention, which Meteor requires if we want to publish this package on Atmosphere for others to use (refer to the *Publishing custom packages to Atmosphere* recipe in this chapter for details).

Once created, we added our functionality, which was very simple. We just called `console.log()` on the client and on the server.

Then, we modified the configuration file, which is always named `package.js`. The following table shows the three sections that this file contains:

Package.describe()	This contains the name, summary, and version number of our package.
Package.onUse()	This lists dependencies and exposes the methods available in our package.
Package.onTest()	This lists dependencies and test methods to be run during testing.

For this recipe, we didn't modify the `Package.describe()` method. Meteor autocreated this section for us and gave us a *version number*, which is required.

Version numbers for packages follow the **Semantic Versioning Specification (SemVer)** specification (3 digits + an optional wrap, such as `1.0.2-rc_beta`). More information on the SemVer specification can be found at `http://semver.org/`

The bulk of our changes occurred in `Package.onUse()`, so we'll go through each item in this method.

The `api.versionsFrom()` method specifies which version of Meteor the core packages used in your package should come from. This comes in handy because Meteor is updated pretty regularly, and some of the dependencies needed to run your package may change in later versions. This method allows you to *freeze* the release versions of the dependency packages you use in your app to prevent compatibility issues.

The `api.addFiles()` method allows us to include files found in our package directory and to specify whether they are client or server-specific. In our case, we used `api.addFiles()` with a `client` parameter to tell Meteor that the `testpack.js` file was client-specific. We then used a `server` parameter to tell Meteor that the `servertestpack.js` file was server-specific.

We then used the `api.export()` method to declare/expose the `TestPack` object. This is what enabled us to use the `TestPack.log()` call in the browser's web console.

Finally, we have the `Package.onTest()` method. It contains two `api.use()` method calls, which declare the package dependencies needed to run the `testpack-test.js` file during testing.

The `api.use()` method isn't exclusive to testing. You can use it in the `Package.onUse()` method as well to include the MDG core or third-party packages.

After completing our modifications, we copied our entire package over to the `packages/` subfolder in our project. This is necessary for any non-deployed package. When you use the `meteor add` command to add a package, Meteor checks for the package in two places: in the online Meteor package repository (Atmosphere) and in the `[project root]/packages/` subfolder. In this case, because our package isn't deployed to Atmosphere, we had a copy of our package in the `packages/` subfolder.

There's more...

Several other options exist for configuring packages (some of which are included in other recipes in this chapter). A complete list of these can be found in the Meteor documentation, found at `http://docs.meteor.com/#/full/packagejs`.

See also

- ▸ The *Using npm modules* and *Publishing custom packages to Atmosphere* recipes in this chapter
- ▸ The *Building custom server methods* recipe in *Chapter 11, Leveraging Advanced Features*

Using npm modules

Node Package Manager (**NPM**) has thousands of modules available. Knowing how to add an npm module for use in your Meteor project gives you access to all of those modules. This recipe will show you how to do this.

Getting ready

You will need to make sure that you have Meteor and Node/npm installed.

You will also need a project that makes use of a custom-built package. We will be using the project from the *Building a custom package* recipe, found in this chapter.

How to do it...

We first need to add a reference to the npm package that we would like to add, which in this case is going to be the `colors` module.

1. Inside your custom package (the one in the `packages/` subfolder of your app), in the `package.js` file, add an `Npm.depends` statement to the end of the file, as shown in the following example:

```
Npm.depends({
```

```
      "colors": "0.6.2"
});
```

2. Now we need to add an `Npm.require` reference to the `colors` module and change our `console.log()` command to use a rainbow of fruit flavors. Change your `server-test.js` file so it looks like the following example:

```
var colors = Npm.require('colors');

Meteor.methods({
  serverlog : function(msg,warn){
    console.log(msg.rainbow);
  }
});
```

3. Save your changes and we are ready to test our updated package. Navigate to `http://localhost:3000` in a browser, open the browser web console, and execute the following command a few times:

```
> TestPack.log('rainbows and unicorns')
```

4. If you switch to your console window, you should see a multicolored response, as shown in the following screenshot:

```
packtmeteor:testpack: updating npm dependencies — colors...
=> Meteor server restarted
=> Meteor server restarted
I20150313-00:12:48.739(-6)? rainbows and unicorns
I20150313-00:12:49.306(-6)? rainbows and unicorns
I20150313-00:12:49.801(-6)? rainbows and unicorns
```

How it works...

The `Npm.depends` declaration in `package.js` tells Meteor that whenever it starts, it needs to go and install the npm modules listed. In this case, we are telling Meteor to go and fetch the `colors` module, version `0.6.2`, from the npm registry.

The `Npm.require` function call in `server-test.js` makes the `colors` module functionality available on the server. Now, any time we make a `console.log()` call, the string passed into the call can have a `.color` reference added to it. In our case, we chose `.rainbow`, which makes every letter from the string printed out to the console appear in a different color.

 To see all the various options available in the npm `colors` module, visit `https://npmjs.org/package/colors`.

There's more...

You can use any npm module you would like in a custom Meteor package. Some of them rely on asynchronous methods and events, so you will have to wrap those modules with specific asynchronous Meteor methods. You can read more about these methods in *Chapter 11, Leveraging Advanced Features*.

See also

▶ The *Using npm packages directly* recipe in *Chapter 8, Integrating Third-party Libraries*

▶ The *Handling asynchronous methods and using asynchronous functions* recipe in *Chapter 11, Leveraging Advanced Features*

Publishing custom packages to Atmosphere

When you've created a useful package and want to share it with the world, Atmosphere is the way to go. This recipe will show you how to upload your custom package to Atmosphere and provides some best practices for maintaining your package moving forward.

Getting ready

To create a quick Atmosphere package, please complete the *Using npm modules* recipe found in this chapter.

You will also need to create a blank repository on GitHub. Assuming you have a GitHub login, navigate to the home page (`https://github.com`) and create a new repository:

Add a title and description to your repository and click on the button marked **Create repository**.

To populate your new Git repository, you will need the Git URL, which can be copied from the home page of your new Git project. It should look something like `https://github.com/strack/packt-testpack.git`.

Remember this URL, as you will be using it to populate the content of your new repository.

How to do it...

To register and upload our package, we need to check our configuration file, upload our code to GitHub, and then deploy our package.

1. To configure `package.js`, open the `package.js` file found in the root folder of your package. In our case, the file is located at `[project root]/packages/testpack/package.js`. We will first modify the summary, as shown in the following example:

   ```
   // Brief, one-line summary of the package.
   summary: 'Demonstration of an Atmosphere Package',
   ```

   Next, we will add the GitHub URL to the `git` property:

   ```
   // URL to the Git repository...
   git: 'https://github.com/strack/packt-testpack.git',
   ```

   You will notice that the documentation property references the `README.md` file, which means that our GitHub documentation will serve a dual purpose. Open `README.md` and add the following line:

   ```
   Demonstration of an Atmosphere Package, deployed to Atmosphere
   ```

2. To push the code to GitHub, save all of your files and navigate to the root folder of your package (not the root folder of your application) in a terminal window. In our case, the root folder is `[project root]/packages/testpack/`. Enter the following lines to populate the GitHub repository:

   ```
   $ git init
   $ git add -A
   $ git commit -m "Created color server console"
   $ git remote add origin https://github.com/strack/packt-testpack.git
   $ git pull origin master -m "initial pull"
   $ git push origin master
   ```

3. To publish to Atmosphere, call `meteor publish` with the following command once it is completed:

   ```
   $ meteor publish --create
   ```

   Voila! You have added your package to Atmosphere.

We deployed all packages directly from the `packages` subfolder of an application. A best practice is to develop and deploy your package on its own, independent of any application. Refer to the *Building a custom package* recipe.

You can see your package live on Atmosphere by navigating to `https://atmospherejs.com` and searching for it by name, as shown in the following screenshot:

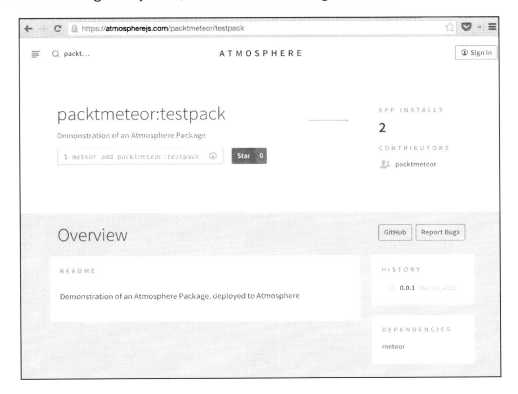

As with any other Meteor package found in Atmosphere, you can add it to any of your projects using the `meteor add` command in the terminal.

How it works...

Atmosphere reads the `package.js` file for the data that needs to be published, checks to make sure all information is accurate, and then publishes a link to your project from a GitHub repository. In this specific case, we added a summary to our file, specified the GitHub URL in the `git` property, and (after creating the GitHub repository) called `meteor publish` to deploy packages.

There's more...

More instructions on how to publish to Atmosphere can be found at `https://atmospherejs.com/i/publishing`.

See also

- ► The *Adding Meteor packages* and *Discovering new packages with Atmosphere* recipes in this chapter

3
Building Great
User Interfaces

In this chapter, we will cover the following topics:

- ▶ Inserting templates with Spacebars
- ▶ Inserting raw HTML using triple braces
- ▶ Creating dynamic lists
- ▶ Building a smooth interface with Bootstrap
- ▶ Creating customized global helpers
- ▶ Creating custom components
- ▶ Using reactivity with HTML attributes
- ▶ Using dynamic templates
- ▶ Animating DOM elements

Introduction

Like everything else in Meteor, UI development is designed to be simple, elegant, and powerful. With just a few imperative commands, you can create sophisticated and dynamic user interfaces, significantly speeding up your prototyping/wireframing efforts.

The recipes in this chapter will walk you through the most common UI- and template-building techniques, which will form the foundation for your Meteor apps moving forward.

Inserting templates with Spacebars

Spacebars is Meteor's templating language. All **Document Object Model** (**DOM**) elements in Meteor are created programmatically using Meteor's default templating engine, **Blaze**. Elements can therefore be created using pure JavaScript. Using JavaScript to create HTML elements, however, isn't exactly quick and easy.

Inspired by the popular HTML templating language **Handlebars**, Spacebars makes it incredibly easy to structure and declare your HTML elements using templates. And, it gives you access to all the reactive and dynamic features of Meteor. This recipe will show you how to create templates using the Spacebars syntax.

Getting ready

You will need Meteor installed and have a project created. We recommend that you have a simple project, similar to the one found in the *Setting up your project file structure* recipe in *Chapter 1, Optimizing Your Workflow*, but any project will do. You will need to locate your `<body>` tag, which is usually found inside your `main.html` file.

How to do it...

To make this recipe just a little bit more useful, we are going to create two templates and nest one inside of the other, using the following steps:

1. First, create a file named `templates.html` and add it to your `client` folder:

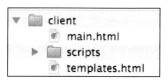

2. Open `templates.html` in an editor, add the following code, and save your changes:

```
<template name="firstTemplate">
    <div id="title">This is my first ever template</div>
    <svg height="200" width="100%" id="shapes">
        {{> one}}
    </svg>
</template>


<template name="one">
    <circle cx="100" cy="50" r="40" stroke="#ffc348"
stroke-width="3" fill="#31be4f" />
</template>
```

3. Next, open your `main.html` file (or the `.html` file that contains your `<body>` tag) and edit your `body` tag by adding the following code:

```
<body>
   {{> firstTemplate}}
</body>
```

4. Save the changes, start Meteor if it isn't already running, and navigate to your Meteor-hosted page in a browser (usually `http://localhost:3000`):

How it works...

We created two templates, with the first one being a very simple `svg` element:

```
<template name="one">
    <circle cx="100" cy="50" r="40" stroke="#ffc348"
stroke-width="3" fill="#31be4f" />
</template>
```

We gave the template a `name` attribute value as `"one"` and added the well-formed HTML `<circle>` element with position and appearance attributes. We also created a parent template, as follows:

```
<template name="firstTemplate">
    <div id="title">This is my first ever template</div>
    <svg height="200" width="100%">
        {{> one}}
    </svg>
</template>
```

This template also has a name (`"firstTemplate"`) and contains a `<div>` element, containing the title of our template. We declared an `<svg>` element, and we inserted our template named `one` between the `<svg>` and `</svg>` tags using the `{{>}}` command.

Finally, in `main.html`, we inserted the `firstTemplate` template between the main `<body>` and `</body>` tags, again using the `{{>}}` command, which is also known as **template inclusion**.

As you can see, the content of our templates consists primarily of HTML tags. This is the fundamental building block of our UI, and it's how we've been creating templates from the very beginning. Anything contained inside double braces (`{{...}}`) is a command meant for Blaze, Meteor's templating engine. In this case, we told Blaze to:

1. Insert the `firstTemplate` template into our `<body>` element.
2. Insert the `one` template into our `<svg>` element, inside `firstTemplate`.

There's more...

You can read all about templates in the official Meteor documentation, found at `http://docs.meteor.com/#/full/templates`.

Inserting raw HTML using triple braces

Occasionally, you will want to insert raw HTML into your Meteor page. This is typically done when you have HTML generated by another process or library. This recipe will show you how to render your raw HTML inside a Meteor template.

Getting ready

You will need Meteor installed and have a project created with at least one template in it. We recommend that you use the files created in the *Inserting templates with Spacebars* recipe found in this chapter.

If you don't have a `templates.js` file in your `client` folder already, you should create one to keep your template `helpers` and `events` logic separate from other JavaScript you may be running.

How to do it...

Identify the name of your root template and open the file containing your template definition. In our case, the root template is named `firstTemplate`, which can be found in our `templates.html` file, which is in our `[project root]/client` folder. Proceed with the following steps to insert raw HTML using triple braces:

1. Insert the following line, just before the `</template>` tag, and save your changes:

```
<template name="firstTemplate">
    ...
    {{{rawInsert}}}
</template>
```

Now, open your `templates.js` file and add the following helper function:

```
Template.firstTemplate.helpers({
  rawInsert: function () {
    return "<div><strong>Raw HTML!</strong></div>";
  }
});
```

2. Save your changes, start Meteor if it isn't already running, and navigate to your Meteor-hosted page in a browser (usually `http://localhost:3000`). You should see the rendered HTML at the bottom of your screen, as shown in the following screenshot:

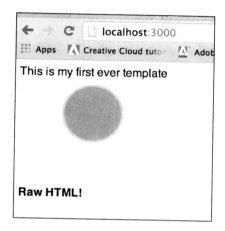

How it works...

We created and then called our `Template.firstTemplate.rawInsert` helper function by adding the `{{rawInsert}}` tag at the bottom of our template and declaring the `rawInsert` helper in our `templates.js` file.

The triple-braced tag informs Blaze that the object returned from the helper will be raw HTML and needs to be rendered as such. Accordingly, Blaze expects a string and will attempt to render it.

To see how Blaze would normally treat raw HTML, change the triple-braced tag to a double-braced tag (`{{rawInsert}}`) save your file, and view the result in your browser, as shown in the following screenshot:

See also

▸ The *Creating dynamic graphs with SVG and Ajax* recipe in *Chapter 7, Using Client Methods*

Creating dynamic lists

The Meteor Spacebars syntax supports the rapid development of lists, tables, and other displays of data through the use of template block tags. Used within templates, block tags can quickly add dynamic lists and even customize the look and feel of each element, based on its unique attributes. This recipe will show you how to use the `#each` block tag to display multiple elements of a collection inside a Blaze template.

Getting ready

We will use the code from the *Inserting templates with Spacebars* recipe, found in this chapter, as our baseline project.

If you haven't already done so, create and save a new file in your `[project root]/client` folder called `templates.js`.

Create and save a new file in your `[project root]/both` folder called `collections.js`.

We will want to make one modification to the HTML in the `templates.html` file. We will change the height of our `<svg>` element from `200` to `800`:

```
<svg height="800" width="100%" id="shapes">
```

Finally, we want to add the `random` package to our project to help us generate some random colors and positions. In a terminal window, navigate to your project root and enter the following command:

```
$ meteor add random
```

How to do it...

To create a dynamic list, proceed with the following steps:

1. First, let's declare a `shapes` collection. Open `collections.js`, add the following code, and save your changes:

   ```
   Shapes = new Mongo.Collection('shapes');
   ```

2. Now, let's add shapes to the page dynamically. Open your `templates.html` file, make the following changes to the `one` template, and save your changes:

   ```
   <template name="one">
       {{#each svgShapes}}
       <circle cx="{{x}}" cy="{{y}}" r="40" stroke="{{border}}"
   stroke-width="3" fill="{{color}}" />
       {{/each}}
   </template>
   ```

3. We will now create the template helper, which returns our dynamic collection. Open `templates.js`, add the following helper function, and then close and save your changes:

   ```
   Template.one.helpers({
     svgShapes: function () {
       return Shapes.find();
     }
   });
   ```

4. We can now dynamically add shapes to the `shape` collection, and they will be rendered on our page. Open the JavaScript console in your browser and enter the following command:

```
> Shapes.insert({x:200,y:50,border:'#123456',color:'#bada55'})
```

You should see a green circle with a dark border appear on the screen, similar to the following screenshot:

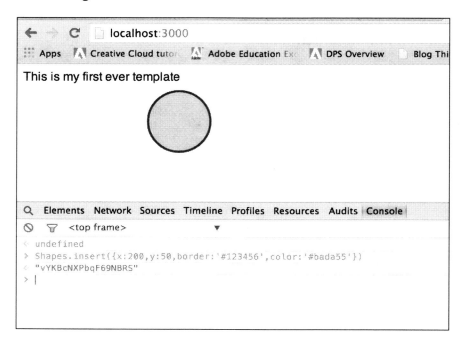

Let's add more circles to prove that our template is rendering all the shapes in the `Shapes` collection.

5. In `templates.js`, add the following code:

```
Template.firstTemplate.events({
  'click svg': function (e,t){
    var xpos,ypos;
    if(e.offsetX==undefined)
    {
      xpos = e.pageX-$('#shapes').offset().left;
      ypos = e.pageY-$('#shapes').offset().top;
    }
```

```
      else
      {
        xpos = e.offsetX;
        ypos = e.offsetY;
      }
          choices = ['#bada55','#B43831', '783BA3',
    '#00AB1B', '#143275', '#FFA700'],
          color = Random.choice(choices),
          border = Random.choice(choices);
      Shapes.insert({x:xpos,y:ypos,border:border,color:color});
      },
      'dblclick': function(e,t){
          Meteor.call('resetShapes');
      }
});
```

6. We now want to display the total number of shapes, so we need to add a shapeCount function to the `Template.firstTemplate.helpers` method call:

```
Template.firstTemplate.helpers({
  shapeCount: function () {
    return Shapes.find().count();
  },
  rawInsert: function () {...
```

We will also need to Modify templates.html to display a count of the shapes collection:

```
<template name="firstTemplate">
    <div id="title">shapes collection count: {{shapeCount}}</div>
```

7. Let's add a `resetShapes` method for good measure. Open/create the `server.js` file, found in your `[project root]/server` folder, and add the following code:

```
Meteor.methods({
    resetShapes: function(){
        Shapes.remove({});
    }
});
```

8. Save all your changes, start Meteor if it isn't already running, and navigate to your Meteor-hosted page in a browser (usually `http://localhost:3000`).

Now, as you click in your browser, new circles will appear and the upper-left part of the screen will display your `shapes` collection count:

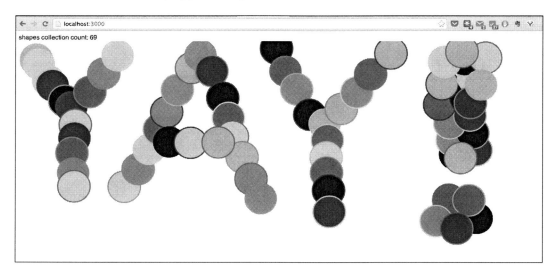

Feel free to add as many shapes as you would like or reset back to zero by double-clicking anywhere on the screen.

How it works...

We created the `Template.one.svgShapes` helper in `templates.js`, which returns a cursor to the `shapes` collection. This sets the data context for our template and is accessible using the `{{#each svgShapes}}` block tag, which we added to our `one` template in `templates.html`.

Because templates and template helpers are reactive computations, they react when the collection is updated. This reaction causes Blaze to re-render the page, using the dynamic template found within the `#each` block tag.

There's more...

Other block helpers exist and they are just as easy to use. Refer to the Spacebars documentation on GitHub for a more detailed explanation, which is available at `https://github.com/meteor/meteor/blob/devel/packages/spacebars/README.md`.

- ▸ The *Implementing a simple collection* recipe in *Chapter 4, Creating Models*
- ▸ The *Creating dynamic graphs with SVG and Ajax* recipe in *Chapter 7, Using Client Methods*

Building a smooth interface with Bootstrap

As a web developer, one of the biggest drains on your time comes from styling your pages. Bootstrap offers an elegant, simple design with enough ready-to-use component styles to get you up and running quickly, without having to get bogged down writing CSS. This recipe will walk you through a few of the Bootstrap component styles and give you a sampling of how easy they are to use.

Getting ready

We will be using the *Creating dynamic lists* recipe found in this chapter as a baseline for our code.

We will also need to add the official Bootstrap package to our Meteor project using Meteor's package repository. Open a terminal window, navigate to the root folder of your project, and enter the following command:

```
$ meteor add twbs:bootstrap
```

 There are other packages that are complementary to the official Bootstrap package. You can find a complete list of these at https://atmospherejs.com/?q=bootstrap.

How to do it...

We will make our title and collection count presentable using the `btn` and `navbar` styles built in to Bootstrap. Proceed with the following steps to build a smooth interface with Bootstrap:

1. First, let's modify our title, adding a sub `<div>` tag and styling it like a Bootstrap button. Open `templates.html`, make the following code changes, and save your file:

```
<div id="title">Shapes Collection Count:
    <div id="resetShapes" class="btn btn-warning">
        {{shapeCount}}
        </div>
    </div>
```

2. After this change, your title should look much more presentable, as shown in the following screenshot:

3. We will now add the `navbar` style to the entire title, giving it a distinct, intentional look. Open `templates.html` again and replace the title `<div>` tag with the following code:

```
<nav class="navbar navbar-default">
    <div class="container-fluid">
        <div class="navbar-header">
            <div id="title" class="navbar-brand">Shapes
Collection Count</div>
        </div>
        <div class="nav navbar-left">
            <div id="resetShapes" class="btn btn-warning
navbar-btn">
                {{shapeCount}}
            </div>
        </div>
    </div>
</nav>
```

4. Save these changes and your page should be updated. The **Shapes Collection Count** section should now appear in a distinct `navbar` style, similar to the following screenshot:

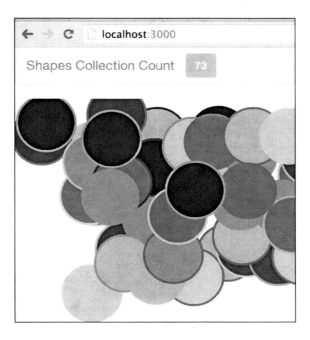

5. Lastly, let's turn our count button into an actual button. Open `templates.js` and change the `dblclick` event to a specific `click` event. This event is placed at the bottom of the `Template.firstTemplate.events` function:

```
Template.firstTemplate.events({
    …
    'click #resetShapes': function(e,t){
        Meteor.call('resetShapes');
    }
})
```

We have now disabled double-click as the method of resetting our `shapes` collection and transferred it to the **Shapes Collection Count** total. By clicking on the orange button, the collection will reset to zero:

How it works...

Changing the look and feel of a page using Bootstrap is simply a matter of adding the correct CSS `class` declarations and structuring our HTML appropriately.

To style the `shapes` collection count, we added the `btn` and `btn-warning` value to the `class` attribute. This allows the Bootstrap CSS to appropriately style the `<div>` tag, making it appear as an orange button.

To style our title, we had to first create the scaffolding for the `navbar` tag. We did this by essentially wrapping our `<div>` tag with a `<nav>` tag. We then appropriately structured the containing tags by adding `nav`, `navbar`, `navbar-header`, and `navbar-left` to the `class` attributes. The other `class` declarations (`navbar-default`, `navbar-brand`, and `navbar-btn`) are strictly style declarations, changing the color/shape but not affecting the overall structure or layout.

There's more...

Bootstrap is very robust and comes with excellent documentation. You can learn more about Bootstrap at `http://getbootstrap.com/`.

See also

▶ The *Adding Meteor packages* and *Discovering new packages with Atmosphere* recipes in *Chapter 2, Customizing with Packages*

Creating customized global helpers

As you begin to really dig into templates, you'll soon discover how truly great template helpers are. You can access data inline and drastically reduce the amount of code you need to write.

You will, however, eventually run into a situation where you find yourself repeating the same logic in multiple, in-template helpers. Wouldn't it be great if there was a way to create global helpers accessible from any template? Well, Meteor has a solution for this too! This recipe will show you how to create global template helpers using the `Template.registerHelper` function.

Getting ready

We will use the codebase from the *Building a smooth interface with Bootstrap* recipe, found in this chapter. Please follow that recipe first or download the corresponding codebase.

How to do it...

We're going to make a global random color generator and add random colors to all the objects on the screen by performing the following steps:

1. Open `templates.html`, found in your `[project root]/client` folder, and make the following changes to the color attributes of the `one` template:

```
<template name="one">
    {{#each svgShapes}}
    <circle cx="{{x}}" cy="{{y}}" r="40"
stroke="{{randColor}}" stroke-width="3"
fill="{{randColor}}" />{{/each}}
</template>
```

2. We will also use the `randColor` helper in our `<div>` title to give it a bit of (random) color. Inside the `firstTemplate` template, look for and modify the `<div>` title as follows:

```
<div class="navbar-header">
                <div id="title" class="navbar-brand"
style="color:{{randColor}}">Shapes Collection Count</div>
```

3. Save your changes and start your Meteor app if it isn't already started. As you view your Meteor page in your browser, you will notice that the circles have all turned black. This is because although we are referencing the global helper, we haven't actually created it yet.

4. So, let's take care of that. Open `templates.js`, found in your `[project root]/client` folder, and add the following function at the bottom:

```
Template.registerHelper('randColor',function(){
    choices = ['#bada55','#B43831', '783BA3', '#00AB1B',
'#143275', '#FFA700'];
    return Random.choice(choices);
});
```

5. Once you save the changes, your page will refresh and the circles will now have a random color, as will the title bar of your app. To prove that it is indeed using the global `randColor` helper, open another browser window, navigate to your page (usually `http://localhost:3000`), and view the results side by side. As you click on the page to add circles or refresh the page, the colors will change at random and will be different from one browser window to the next, as shown in the following screenshot:

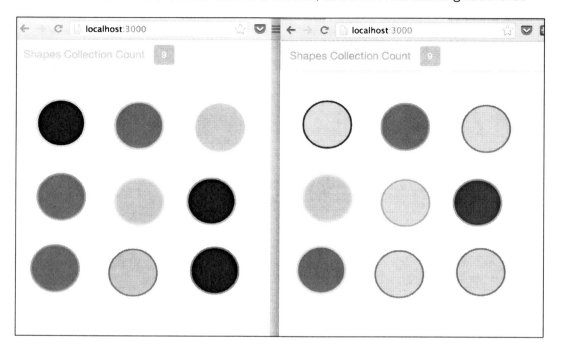

How it works...

The `Template.registerHelper` function declares a helper that can be seen in context with any template. Think of it as a way to declare global functions, accessible within the Spacebars syntax.

The first argument of `Template.registerHelper` is a string value, which contains the name of our helper (the name to be used to reference it inline, inside our templates). When deciding on a name for a global helper, keep in mind that it is indeed global. It should therefore be unique, to prevent conflicts, or the value could be overridden by a template-specific helper. Our example is very simple, so we can get away with `randColor`; however, as you build more sophisticated templates, it's a good idea to give your helpers more distinct names. The value returned is obviously a randomly selected color, using the same technique that we used in the original `firstTemplate` click event handler.

We then used the global helper in two different templates. First, we replaced `{{color}}` and `{{border}}` in the circle's `svg` declaration with `{{randColor}}`, causing our circles to appear with a random color every time. Finally, we added a `style="color:{{randColor}}"` attribute to our `<div>` title, which randomly assigns a text color upon page refresh.

There's more...

There are obviously some very advanced techniques you can accomplish with global helpers, using other template-related methods such as `Template.instance()` and `Template.currentData`. All of these can't be covered in this recipe, but we encourage you to explore the Meteor documentation to familiarize yourself with what global helpers can do.

 For a good overview of the available template utilities, consult the Meteor documentation at `http://docs.meteor.com/#/full/templates_api`.

See also

▸ The *Inserting templates with Spacebars* and *Using reactivity with HTML attributes* recipes in this chapter

Creating custom components

Adding and using templates in Meteor is a great way to speed up your workflow. Using Meteor's built-in content block helpers can further streamline your workflow by allowing nested and deferred template calls. In essence, you can combine and nest templates to create your own "components". This recipe will show you how to build a basic Spacebars custom block helper using `Template.contentBlock`.

Getting ready

We will use the codebase from the *Building a smooth interface with Bootstrap* recipe found in this chapter. Please follow that recipe first, or download the corresponding codebase.

How to do it...

Proceed with the following steps to create custom components:

1. We need to make the template-specific `shapeCount` helper global so we can use it inside our component. In `templates.js`, delete the `shapeCount` function found in the `Template.firstTemplate.helpers()` method call, and add the following function to the bottom of the page:

```
Template.registerHelper('shapeCount',function (){
  return Shapes.find().count();
});
```

2. Now, we will create our component. We will first create a `navbutton` template, which will use the newly created `shapeCount` helper. Create a new template file, named `navbar.html`, in your `[project_root]/client` folder. Open this file in a text editor and add the following template code:

```
<template name="navbutton">
    <div class="nav navbar-left">
        <div id="resetShapes" class="btn btn-warning
        navbar-btn">
            {{shapeCount}}
        </div>
    </div>
</template>
```

3. To create a custom `navbar` block tag, add the `navbar` template in the same file, complete with a `Template.contentBlock` reference, as follows:

```
<template name="navbar">
    <nav class="navbar navbar-default">
        <div class="container-fluid">
            <div class="navbar-header">
                <div id="title" class="navbar-brand">Shapes
                Collection Count</div>
            </div>
            {{> Template.contentBlock}}
        </div>
    </nav>
</template>
```

4. Our component is now complete! Let's use it in our code. Open `templates.html` and completely remove the `<nav>` element block, including the code inside the `firstTemplate` template. The only element left after this change will be the `<svg>` element. Just above the `<svg>` element, we are going to call our `navbar` template using the `{{#[template name]}}` block tag, as follows:

```
<template name="firstTemplate">
    {{#navbar}}
      {{> navbutton}}
    {{/navbar}}
    <svg>
```

5. Save all your changes, start your Meteor instance if it isn't already running, and view the results in your browser. You will notice that nothing has changed. We have the same functionality as before; only now, we have created a custom Spacebars component (formally, a custom block helper), and we could add more components to the `navbar` tag as needed or enter explicit HTML, for example, replacing `{{> navbutton}}` with `<div>{{shapeCount}}</div>` will display the **Shapes collection count** without the use of the `navbutton` template, similar to the following screenshot (not very pretty, but you get the point):

If you inspect the element in your browser, you will notice that manually entered `<div>...</div>` has been inserted in the placeholder block, similar to the following example:

```
<nav class="navbar navbar-default">
  ...
    <div>15</div>
  ...
</nav>
```

How it works...

The key to building block helpers resides in the `Template.contentBlock` function. We created a new `navbar` template and used `{{> Template.contentBlock}}` inside that template to specify a placeholder. This placeholder (called a **content block**) can be specified later, rather than having to be specified explicitly inside the `navbar` template. This simple addition of a content block turns our `navbar` template into a *component*.

Once we created our block helper, along with the template meant to go inside the block helper, we added a `Spacebars` block tag with `{{#navbar}}` and the ending `{{/navbar}}` calls. Inside this block, we called our new `navbutton` template using `{{> navbutton}}`, which is inserted in the `{{> Template.contentBlock}}` placeholder. At runtime, all these template functions get executed in order, and Blaze renders the actual HTML DOM elements.

There's more...

Custom block helpers can also utilize the `#if`, `#else`, and `#unless` logic through the use of `UI.elseBlock`. Using these commands, you can create reusable, dynamic block helpers and templates, further streamlining your development process.

 For a thorough walkthrough of all the options available, see the GitHub documentation on Spacebars, found at https://github.com/meteor/meteor/blob/devel/packages/spacebars/README.md.

See also

> ▶ The *Inserting templates with Spacebars* and *Creating customized global helpers* recipes in this chapter

Using reactivity with HTML attributes

One of the hidden gems in Meteor is the extremely granular control you have over how HTML is rendered. Blaze was designed in such a way that you can modify, add, or remove HTML element attributes dynamically without affecting anything else in the DOM! This recipe will walk you through the use of dynamic, reactive data inside element attributes.

Getting ready

We will use the codebase from the *Creating custom components* recipe, the previous recipe in this chapter. Please follow that recipe first or download the corresponding codebase.

How to do it...

Proceed with the following steps to use reactivity with HTML attributes:

1. We first need to create a new `navcolor` template. Open `navbar.html` in your `[project root]/client` folder and add the following code:

    ```
    <template name="navcolor">
        <div class="nav navbar-form navbar-right">
            <input type="checkbox" id='bgCheck'
            checked="{{useBG}}"/>
            <input type="text" id='bgColor'
            placeholder="#bgcolor" value="{{bgColor}}" />
        </div>
    </template>
    ```

2. We now need to add our new template to our `navbar` content block so that we can input a new background color and turn it on and off. Open `templates.html` (also in the `client` folder) and modify the `firstTemplate` template, adding a template call just below the `{{> navbutton}}` call, similar to the following:

    ```
    {{#navbar this}}
        {{> navbutton}}
        {{> navcolor}}
    {{/navbar}}
    ```

3. On the very next line, add a `style` attribute to the `<svg>` element so that we can change the background color, like so:

    ```
    <svg height="800" width="100%" id="shapes"
    style="background-color:{{bgColor}}">
    ```

4. In the preceding code, we have set up references to two helper functions: `bgColor` and `useBG`. We will now create these global template helpers. Open `templates.js` and append the following two functions:

    ```
    Template.registerHelper('bgColor', function () {
        if (Session.equals('useBG', true)) {
            return Session.get('bgColor');
        } else return null;
    });


    Template.registerHelper('useBG', function(){
        return Session.get('useBG');
    });
    ```

5. If we save these changes and open the web console in your browser, we can now programmatically change and toggle the background color. In the web console, execute the following two lines:

```
> Session.set('bgColor','lightgrey')
```

```
> Session.set('useBG',true)
```

These three things should have changed on your screen:

❑ The background should now be light grey in color

❑ The checkbox to the top-right of your `navbar` tag should be checked

❑ The word **lightgrey** should now appear in the top-right text box

Your screen should now look similar to the following screenshot:

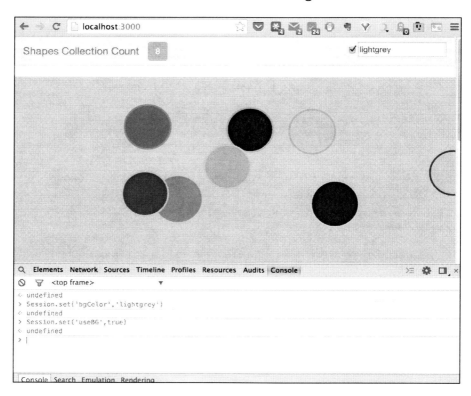

6. All that's left is to hook up events to the checkbox's and textbox's `<input>` elements. Create a new file named `navbar.js` in your `[project_root]/client` folder and add the following `events` handler declarations:

```
Template.navcolor.events({
  'click #bgCheck': function (e, c) {
    Session.set('useBG', e.currentTarget.checked);
  },
  'change #bgColor, keyup #bgColor': function (e, c) {
    if (!Session.equals('bgColor',
    e.currentTarget.value)) {
      Session.set('bgColor', e.currentTarget.value);
    }
  }
});
```

7. Save your changes and your elements will now affect the background. Checking/unchecking the checkbox will toggle the background color, and changing the value in the textbox will dynamically change the displayed background.

8. We want to observe the effect this has on the DOM. Open the `developer` panel in your browser and locate the `<svg>` element. As you toggle the background on and off using the checkbox, observe the attribute list inside the top `<svg>` tag. You'll notice that the `style` attribute appears and disappears, depending on the state of the checkbox, similar to the following screenshot:

As you can see, the attribute doesn't just become empty. It is removed altogether. You will also notice that when this happens, neither the screen nor the elements view are refreshing. That's because the DOM is not being rebuilt. The attribute is being added and removed, according to the state of `{{bgColor}}`. Similarly, when you modify the value in the textbox, nothing else is affected (no screen refreshes, or lost states).

How it works...

With the introduction of the Blaze templating engine, Meteor stopped manipulating strings and started interacting with DOM trees / DOM elements directly. This change simplifies the development process in comparison to other templating libraries because DOM elements don't have to be re-rendered every time there is a change to the HTML.

In the case of the `style` attribute, the only argument inside the attribute is a reference to the `bgColor` helper function. If the value from a helper function or data context is `null`/`undefined`, and if that value is the only value in an attribute, Blaze automatically removes the attribute, rather than rendering it with no value in it.

So, in this case, when the `{{bgColor}}` helper function returned `null` (when `Session.useBG` is `false` or `undefined`), Blaze was removing the `style` attribute from the `<svg>` element.

See also

▸ The *Inserting templates with Spacebars* recipe in this chapter

▸ The *Using the Session object* recipe in *Chapter 4, Creating Models*

Using dynamic templates

Meteor has yet another templating trick up its sleeve! In addition to custom code blocks, reactive data contexts, and all the other various template niceties, Meteor also allows you to dynamically switch between rendered templates. This recipe will show you how to dynamically render templates, using the `Template.dynamic` helper.

Getting ready

We will use the codebase from the *Creating custom components* recipe found in this chapter. Please follow that recipe first or download the corresponding codebase.

How to do it...

We will add a dynamic template that will switch our shapes from circles to squares, when rendered. Proceed with the following steps to use dynamic templates:

1. First, we need to create our alternate template. Inside `templates.html`, located in your `[project root]/client` folder, add the following template, just below the declaration for the existing `one` template:

```
<template name="two">
    {{#each svgShapes}}
        <rect x="{{x}}" y="{{y}}" width="80" height="80"
stroke="{{border}}" stroke-width="3" fill="{{color}}" />
    {{/each}}
</template>
```

2. We will need a data context for this template. Fortunately, we can reuse the `Shapes` collection. Open `templates.js`, make a copy of the `svgShapes` function, and add it to a new `Template.two.helpers()` method call, as follows:

```
Template.two.helpers({
  svgShapes: function () {
    return Shapes.find();
  }
});
```

Now, we will add logic to toggle between the `one` and `two` templates, based on the `Session.curTemplate` variable. At the bottom of `templates.js`, add the following `helpers()` method call:

```
Template.firstTemplate.helpers({
  curTemplate: function () {
    var curTempl = Session.get('curTemplate');
    if (!curTempl) {
      curTempl = 'one';
      Session.set('curTemplate', curTempl);
    }
    return curTempl;
  }
});
```

3. All that's left to do is to add the dynamic template declaration and create an easy way to toggle between the templates. Let's take care of the declaration first. Open `templates.html` and modify the double brackets inside the `<svg>` element as follows:

```
<svg height="800" width="100%" id="shapes">
    {{> Template.dynamic template = curTemplate}}
</svg>
```

4. Now, we will add some toggle buttons and hook up the events to change the value of the `Session.curTemplate` variable. Open `navbar.html` and add the following template at the bottom:

```
<template name="navshapes">
    <div class="nav navbar-right">
        <button id="btnCircles" class="btn btn-success navbar-
btn">one</button>
        <button id="btnSquares" class="btn btn-danger navbar-
btn">two</button>
    </div>
</template>
```

5. We need to include the `navshapes` template in our block helper. Open `templates.html` and add the following template inclusion just before the `{{/navbar}}` block tag:

```
{{#navbar}}
   ...
   {{> navshapes}}
{{/navbar}}
```

6. One last addition, to hook up the events, and we're ready to roll. Create a `navbar.js` file in your `[project root]/client` folder and add the following code:

```
Template.navshapes.events({
   'click button.btn': function(e,c){
      Session.set('curTemplate',e.currentTarget.textContent);
   }
});
```

7. Save all your changes, start your Meteor project if it isn't already running, and navigate to your project in a browser (usually `http://localhost:3000`). You will see two buttons at the top-right corner of the screen. Click on them, back and forth, to see the shapes on the screen toggle between circles and squares, similar to the following screenshot:

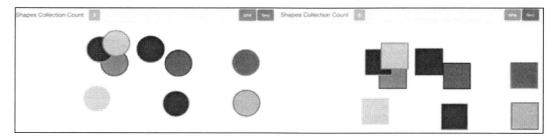

How it works...

`Template.dynamic` takes a `template` argument and renders the template with the appropriate name. Because we make the template argument dynamic and reactive, using the `curTemplate` helper, the rendered template will change as the value of `Session.curTemplate` changes. This ability to dynamically render templates is the basis for the popular Meteor package `iron:router`. It can be used in multiple situations where you would like to switch out templates, based on reactive data sources.

There's more...

Iron Router takes dynamic templates to an entirely new level. The documentation for Iron Router can be found at `https://github.com/iron-meteor/iron-router/blob/devel/Guide.md`.

See also

- ▶ The *Creating a multipage application with Iron Router* recipe in *Chapter 2, Customizing with Packages*
- ▶ The *Creating custom components* recipe in this chapter
- ▶ The *Using the Session object recipe* in *Chapter 4, Creating Models*
- ▶ The *Creating a complete app with Iron Router* recipe in *Chapter 12, Creating Useful Projects*

Animating DOM elements

Meteor has a very elegant way of rendering DOM elements in our web apps, but until now, this hasn't included animations. Fortunately for us, Meteor now supports animations, including animations when an element is first added to the DOM. This recipe will walk you through how to use standard CSS animation techniques inside Meteor.

Getting ready

We will use the codebase from the *Using dynamic templates* recipe found in this chapter. Please follow that recipe first or download the corresponding codebase.

How to do it...

We will animate the shapes from our previous recipe, demonstrating animation both before and after the elements are first created and rendered.

Because we used SVG elements instead of DOM elements, we need to modify jQuery to be able to use `.addClass` and `.removeClass`. Fortunately, there is a custom package available that will add SVG support and add Meteor UI event support at the same time.

1. In a terminal window, navigate to the root folder of your project and execute the following line:

```
$ meteor add appmill:animation-hooks
```

This will install the `animation-hooks` package, which includes support for SVG in jQuery.

2. We will now add a very simple hover animation effect. Open or create a `style.css` file in your `[project root]/client/lib/styles` folder and add the following code:

```css
circle,rect {
    opacity:1;
    transition:all 500ms 0ms ease-in;
}

circle:hover, rect:hover{
    opacity:0;
}
```

3. Save your changes, start your Meteor project if it isn't already started, and navigate to your project URL in a browser (usually `http://localhost:3000`). If you don't have shapes on your screen, click to add some and then hover over the shapes. As you hover, you will notice that the shapes will fade out slowly, and as you move the mouse away, the shapes will fade in slowly until they return to full opacity. Now we will use jQuery to move all the shapes on the screen at once. Inside `navbar.html`, add the following template at the bottom:

```html
<template name="navoffset">
    <div class="nav navbar-right">
        <button id="btnNegative" class="btn btn-danger navbar-btn"
data-offset="-">red</button>
        <button id="btnPositive" class="btn btn-info navbar-btn"
data-offset="">blue</button>
    </div>
</template>
```

4. Inside `templates.html`, add a call to the new `navoffset` template, just before the `navshapes` declaration:

```
{{#navbar this}}
{{> navbutton}}
{{> navoffset}}
{{> navshapes}}
{{/navbar}}
```

We now add the code for the `button` events by modifying `navbar.js`, adding the following function at the bottom:

```js
Template.navoffset.events({
  'click button.btn': function(e,c){
    var shapes = ($('rect').length)? $('rect'):$('circle');
    if (shapes.length==0) return;
```

```
        var offset = e.currentTarget.dataset.offset;
        _.each(shapes,function(d,i){
          var randVal = Math.ceil(Math.random()*200)+'px';
          var randOffset = offset+randVal;
          var translate = ('translate('+randOffset+','+randOffs
et+')');
          $(d).css('transform',translate);
        });
      }
    });
```

5. We also want to add a little bit of polish to our `nav` buttons, so add the following CSS to the `style.css` file, at the bottom:

```
div.nav {
    margin-left: 20px;
}
```

6. Save all these changes and your web page should now contain two new buttons, labeled **red** and **blue**. As you click on these buttons alternately, all the shapes on the screen will move their location randomly, back and forth diagonally across your screen.

7. We will now use the built-in animation hooks, called `_uihooks`, to animate shapes as they are added dynamically to the DOM. Open `templates.html` and make the following modifications to both the `one` and `two` templates:

```
{{#each svgShapes}}
  {{#Animate}}
    <circle class="shape animate" ...
  {{/Animate}}
{{/each}}
...
{{#each svgShapes}}
  {{#Animate}}
    <rect class="shape animate" ...
  {{/Animate}}
{{/each}}
```

8. We have one final step and that is to add the initial *before* state to the shapes, via our `.animate` CSS declaration. Open `style.css` and add the following declaration at the bottom:

```
rect.animate, circle.animate {
    transform: translate(-300px,-100px);
    opacity:0;
}
```

9. Save your changes and test out the new animations functionality by either adding new shapes to the screen (clicking anywhere), or by changing the shapes from circles to squares, and back again (clicking on the **one** and **two** buttons). As you click, you will see the shape(s) fade in and move into place from the left.

How it works...

Because Blaze now renders objects according to the DOM, rather than rendering according to text-based HTML tags, it is aware of the styles and conditions of the created elements, for example, because we added the `opacity:0` style to our `:hover` shape elements in `style.css`, elements underneath the mouse will fade out and stay faded out, even when we click on / add new shapes. Using jQuery, we can programmatically add styles and transformations, as we did in `navbar.js` with the `.css()` functions. Blaze will respect these changes as well because programmatic changes to the CSS/DOM are remembered, even when new elements are added.

The `_uihooks` declaration contains three event handlers:

`insertElement`	This is fired before a DOM node is rendered so that we can manipulate its position, map where the node will go when animated, and then animate the node as it is rendered.
`removeElement`	This is fired before a DOM node is removed. We check to see whether there is an outgoing animation and animate the node if so. Otherwise, we just remove it.
`moveElement`	This is fired when a DOM node changes the indexed position in the DOM. We can add any animations before, and then during the index change, to create an animation effect.

For our sample, we only need to worry about inserting and removing elements. Each element has the CSS `animate` class assigned to it, by virtue of the template, which offsets the intended position by (-300,-100). The way we animate is by having the element appear on the screen in the offset position (with the `animate` class in effect), and then by removing the `animate` class, which triggers a transition/animation because the element moves to its intended position. Thanks to `_uihooks` and the `insertElement` event handler, we can programmatically remove `class` declarations to elements, right after they are initially rendered, causing them to animate. This makes the shapes seem to fade in from the top-left. Similarly, we can then add them back right before the elements are removed in order to perform an outgoing animation.

We declare which elements will be affected by wrapping the elements in the `{{#Animate}}`...`{{/Animate}}` block helpers, which causes the `insertElement` and `removeElement` handlers to fire on the wrapped elements.

There's more...

We expect some changes as Meteor continues to improve animation support, although the major functionality is already there. Meanwhile, you can walk through how `_uihooks` works by adding breakpoints to the client source, in the `packages/appmill:animations-hooks/animation-hooks.js` file, similar to the following screenshot:

```
 9
10  Template['Animate'].rendered = function(){
11      var animationElements = this.findAll('.animate');
12
13      // HACK: initial animation rendered, as insertElement, doesn't seem to fire
14      _.each(animationElements, function(item){
15          var $item = $(item);
```

You can also get a (slightly) more thorough explanation at `https://github.com/strack/meteor-animation-hooks`.

See also

▸ The *Using reactivity with HTML attributes* recipe in this chapter

4

Creating Models

In this chapter, we will cover the following topics:

- ► Implementing a simple collection
- ► Using the Session object
- ► Sorting with MongoDB queries
- ► Filtering with MongoDB queries
- ► Creating upsert MongoDB queries
- ► Implementing a partial collection

Introduction

The Meteor data model is designed to be very easy to develop. Gone are the days of worrying about lengthy SQL statements, database drivers, and rigidly structured database tables. In its place is a straightforward, JSON-based document model that lets you focus on the functionality of your application. This chapter contains the most common recipes to interact with MongoDB and the reactive model context inside Meteor.

Implementing a simple collection

Collections are the medium of communication between the client and the server, with changes being pushed down to the client and requests being pushed up to the server. This recipe will show you how and where to declare a collection for use on both the client and the server.

Getting ready

First, you will need Meteor installed and have a project created. To create a standard project file structure, please see the *Setting up your project file structure* recipe in *Chapter 1, Optimizing Your Workflow*.

For this particular exercise, you will also need to have the `autopublish` and `insecure` packages installed (which are installed by default). If you need to add them, please see the *Adding Meteor packages* recipe in *Chapter 2, Customizing with Packages*.

How to do it...

To implement a simple collection, proceed with the following steps:

1. Create a new file in your `both` folder, called `simple.js`.

2. Open the `simple.js` file in an editor, and declare a MongoDB comments collection by entering the following:

```
Comments = new Mongo.Collection('comments');
```

3. Now, open the `main.js` file in your client's `scripts` folder (`[project root]/client/scripts/main.js`), add an action to the `click button` event handler, which will insert a record into the `Comments` collection:

```
Template.hello.events({
  'click button': function () {
    // increment the counter when button is clicked
    Session.set('counter', Session.get('counter') + 1);
    Comments.insert({text:'This is comment #'
    + (Comments.find().count()+1)});
  }
});
```

4. We need to add a comments helper as well. Locate the `Template.hello.helpers` method and add the following helper to the beginning:

```
Template.hello.helpers({
  comments: function () {
    return Comments.find();
  },
  . . .
  });
```

5. Save these changes.

6. Open your `main.html` page (`[project root]/client/main.html`), add a `{{ #each..}}` template fragment to the `hello` template as specified in the following example, and save your changes:

```
<template name="hello">
  {{#each comments}}
  <div>{{text}}</div>
  {{/each}}
  ...
</template>
```

7. Now, open a terminal window, navigate to the `[root]` folder of your project, and start up Meteor:

```
$ cd [project root]
$ meteor
```

8. In a web browser, navigate to `http://localhost:3000/` and click on the button on the screen several times. The result should add comments with each click, similar to this:

> # Hello World!
>
> This is comment #1
> This is comment #2
> This is comment #3
> This is comment #4
> Welcome to FileTemplate. [Click]

How it works...

The declaration in `simple.js` is read by both the client and the server:

```
Comments = new Mongo.Collection('comments');
```

This instantiates the model and manifests as a collection called `Comments`.

The changes to `main.js` consist of an extra action in the `click` event:

```
Comments.insert({text:'This is comment #' +
(Comments.find().count()+1)});
```

This adds a comment object to the `Comments` collection on the client, which is quickly propagated to a minimongo on the client and then to MongoDB on the server. The UI is updated instantly because of the second change in `main.js`:

```
comments: function () {
   return Comments.find();
 }
```

The `comments` helper is a **reactive computation**, which means that it reruns itself every time there is a change in one of the **reactive contexts** (observed properties) it contains. In this example, `Comments.find()` is a reactive context, and therefore, whenever there is a change in the `Comments` collection, this `comments` helper will rerun.

Provided that the MongoDB collection (server side) ratifies the change, the UI will stay updated. If there was a conflict or some problem with the transaction, the server will send a corrective message, and Minimongo will be updated with the correct state. But, in this case, since we have no conflicts or latency, the change stuck, and comments are added after each click.

This template is reactive, which means when a change is found in the `Comments` collection, this function will be updated, and Blaze will re-render the `{{#each...}}` template block added to `main.html`:

```
{{#each comments}}
  <div>{{text}}</div>
  {{/each}}
```

See also

▶ The *Creating dynamic lists* and *Using reactivity with HTML attributes* recipes in *Chapter 3, Building Great User Interfaces*

Using the Session object

The **Session object** is a global client-side object, and as such, is part of the client model. Though it's not part of any collection, the Session object can be used in a reactive context, which means you can use it to make reactive methods rerun whenever it is changed. This recipe will show you how to use the Session object to update the elements on your page.

Getting ready

You will need to have Meteor installed and a project created. To create a standard project file structure, please see the *Setting up your project file structure* recipe in *Chapter 1, Optimizing Your Workflow*. A quick default project will work just as well for this recipe.

How to do it...

To use the Session object, proceed with the following steps:

1. Open the `main.js` file in your client's `scripts` folder (`[project root]/client/scripts/main.js`) and add a `greeting` helper to the beginning of `Template.hello.helpers`, as follows:

```
Template.hello.helpers({
  greeting: function() {
    return Session.get('greeting')||'Welcome to Chapter 4';
  },
  ...
```

2. Open `main.html` and add the greeting to your `hello` template, as follows:

```
<template name="hello">
  <h3>{{greeting}}</h3>
```

3. If Meteor is not already running, initiate it by navigating to your project root folder in a terminal window and run the `meteor` command:

```
$ cd [project root]
$ meteor
```

4. Now, open a browser, navigate to `http://localhost:3000/`, and open your web console.

5. In the web console, enter and execute the following command:

```
> Session.set('greeting','I just changed the Session Object')
```

The greeting on your screen should have changed from **Welcome to Chapter 4** to **I just changed the Session Object**, as shown in the following screenshot:

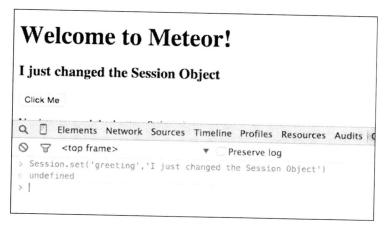

How it works...

Adding a call to `Session.get` inside the `greeting` template helper tells Meteor to look for a value placed in the greeting key of the `Session.keys` collection. As the collections are reactive contexts in Meteor, changes made in the `Session` collection (even when executed through the web console) are instantly reflected in the UI.

 The `Session` object is literally a *Session* object. It lasts only until the next manual page refresh. If you want something more permanent, you will need to use offline storage or a MongoDB collection. Make sure to include this fact in your design/development plans.

There's more...

As of `0.9.1`, Meteor also provides single reactive variables. They can be used in place of the `Session` object, have a cleaner syntax, can be any type of object, and support checking for changes before a reactive invalidation is triggered.

To use reactive variables, add the `reactive-var` package to your Meteor project:

```
$ meteor add reactive-var
```

You can then declare and use a variable instead of the `Session` object:

```
greeting = ReactiveVar("Welcome to Chapter 4");

greeting: function () {
    return greeting.get();
}
```

This variable (declared properly) can be manipulated in the same way as the Session object, with cleaner syntax. The following command entered in the web debug console will change the display accordingly:

```
> greeting.set('I just changed the reactive variable')
```

The preceding command will result in something similar to the following screenshot:

Hello World!

I just changed the reactive variable [Click]

- ▶ The *Using reactivity with HTML attributes* recipe in *Chapter 3, Building Great User Interfaces*
- ▶ The *Creating and consuming a reactive* value and *Updating Blaze template without Mongo* recipes in *Chapter 6, Mastering Reactivity*

Sorting with MongoDB queries

There are many times when you will need to sort a collection. Most recent comments, alphabetized lists, and bank transactions by amount are all good examples. This recipe will show you how to sort MongoDB collections, using the options in your `find()` request.

Getting ready

We will be using the *Implementing a simple collection* recipe found in this chapter as a baseline. please follow that recipe in preparation for this activity.

How to do it...

To perform sorting with MongoDB queries, proceed with the following steps:

1. In your `main.html` file (located at `[project root]/client/main.html`), make the following modification to the `{{#each...}}` template fragment:

```
{{#each comments}}
  <div>{{text}}{{number}}</div>
  {{/each}}
  {{greeting}}
```

2. Next, modify the `Comments.insert` action inside the `click` event handler, found in `[project root]/client/script/main.js`:

```
Template.hello.events({
    'click button' : function () {
      // template data, if any, is available in 'this'
      if (typeof console !== 'undefined')
        console.log("You pressed the button");
        Comments.insert({text:'This is comment #',
        number:Random.hexString(3)});
    }
});
```

3. Finally, inside `main.js`, modify the `find()` arguments to specify a `sort` comments by its `number` in descending order (`-1`):

```
Template.hello.helpers({
  ...
  comments: function () {
  return Comments.find({},{sort:{number:-1}});
  },
  ...
});
```

4. Save all the changes and run Meteor if necessary. Navigate to `http://localhost:3000/`, click on the button on the screen several times, and watch as the comments are sorted by a comment number:

> # Hello World!
>
> This is comment #cd0
> This is comment #884
> This is comment #78f
> This is comment #664
> This is comment #560
> This is comment #50d
> This is comment #124
> Welcome to Chapter 4. `Click`

How it works...

The crux of this recipe is found in the `find()` method arguments. We modified how the number was being stored by adding a random number so that if we do nothing else, the comments will appear out of order. But by adding `{sort:{number:-1}}` to the `comments` helper, we are giving results to Blaze that are sorted in descending order by the randomly generated `number` property. To sort in ascending order, use `1` as your parameter. To sort in descending order, use `-1`.

The rest of the changes are to support the sorting change. First, `main.js` was modified so that the `number` property could be assigned at random and added to the comment object when it is inserted into the `Comments` collection:

```
Comments.insert({text:'This is comment #',
number:Random.hexString(3)});
```

The last change is made to `main.html` to display the new `number` property in the UI:

```
<div>{{text}}{{number}}</div>
```

There's more...

You can perform complex sorts using multiple properties if the need arises. To do so, simply add the additional property key to the `sort` option, with either an ascending (`1`) or descending(`-1`) value, similar to the following:

```
return Collection.find({},{sort:{prop1:-1, prop2:1}});
```

See also

▶ The *Inserting templates with Spacebars* recipe in *Chapter 3, Building Great User Interfaces*

Filtering with MongoDB queries

Whether you're performing searches, organizing records, or narrowing down results, sooner or later, you'll want to filter the results of your collections. This recipe shows you how to limit the number of records in a collection, using MongoDB's `find` method options.

Getting ready

We will use the project created in the *Sorting with MongoDB queries* recipe, found in this chapter. Please complete that recipe, and use the files as a baseline for this recipe.

How to do it...

To filter MongoDB queries, proceed with the following steps:

1. Make the following change to the `comments` helper function in `[project root]/client/scripts/main.js`:

```
Template.hello.helpers({
  ...
  comments: function () {
    return Comments.find({number:/[2468]/},{sort:{number:-1}});
  },
  ...
});
```

2. Save `main.js` and start Meteor if necessary. Navigate to `http://localhost:3000/`; click the button on the screen several times and watch as only the comments that contain an even number are displayed. Your results after multiple clicks should look similar to the following screenshot:

> # Hello World!
>
> This is comment #e68
> This is comment #c54
> This is comment #8d0
> This is comment #458
> This is comment #403
> Welcome to FileTemplate. [Click]

3. Change the regular expression in `main.js` to only show comments that contain an odd number by making the following change to the query:

```
return Comments.find({number:/[13579]/},
{sort:{number:-1}});
```

4. Save your changes and observe the change to your UI, which should look similar to the following screenshot:

> # Hello World!
>
> This is comment #c54
> This is comment #9a0
> This is comment #7c3
> This is comment #458
> This is comment #403
> This is comment #319
> Welcome to FileTemplate. [Click]

How it works...

By adding a selector to the `find()` statement in the query, the collection is paired down to match whatever is specified in the selector. In this case, the selector was a regular expression, which returned results only if the `number` property contained at least one even number, and subsequently, if the `number` property contained at least one odd number.

Notice that this didn't change the `{sort:{number:-1}}` predicate in any way and that it works exactly the same, regardless of how we changed the query.

There is a healthy range of selectors that you can use to limit/filter your collection. For a complete list, check out the MongoDB query operators list found at `http://docs.mongodb.org/manual/reference/operator/query/`.

There's more...

Moving the filter to the server side provides security and performance advantages as the non-matching results are never sent down the wire to the client in the first place. In fact, `find()` is most commonly found on the server, using the Meteor publish and subscribe functionality. For an example of `find()` being used on the server, please see the *Implementing a partial collection* recipe found in this chapter.

See also

- The *Implementing a partial collection* and *Sorting with MongoDB queries* recipes in this chapter

Creating upsert MongoDB queries

As you are developing applications, on occasion, you will run into a situation where you need to either update an existing record, or insert a record if it doesn't exist already. This is done traditionally using conditional operators such as `if`.

Through MongoDB, Meteor removes the burden of checking by allowing you to upsert (update + insert) records using a simple syntax. This recipe will show you how.

Getting ready

We will again use the project created in the *Sorting with MongoDB queries* recipe, found in this chapter. Please create a fresh copy of this recipe, and use the files as a baseline for this recipe.

We will also be using the official `momentjs` package. To add the `momentjs` package, navigate to your project's root folder in a terminal window. Once there, execute the following command:

```
$ meteor add momentjs:moment
```

This will add the `momentjs` package, and you're now ready to complete this recipe.

How to do it...

We first need to increase the likelihood of duplicate records and identify the time at which each comment was inserted or updated. Proceed with the following steps to create upsert MongoDB queries:

1. Open the `[project root]/client/scripts/main.js` file and modify `Template.hello.events` as follows:

```
'click button': function () {
...
Session.set('counter', Session.get('counter') + 1);
var newC = {
  text:'This is comment #',
  number:Random.hexString(1),
  time: moment().format('ll, hh:mm:ss')
};
Meteor.call('commentUpsert',newC);
}
```

2. We will now create a server method for the `upsert` function. By default, Meteor only allows modifications on the client by `_id`, and since an `_id` value may not exist, we need to create a server method for our `upsert` function. Open `[project root]/server/server.js` and add the following method to the bottom of the file:

```
Meteor.methods({
  commentUpsert: function(newC){
    Comments.upsert({number:newC.number},{$set:newC});
  }
});
```

3. Finally, we will modify `[project root]/client/main.html` to display the timestamp on each comment in the `comments` collection:

```
{{#each comments}}
  <div>{{text}}{{number}} at: {{time}}</div>
{{/each}}
```

4. Save your changes, start the Meteor if it is not already running, and navigate to `http://localhost:3000/`.

5. Continuously, click on the button on the screen, and observe how, instead of new records being added on each and every click, if a record already exists, the record's timestamp is updated.

How it works...

In `server.js`, we created a method by declaring the `commentUpsert` method inside `Meteor.methods`.

This method receives a new comment object (`newC`) as an argument and calls `upsert` on the `Comments` collection. The first argument (the selector) tells MongoDB to look for any entries that match the `number` property found in the `newC` object. The second argument (the modifier) tells MongoDB which fields to insert/update on the `upsert` object.

If a match is found, the fields are updated. If no match is found, a new record is inserted, with the `newC` object providing the values.

In `main.html`, we simply added the new `time` property to the display:

```
<div>{{text}}{{number}} at: {{time}}</div>
```

In `main.js`, we first remove the `Comments.insert()` statement. We then create the `newC` object, populating it with a random number, some text, and a timestamp using `moment().format()` to convert the timestamp into a readable format. Finally, we make a call to the `commentUpsert` server-side method, with a `Meteor.call` statement.

The result confirms that our `upsert` function is working properly, as each new comment (with a new `number` property) is added to our list, and each existing comment (with an already existing `number` property) has its timestamp updated.

There's more...

Meteor simplifies things a bit by adding the actual `upsert` function, rather than setting `{upsert:true}` inside a traditional MongoDB `update` query. Both `update` or `upsert` can be used in Meteor, and it's really up to you to choose.

 Extensive documentation exists on updating and upserting records in a MongoDB collection. You can find more details at `http://docs.mongodb.org/manual/reference/method/db.collection.update/`.

See also

▶ The *Building custom server methods* recipe in *Chapter 11, Leveraging Advanced Features*

Implementing a partial collection

Partial collections are collections sent down the wire from the server that contain only part of the information available on each record. This is useful for hiding properties or fields, and also for paring down the size of records containing a lot of information. In other words, partial collections can help with security and performance. This recipe will show you how to implement a partial collection on the server.

Getting ready

Let's use the *Creating upsert MongoDB queries* recipe found in this chapter as a baseline for this recipe. Create a fresh copy of this recipe and then proceed to the other preparations.

Let's spruce things up just a bit as well while we're at it. In a terminal window, navigate to the root project folder and execute the following command:

```
$ meteor add twbs:bootstrap
```

This will add the bootstrap CSS framework. We now want to take advantage of bootstrap, so open up your main.html file (found in [project root]/client/) and make the following changes to the hello template:

```html
<template name="hello">
  . . .
  <div class="btn-group-vertical">
    {{#each comments}}
    <div class="btn btn-default">{{text}}{{number}}
      <span class="label label-warning">
        {{time}}
      </span>
    </div>
    {{/each}}
  </div>
  <p><button>Click Me</button></p>
  . . .
</template>
```

These changes will use some of the default `bootstrap` component styles to make our display look similar to the following screenshot:

We now need to remove the `autopublish` default Meteor package. In the terminal window, execute the following command:

```
$ meteor remove autopublish
```

This will temporarily *break* your application; in that no records from the `Comments` collection are being sent down the wire to the client, so no records will be displayed in the UI. Don't worry, we'll fix this!

You are now ready to move on to the recipe.

How to do it...

First, since we removed `autopublish`, we need to prepare the client to subscribe to the `comments` data stream. To implement a partial collection, proceed with the following steps:

1. Open `[project root]/client/scripts/main.js` and add the following code to the very top of the document:

   ```
   Meteor.subscribe('comments');
   ```

2. While we have `main.js` open, let's also change what we sort, by making the following change to the `comments` helper function and save your changes:

   ```
   comments: function () {
     return Comments.find({},{sort:{time:-1}});
   },
   ```

3. Next, we need to have the server publish the `Comments` data collection. We'll simultaneously remove the text field from the response stream, implementing a **partial collection**. Open `[project root]/server/server.js`, add the following code, and save your changes:

   ```
   Meteor.publish ('comments',function(){
     return Comments.find({} , {fields:{text:false}});
   });
   ```

We can now immediately see that the text field is no longer being displayed in the UI, as shown in the following screenshot:

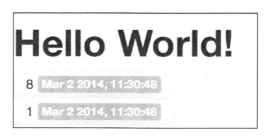

4. Let's clean up our UI a little bit now and make it obvious that the records are being reordered. Open `main.html` again, make the following changes, and save the file:

```
<div class="btn btn-default">{{time}}
  <span class="label label-warning">
    {{number}}
  </span>
</div>
```

Now, when you click on the button to update the `time` property, the timestamp will be updated, and the ordering of the records will change with each click (click several times to really see the effect in action):

The crux of this recipe is found inside `server.js` where we added the `fields` field specifier to the MongoDB query (in the `Meteor.publish(...)` statement):

```
Meteor.publish ('comments',function(){
  return Comments.find({} , {fields:{text:false}});
})
```

This field specifier tells the MongoDB query to exclude the text field/property from the results. Once this change has been made, `main.html` still tries to call `{{text}}` in the template, but since it's null, it doesn't appear. We then removed the call to display `{{text}}` altogether, because it wasn't needed.

There's more...

The `fields` field specifier can be made **exclusive**, as we have seen in the preceding section, by only listing the fields we don't want to see. To do this, simply use the `:false` (or `:0`) parameter for each field you don't want to see, and the rest of the fields will be included by default. For example:

```
record.find({} , {fields:{f1:false , f2:false}});
```

The field specifier can also be made **inclusive**, which means that only the fields specified will be included by using the `:true` (or `:1`) parameter. This would look similar to the following code:

```
record.find({} , {fields:{f3:true , f4:true}});
```

 To read more about the `fields` field specifier, check out the official Meteor documentation at `http://docs.meteor.com/#/full/fieldspecifiers`.

See also

▶ The *Basic safety – turning off autopublish* recipe in *Chapter 9, Securing Your Application*

5
Implementing DDP

In this chapter, we will cover the following topics:

- ▶ Reading the DDP stream
- ▶ Using client-only collections
- ▶ Implementing a multiserver DDP
- ▶ Integrating DDP with other technologies

Introduction

Fundamental to Meteor is the concept of real-time applications, with the client and server interacting with each other using the principle of **data on the wire**. The folks at Meteor have developed a protocol for this real-time client-server communication, called the **Distributed Data Protocol** (**DDP**). As with everything else in Meteor, DDP is a discreet (albeit core) library, which you can use separately. The recipes in this chapter will show you how DDP works and give you some ideas about what you can do with it outside of its default use in Meteor.

Reading the DDP stream

To truly understand what is going on with DDP (and for debugging purposes) it's useful to be able to read the DDP stream. Seeing DDP in action can not only help with the debugging process, but can also help you to better understand how flexible and useful this protocol is. This recipe will show you how to use Arunoda Susiripala's most excellent DDP Analyzer.

Getting ready

You will need Meteor, Node, and npm installed. For installation instructions, visit the following URLs:

- Node—`http://nodejs.org`
- npm—`https://www.npmjs.com/`

You will also need a project. You can use pretty much any project you like. Because it offers a decent, controllable amount of client-server communication (in other words, DDP streams), we will use the `todos` example application. Note that you can also use your own Meteor project if you like. We are only using this as an example because it's convenient and because we can control the flow of data.

To install the `todos` example, open a terminal window, navigate to a directory of your choice, and enter the following command:

```
$ meteor create --example todos
```

Go ahead and start your Meteor application by entering the following commands:

```
$ cd todos
$ meteor
```

You are now ready to install and run the DDP Analyzer on the `todos` app.

How to do it...

1. First, we need to install the DDP Analyzer. In a terminal window, enter and execute the following command:

   ```
   $ npm install -g ddp-analyzer
   ```

   Note that you may need to use `sudo` when using the `-g` operator to make the Analyzer available from anywhere and to make sure it has proper permissions. After a brief installation process, the Analyzer will be installed and ready to be used.

2. Start the Analyzer proxy by entering the following command:

   ```
   $ ddp-analyzer-proxy
   ```

   You will get a message similar to the following:

   ```
   DDP Proxy Started on port: 3030

   ================================

   Export following env. variables and start your meteor app
     export DDP_DEFAULT_CONNECTION_URL=http://localhost:3030
     meteor
   ```

3. We now need to restart our Meteor instance with the environmental variable mentioned in the preceding step. In your terminal window, stop the `meteor` if it is still running and enter the following commands:

```
$ export DDP_DEFAULT_CONNECTION_URL=http://localhost:3030
$ meteor
```

4. Once the `meteor` starts the backup, navigate to `http://localhost:3000` in a browser and the DDP Analyzer will be ready for action.

5. Perform several tasks, such as adding new `todo` items, completing/editing existing items, and so on.

6. Take a look at the DDP stream in the terminal window where you started the DDP Analyzer. It will look similar to the following screenshot:

```
1  IN    2  {"msg":"added","collection":"lists","id":"5ZvEgXMZM8TA5hw6W","fields":{"name":"List A","incompleteCount":0}}
1  IN    0  {"msg":"updated","methods":["5"]}
1  OUT   86 {"msg":"sub","id":"xSw7uXy4SwdkCDXS9","name":"todos","params":["5ZvEgXMZM8TA5hw6W"]}
1  OUT   1  {"msg":"unsub","id":"P4hi9sw6NQoborLaC"}
1  IN    9  {"msg":"ready","subs":["xSw7uXy4SwdkCDXS9"]}
1  IN    0  {"msg":"removed","collection":"todos","id":"kSz9oNBos5izsM6AL"}
1  IN    0  {"msg":"removed","collection":"todos","id":"EYYr8fZvJWLBoXuMk"}
1  IN    0  {"msg":"removed","collection":"todos","id":"FTrsdR3aCzc2QpqQm"}
1  IN    0  {"msg":"removed","collection":"todos","id":"5rhu6kczXSsRXidfj"}
1  IN    1  {"msg":"removed","collection":"todos","id":"bNbaSxF7rsJXhDPDC"}
1  IN    0  {"msg":"removed","collection":"todos","id":"TkNAs64k4hKwbizH9"}
1  IN    0  {"msg":"removed","collection":"todos","id":"XTMjtXX9pqeNsWQKr"}
1  IN    0  {"msg":"nosub","id":"P4hi9sw6NQoborLaC"}
1  IN  501  {"msg":"ping"}
1  OUT   7  {"msg":"pong"}
1  OUT 11698 {"msg":"method","method":"/lists/update","params":[{"_id":"5ZvEgXMZM8TA5hw6W"},{"$set":{"name":"Stuff for Chapter 5"}},{}],"id":"6"}
1  IN    4  {"msg":"result","id":"6","result":1}
1  IN    2  {"msg":"changed","collection":"lists","id":"5ZvEgXMZM8TA5hw6W","fields":{"name":"Stuff for Chapter 5"}}
1  IN    0  {"msg":"updated","methods":["6"]}
1  OUT 6140 {"msg":"method","method":"/todos/insert","params":[{"listId":"5Zv
```

You will be able to see all the messages intended for the clients. The numbers in yellow tell you which client it was sent to/from. Messages preceded by **IN** indicate that the message was sent from the server to the client. If the message is preceded by **OUT**, this indicates the message and outbound request from the client to the server. The messages are in plain text following the color-coded texts.

With the DDP Analyzer, you can really get under the hood, seeing exactly how DDP works. You'll quickly realize how flexible and simple the protocol is, and you will gain a better understanding of what you can do with it inside your Meteor (or other) applications.

How it works...

DDP, oversimplified, is a series of messages between two end points. The messages show updates, additions, and deletions, and are transmitted over websockets. This means the messages can be sent in real time, rather than waiting for the traditional client request polling. This cuts down on traffic (chatter) and ensures that the messages are delivered as quickly as possible.

The DDP Analyzer uses the DDP protocol and listens in on the streaming conversation between your browser and the Meteor application. When you changed the port that DDP executes through using the `DDP_DEFAULT_CONNECTION_URL=` command, you rerouted your app through port `3030`. The DDP Analyzer listened on this port, proxied the connection to port `3000`, and logged all the traffic approaching it in the terminal window.

There's more...

Once you have finished, be sure to either open a new terminal window or change your environment variable back to port `3000` using the following command:

```
$ export DDP_DEFAULT_CONNECTION_URL=http://localhost:3000
```

If you don't, your application will stop working because DDP is still running through port `3030`.

See also

▶ The *Using the web console* recipe in *Chapter 1, Optimizing Your Workflow*

Using client-only collections

To truly understand how DDP works, it's helpful to try *rolling your own* as far as communicating with data over the wire is concerned. The best way to do this (and a quite helpful recipe to boot!) is to let the client continue to take advantage of the built-in Mongo collections and programmatically send updates from the server based on some simple logic. This recipe will walk you through creating a client-only collection and manipulating this collection with calls on the server side.

Getting ready

We are going to need a sample project to use as a baseline. For this baseline, we will quickly create a bookmark application. No bells and whistles, just a simple list of bookmark titles and URLs.

To do this, we first need our default template scaffolding. Please create a new project called `bookmarks` using the *Setting up your project file structure* recipe in *Chapter 1, Optimizing Your Workflow*, as your starting file structure.

We need to add and remove some Meteor packages. Start by removing the `autopublish` package. Open a terminal window, navigate to the root folder of your project, and execute the following command:

```
$ meteor remove autopublish
```

Next, let's add the `bootstrap` package. Execute the following command in your terminal window:

```
$ meteor add twbs:bootstrap
```

We will now add the HTML and JavaScript needed to create our `bookmarks` program.

Replace the contents of your `[project root]/client/main.html` file with the following:

```html
<head>
    <title>Chapter 05</title>
</head>
<body>
    {{> urls}}
</body>
<template name="urls">
    <div class="url-container">
      {{#each bookmarks}}
      <div class="bookmark panel {{selected}}">
        <div class="panel-heading">
          <button type="button" class="close"><span
          class="glyphicon glyphicon-remove"></span>
          </button>
          {{#if editing}}
            <h3 class="panel-title"><input type="text"
            value="{{title}}"></h3>
          {{else}}
          <h3 class="panel-title"> {{title}}</h3>
            {{/if}}
        </div>
        <div class="panel-body">
          {{#if src}}
            <a href="{{src}}">{{src}}</a>
          {{else}}
            <div class="input-group">
              <input type="text" class="form-control"
              placeholder="enter URL here" />
```

```
          </div>
        {{/if}}
       </div>
      </div>
     {{/each}}
     <input type="button" class="btn btn-primary" id="btnNewBM"
     value="add" />
    </div>
  </template>
```

Next, in your `[project root]/client/scripts` folder, add the following to `main.js`:

```
Meteor.subscribe('urls');
```

Then, create a `templateHelpers.js` file in the same `scripts` folder and add the following `helpers` function:

```
Template.urls.helpers({
    bookmarks: function () {
      return URLs.find();
    },
    title: function () {
      return this.title || this.src;
    },
    editing: function () {
      return Session.equals('selMark', this._id) &&
      Session.equals('editMark', this._id);
    },
    selected: function () {
      return Session.equals('selMark', this._id) ? "panel-warning"
: "panel-success";
    },
    src: function () {
        return this.src || false;
    }
});
```

In the same `templateHelpers.js` file, add the following `events` function:

```
Template.urls.events({
    'click .bookmark': function (e) {
        Session.set('selMark', this._id);
    },
    'dblclick .bookmark': function (e) {
        Session.set('editMark', this._id);
    },
    'blur .panel-title > input': function (e) {
```

```
            if (e.currentTarget.value !== this.title) {
                Meteor.call('updateTitle', this._id, e.currentTarget.
value, function (err, succ) {
                    console.log(succ);
                });
            }
            Session.set('editMark', null);
        },
        'keypress .panel-title > input': function (e) {
            if (e.keyCode == 13 && e.currentTarget.value !== this.title) {
                Meteor.call('updateTitle', this._id, e.currentTarget.
value, function (err, succ) {
                    console.log(succ);
                    Session.set('editMark', null);
                });
            }
        },
        'click #btnNewBM': function (e) {
            URLs.insert({
                title: 'new bookmark'
            });
        },
        'blur .input-group > input': function (e) {
            if (e.currentTarget.value !== this.src) {
                Meteor.call('updateSRC', this._id, e.currentTarget.value,
function (err, succ) {
                    console.log(succ);
                });
            }
        },
        'keypress .input-group > input': function (e) {
            if (e.keyCode == 13 && e.currentTarget.value !== this.src) {
                Meteor.call('updateSRC', this._id, e.currentTarget.value,
function (err, succ) {
                    console.log(succ);
                });
            }
        },
        'click .close': function (e) {
            Meteor.call('removeBM', this._id, function (err, succ) {

            });
        }
    });
```

Now, we need a bit of styling. Open the `style.css` file found in your `[project root]/libs/styles` folder and replace the existing styles with the following:

```css
/* CSS declarations go here */
body {
    font-size:1.5rem;
}

.url-container{
    background-color: rgb(255, 255, 255);
    border-color: rgb(221, 221, 221);
    border-width: 1px;
    border-radius: 4px 4px 0 0;
    -webkit-box-shadow: none;
    box-shadow: none;
    position: relative;
    padding: 45px 15px 15px;
    margin: 20px;
    margin-left:auto;
    margin-right:auto;
    max-width: 90%;
    border-style:solid;
}

.input-group {
    width:90%;
}
```

We need to declare our URLs collection, so create a `collections.js` file in your `[project root]/both` folder and add the following `Mongo.Collection` declaration and `String.prototype` function:

```js
URLs = new Mongo.Collection("urls");

if (typeof String.prototype.startsWith != 'function') {
    String.prototype.startsWith = function (str){
        return this.slice(0, str.length) == str;
    };
}
```

Finally, we add some server logic. Open `[project root]/server/server.js` and replace any existing code with the following:

```
Meteor.publish('urls',function(){
    return URLs.find();
});


Meteor.methods({
    updateTitle: function(id,title){
        var bmark = URLs.findOne(id);
        if (!bmark) return;
        if (title&& title!==bmark.title){
            URLs.update(id,{$set:{title:title}});

            return "updated";
        }
        return "same title";
    },
    updateSRC: function(id,src){
        var bmark = URLs.findOne(id);
        if (!bmark) return;
        if (src&& src!==bmark.src){

            //Adding the http if it doesn't already have it...
            src = src.startsWith('http')? src: 'http://'+src;
            URLs.update(id,{$set:{src:src}});

            return "updated";
        }
        return "same src";
    },
    removeBM: function(id){
        URLs.remove(id);
        return "removed";
    }
});
```

Save all your changes, start up your `meteor` instance, and navigate to your project in a browser (usually `http://localhost:3000`). If everything went correctly, you will now have a working `bookmarks` app, where you can add URLs and (by double-clicking) add/change the titles for the bookmarks. The following screenshot is a sample of how the browser will look when it is complete:

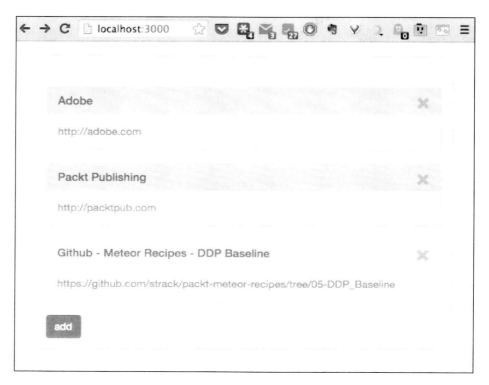

How to do it...

We are going to add a counter at the bottom of our `bookmarks` page. This counter will tell us how many secure and non-secure links we have (determined by whether the link starts with `https`).

1. First, we will add the client-only collection called `bmcounts` and subscribe to it. If we declare the collection anywhere in the `clients` folder, the server will not be able see it. Hence, it will be a client-only collection. Open the `main.js` file in your client `scripts` folder (`[project root]/client/scripts/main.js`) and add the following two lines around the existing `Meteor.subscribe('urls')` command, as follows:

```
BMCounts = new Mongo.Collection("bmcounts");
Meteor.subscribe('urls');
Meteor.subscribe('bmcounts', new Mongo.ObjectID());
```

2. While we are in the `scripts` folder, let's open the `templateHelpers.js` file and add the reactive `Template.helpers` function which we'll need to display the counts. Add the following function to the bottom of the file:

```
Template.linkcount.helpers({
    BMCount: function(){
        return BMCounts.findOne();
    }
});
```

3. Now let's add the HTML template. Open `main.html`, found in your `client` folder, and add the following code around the `<body>` tag:

```
<body>
    {{> urls}}
    {{> linkcount}}
</body>
<template name="linkcount">
    {{#with BMCount}}
    <div id="counts">
        <button class="btn btn-lg btn-info">
            <span class="glyphicon glyphicon-link"></span>
            {{unsecureCount}} /
            <span class="glyphicon glyphicon-lock"></span>
            {{secureCount}}
        </button>
    </div>
    {{/with}}
</template>
```

4. We'll pretty up our counter a bit with some CSS as well. Open your `style.css` file, found in your `lib/styles` director, and add the following CSS declaration:

```
#counts{
    position:relative;
    float:right;
    margin-right:50px;
}
```

5. We have some real work to do now on the server side. We need to count and sort the bookmarks as they are added, removed, or changed. Open your `server.js` file, found in your `server` folder, and add the following `Meteor.publish` function:

```
Meteor.publish('bmcounts', function (id) {
    var self = this;
    var count = 0;
    var secCount = 0;
    var initializing = true;
```

```
        var handle = URLs.find().observeChanges({
          //TODO: Added
          //TODO: Removed
          //TODO: Changed
        });
        initializing = false;
        self.added("bmcounts", id, {
          unsecureCount: count,
          secureCount: secCount
        });
        self.ready();
        self.onStop(function () {
          handle.stop();
        });
    });
```

6. Inside the preceding code block, we have three TODO comments. We first need to create the added listener. Directly under the //TODO: Added comment, add the following code:

```
//TODO: Added
added: function (idx, doc) {
  if (doc.src && doc.src.toLowerCase().startsWith('https')) {
    secCount++;
    if (!initializing)
      self.changed("bmcounts", id, {
        secureCount: secCount
      });
  } else {
    count++;
    if (!initializing)
      self.changed("bmcounts", id, {
        unsecureCount: count
      });
  }
},
```

7. Next is the removed listener. Directly under the //TODO: Removed comment, add the following code:

```
//TODO: Removed
removed: function (idx, doc) {
    //really inefficient...
    var bms = URLs.find().fetch();
    secCount = _.filter(bms,function(bm){
      return bm.src && bm.src.toLowerCase().startsWith('https');
```

```
    }).length;
    count = bms.length - secCount;
    self.changed("bmcounts", id, {
      unsecureCount: count,
      secureCount: secCount
    });

  },
```

8. Finally, the `changed` listener. Add the following code directly under the `//TODO:
   Changed` comment:

```
//TODO: Changed
changed: function (idx, doc) {
  if (doc.src && doc.src.toLowerCase().startsWith('https')) {
    secCount++;
    count--;
    self.changed("bmcounts", id, {
      unsecureCount: count,
      secureCount: secCount
    });
  }
}
}
```

9. Save all your changes, start your `meteor` instance if it isn't already started, and
   navigate to your project in a browser (usually `http://localhost:3000`). You
   should see a small information button at the bottom-right corner of your screen with a
   count of secure and non-secure links. Add some new links, delete others, and watch
   the count change instantly in your browser, similar to the following screenshot:

How it works...

All of the client-side code we just added is exactly the same as it would be for a regular Mongo collection. As far as the client is concerned, everything is normal.

On the server, however, we'd need to manually update the DDP stream with the `.added` and `.changed` messages, based on the changes made to the `URLs` collection.

To accomplish this, we start by using the function passed as an argument in the `Meteor.publish()` function arguments:

```
Meteor.publish('bmcounts', function (id) {
   ...
});
```

This function is rerun every time a client subscribes to the DDP stream. Inside the function, we create a `handle` using the `Mongo.Cursor.observeChanges()` function:

```
var handle = URLs.find().observeChanges({
   ...
});
```

Inside the `observeChanges` function, if a document is added (except when initializing), we check whether the `src` property begins with `https` to see whether we can increment the `secCount` (secure count) variable; otherwise, we'll just increment the normal `count` variable.

If a document is removed, we have to do a bit of trickery, but we will recalculate the `secCount` and `count` variables.

If a document's `src` variable is changed, we will perform the same check as we did in `added` and move the increment from `count` to `secCount`.

These three situations will happen as the `URLs` collection changes in real time. Therefore, after each change, we will call the `self.changed()` function, which sends a message to the client via DDP, mimicking the automatic change messages that would be sent if we were modifying the `bmcounts` collection normally.

You will notice that the `bmcounts` collection is never used on the server. Instead, we send messages to the client through the `"bmcounts"` subscription channel, as in the following example:

```
self.changed("bmcounts", id, {
   ...
});
```

This is an important distinction. The client does not subscribe to the actual MondoDB collection. Instead, it subscribes to a DDP messaging channel. In this case, we're letting the client do the heavy lifting for us by sending the "bmcounts" subscription messages into the bmcount client-only collection. In essence, the server is sending data changes over the wire, and the client, being none the wiser, is treating the messages as actual data changes.

The rest of the method is cleanup for when a client unsubscribes, using handle.stop() to complete the initialization. It includes making a self.added() call, which does the same thing as a self.changed() call (mimics a data change and sends it over the wire to the subscribed clients). The final step in initialization is to call self.ready(), which lets the subscribed client know that all the initial data changes have been sent.

See also

> ▸ The *Implementing a partial collection* recipe in *Chapter 4, Creating Models*
> ▸ The *Basic safety – turning off autopublish* recipe in *Chapter 9, Securing Your Application*

Implementing multiserver DDP

The fun doesn't stop with a single client and server DDP connection. Oh no! Indeed, Meteor has invited everybody to the DDP party, and in this recipe, we're going to see how two Meteor servers can speak to each other using DDP.

Getting ready

We will be using the code base from the *Using client-only collections* recipe, found in this chapter. Please create an instance of this project and start your meteor server.

For this project, we will change the color of the bookmark titles, based on whether the links are secure or not; so we need to make one change to our first project to make the color dependent on the secType property (which we will create in this recipe). Open the templateHelpers.js file, found in the [project root]/client/scripts folder of the first project. Locate the Template.urls.helpers section and make the following change to the selected function:

```
Template.urls.helpers({
    ...
    selected: function () {
        return Session.equals('selMark', this._id) ? "panel-warning" :
this.secType;
    },
    ...
```

As we will be implementing another Meteor server instance, we will also need to create a new Meteor project. In a terminal window, navigate to a location outside your root project folder, and enter the following commands in the terminal window:

```
$ meteor create typecheck
$ cd typecheck
$ meteor remove autopublish
$ meteor --port 3030
```

This will properly initialize our second server instance and start it up on port `3030`.

We're now ready to get our second Meteor project talking to our first project!

How to do it...

We're going to change the color of the bookmark titles using a new bookmark property called `secType`. Our new (second) project will check bookmarks as they come across the DDP wire and add a `secType` property if needed. Let's get started.

1. First, we will want to make use of the `String.startsWith()` function we're familiar with from the *Using client-only collections* recipe. Add the following prototype modifier to the bottom of the `typecheck.js` file, found in your second project's root folder:

   ```
   if (typeof String.prototype.startsWith != 'function') {
       String.prototype.startsWith = function (str){
           return this.slice(0, str.length) == str;
       };
   }
   ```

2. Now, we want to create a server-only file so that we can concentrate on the task at hand. Create a `server` folder in your project root and then create and open a file named `DDPChecker.js` for editing.

3. In the `DDPChecker.js` file, add the following code to connect and subscribe to the `urls` collection from our first project:

   ```
   conn = DDP.connect("http://localhost:3000");
   URLs = new Mongo.Collection("urls",conn);
   conn.subscribe("urls");
   ```

4. Now, we create a function that checks a record to see whether the `secType` variable has been set or not. If it hasn't and if there's an `src` property to check, it will update the record with the appropriate `secType` variable. Add the following function to the bottom of `DDPChecker.js`:

   ```
   function checkSecType(idx,doc){
       if (!doc.src || doc.secType)
           return;
   ```

```
            if (doc.src.toLowerCase().startsWith('https'))
                doc.secType = 'panel-success';
            else
                doc.secType = 'panel-danger';
            URLs.update(idx,doc);
        }
```

5. The last piece of the puzzle is to add a call to the `checkSecType` function we just created, whenever a record is added or changed. We do this by calling the `observeChanges` function and the `URLs.find()` cursor. Add the following code to the bottom of `DDPChecker.js`:

```
URLs.find().observeChanges({
    added:checkSecType,
    changed:checkSecType
});
```

6. Open a browser and navigate to your project (usually `http://localhost:3000`). The colors of each bookmark should correspond to the security types of the bookmark links, similar to the following screenshot:

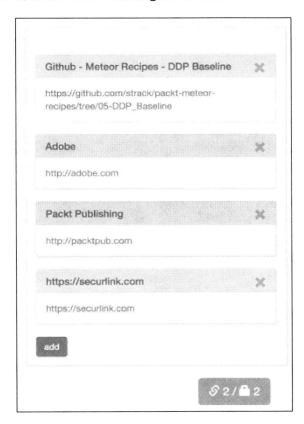

How it works...

Inside our second project, we are declaring the `URLs` collection and subscribing to changes just like we would in a normal `client` app. The difference here is that we're establishing a connection to an existing Meteor server, using the `DDP.Connect()` function:

```
conn = DDP.connect("http://localhost:3000");
URLs = new Mongo.Collection("urls",conn);
```

We passed the handle to this connection as an argument, called `conn`, when we declared our `URLs` collection. This tells Meteor that we're interested in the collection (more accurately, the DDP messages) coming from our first server.

To avoid redundant code, we created the `checkSecType` function, which listens to the changes made to the `URLs` collection and sets the `secType` property to correspond with the security type of the `src` property. We then use the `checkSecType` function as the event handler for both `added` and `changed` events coming through the DDP wire via `observeChanges`.

There's more...

Using DDP as a client isn't unique to Meteor. You can use DDP with nearly any technology. You'll see an example in the *Integrating DDP with other technologies* recipe, found later in this chapter.

See also

▶ The *Implementing a partial collection* recipe in *Chapter 4, Creating Models*
▶ The *Integrating DDP with other technologies* recipe in this chapter

Integrating DDP with other technologies

The party never stops with DDP! DDP libraries are available for most major programming languages and platforms, and you can very quickly get your client, server, or even hardware devices talking to your Meteor server without much effort. This recipe will show you how to connect to a Meteor server using DDP from a `Node.js` program.

Getting ready

We'll want to use the code base from the *Using client-only collections* recipe, found in this chapter. Please create an instance of that project and start your `meteor` server.

You will need Node and npm installed to complete this recipe. They are installed with Meteor by default. However, if you need instructions on how to install Node.js and npm, they can be found on the following websites:

- Node—http://nodejs.org
- NPM—https://www.npmjs.com/

We will also need to make sure that the ddp npm module is installed. Open a terminal window and execute the following command:

```
$ npm -g install ddp
```

 When installing npm modules globally, you may need to use the sudo command, similar to the following command:
```
$ sudo npm -g install ...
```

How to do it...

We will create a Node service that will check the src properties for records in our URLs collection to make sure they're secure (HTTPS). If they aren't secure, the Node service will call our Meteor updateSRC method and change the src properties to be secure. To integrate DDP with other technologies, perform the following steps:

1. We first create the project folder. In a terminal window, create a nodecheck folder and cd to this directory, and add the ddp npm module by executing the following commands:

   ```
   $ mkdir nodecheck
   $ cd nodecheck
   $ npm install ddp
   ```

2. We now want to create our service. Create a file in the nodecheck directory named main.js. Open it for editing and declare the DDP connection by adding the following code:

   ```
   var DDPClient = require("ddp");

   var ddpclient = new DDPClient({
       host: "localhost",
       port: 3000,
       path: "websocket",
       ssl: false,
       autoReconnect: true,
       autoReconnectTimer: 500,
   ```

```
            maintainCollections: true,
            ddpVersion: '1'
    });
```

3. We now want to connect to our Meteor server using the `.connect()` function and display the result of a successful subscription in the console window. Append the following code to `main.js`:

```
ddpclient.connect(function (error) {
        if (error) {
            console.log(error);
        } else console.log('successful connection');

        ddpclient.subscribe('urls', [], function () {
            var urls = Object.keys(ddpclient.collections.urls);
            console.log(urls);
        })
});
```

4. Finally, we will listen to the messages coming across the DDP wire using the `.on()` function. We will check all the `added` and `changed` messages and replace the URL with a secure URL where needed, using the `.call()` function to invoke the remote Meteor server `updateSRC` method. Append the following code to `main.js`:

```
ddpclient.on('message', function (msg) {
        var message = ddpclient.EJSON.parse(msg);
        switch (message.msg) {
        case "added":
        case "changed":
            var url = message.fields.src;
            if (url) {
                if (!url.startsWith('https')) {
                    message.fields.src = url.replace('http:',
'https:');

                    ddpclient.call('updateSRC',
                        [message.id, message.fields.src],
                        function (err, success) {
                            if (!err) console.log(success);
                        })
                }
            }
            break;
        default:
            break;
        }
});
if (typeof String.prototype.startsWith != 'function') {
```

```
    String.prototype.startsWith = function (str) {
        return this.slice(0, str.length) == str;
    };
}
```

Okay, we're now ready to run our Node service. Save all your changes, and make sure you have an instance of your original Meteor project open in a browser (usually `http://localhost:3000`) so that you can see the changes. They'll happen quickly, so don't blink!

5. In a terminal window, navigate to your `nodecheck` folder and enter the following command:

   $ node main.js

   In your web browser, every link that was previously using `http` will now be using `https`. If you add another link and intentionally try to enter the link as `http`, the running node service will immediately change it to `https`. If you look in the terminal window where you ran the node `main.js` command, you'll see the word **updated** for every converted link and your web browser will look something like the following screenshot:

How it works...

The Meteor server is listening for client subscription requests using DDP. Since we are using a DDP `client` library built for Node (using the `ddp` npm module), we are able to declare our connection using the new `DDPClient()` function, connect and subscribe to the `urls` channel, and monitor all messages coming through DDP using the `.on()` function:

```
var ddpclient = new DDPClient({
  host: "localhost",
  port: 3000,
  ...
});
ddpclient.connect(function (error) {
  ...
  ddpclient.subscribe('urls', ... );
  ...
});
ddpclient.on('message', function (msg) {
  ...
});
```

Finally, if we want to make a modification, we can do so by invoking the Meteor server's remote `methods` using the `.call()` function:

```
ddpclient.call('updateSRC', ... );
```

You'll notice that we had to do nothing on the Meteor server side to get this to work. That's the beauty of DDP; the protocol is the same for any compatible DDP library. As long as both systems are using the DDP protocol, the languages, hardware, and operating systems of the systems are immaterial and don't affect communications between the servers.

As you can tell, the DDP protocol is quite powerful because it's simple and clean. There are many other aspects to DDP, for which you will want to consult the Meteor and the corresponding GitHub documentation.

There's more...

You can see a fairly up-to-date list of available DDP clients by visiting Meteoropedia at http://www.meteorpedia.com/read/DDP_Clients.

See also

- ▶ The *Using client-only collections* and *Implementing multiserver DDP* recipes in this chapter

6

Mastering Reactivity

In this chapter, you will learn the following topics:

- ▶ Creating and consuming a reactive value
- ▶ Using Ajax query results in ReactiveVar
- ▶ Making a custom library reactive
- ▶ Updating Blaze templates without Mongo
- ▶ Using inline data to modify UI elements reactively
- ▶ Integrating the jQuery UI

Introduction

Reactive programming is an emerging development methodology, where changes to data automatically trigger changes to the rest of the system. This allows you, the developer, to write code declaratively and let the reactive elements manage any changes. Meteor is, perhaps, the best and most fully developed implementation of reactive programming available today. By understanding the core concepts of reactive programming, you can use the `Tracker` (formerly `Deps`) library to create simple, declarative code while avoiding the usual pitfalls associated with reactive and asynchronous JavaScript programming. The recipes in this chapter will give you simple, clear examples of how the major components of Meteor's reactive model work.

Creating and consuming a reactive value

`Tracker`, simply put, is Meteor's variable tracking system. It is used to manage reactive values, data structures, and computations (functions that consume reactive values). This recipe will show you how to create reactive values, and perform computations on those values, using `Tracker.autorun()`. In other words, it will teach you how reactive programming works inside Meteor. This recipe will come in handy as a foundation for more complex functionalities.

Getting ready

For the sake of simplicity, we will be using a default Meteor project, with the `reactive-var` package added to it. Open a terminal window, navigate to where you would like to create your root project, and execute the following commands:

```
$ meteor create reactiverecipes
$ cd reactiverecipes
$ meteor add reactive-var
$ meteor
```

You are now ready to start using reactive variables.

How to do it...

We are going to modify the text of a button, based on a reactive variable; so we will need to create the button and hook up the reactive context.

1. Open your project in your favorite text editor and edit the `reactiverecipes.html` file, adding an ID to the `<button>` element, as shown in the following example:

    ```html
    <button id='btnReact'>Click Me</button>
    ```

2. Now, open `reactiverecipes.js` and add the following lines of code just below the `if (Meteor.isClient)` condition:

    ```js
    if (Meteor.isClient) {
        btnText = new ReactiveVar('Click Me');
        Tracker.autorun(function () {
            $('#btnReact').text(btnText.get());
        });
    ```

3. Finally, add the following line inside the `Template.hello.events` declaration, just below the `Session.set()` function in the `'click button'` function:

    ```js
    Session.set("counter"...);
    btnText.set('Again!');
    ```

4. Save your changes and navigate to `http://localhost:3000` in a browser. Once there, click on the button labeled **Click Me** and watch the text change to **Again!**:

You can manually change the value of the button text by opening a console window in your browser and using the `btnText.set()` command, as shown in the following example:

```
> btnText.set('Pretty please...')
```

The button text will change to whatever value you set it to, instantly.

How it works...

The preceding example seems oversimplified, but we have two things to say about that.

First, it's simple because Meteor was built to make your code very simple and easy to follow. This makes your development and debug efforts significantly less time consuming.

Notice how the process of declaring a reactive variable is made up of one line of code. When we added the `btnText = new ReactiveVar('Click Me')` statement, we were simply declaring a variable (and initializing its value to `'Click Me'`), but we know by the declaration that it is a reactive variable.

Next, we encapsulated an extremely straightforward jQuery statement inside a `Tracker.autorun()` block. This block is called a **reactive computation**. Reactive computations run once initially and then rerun (are recomputed) whenever a change is made to any reactive variables contained inside. So, in this example, we told `Tracker` to monitor the value of `btnText`(a reactive variable) and automatically run (hence the term `autorun`) the code block again when it would change.

Notice that we don't have to worry about any time conditions, such as "is this the first run?" or "okay, when there's a change...." We just simply declare the jQuery statement and let `Tracker` figure out the timing for us.

This is what the term **transparent reactive programming** means. There is one set of code for the initialization and another set of code for changes. Besides the variable declarations, your entire code base can be written as normal, plain old JavaScript.

Second, what it's doing under the hood is anything but simple! To create this frontend simplicity for you, the programmer, Meteor implements reactive providers and reactive computations.

We'll sacrifice a bit of fidelity to make the concept simpler to understand. When `Tracker.autorun` is called, it does four things:

- It creates a computation
- It sets `Tracker.currentComputation` to that computation
- It calls the function that was passed to it
- It sets `Tracker.currentComputation` to `null`

A computation is essentially an event handler function and contains a reference to the function that was passed to `Tracker.autorun`. The event that the computation is waiting for is a call to the `computation.invalidate` method. When the `invalidate` method is called, the computation reruns the function it contains.

Now we come to the function. The function passed to `Tracker.autorun` is considered a reactive function if it contains **reactive providers**. A reactive provider is an object that has functions to get and set some value, and keeps track of dependencies. When the `get` function is called, it does three things:

1. It checks to see whether `Tracker.currentComputation` has a value.
2. If it does, the computation is added to an internal list.
3. It returns the value of the variable that the getter requested.

Both steps 1 and 2 are performed by making a call to `depend()`, which is a method found on a dependency object. The `reactive-var` library automates this part, so you don't have to call the `depend()` method directly. All you have to do is use the reactive variable!

Likewise, when the `set` function is called, it does two things:

- It changes the value of the internal variable
- For every computation in the internal list, the `invalidate()` method is called

The `invalidate()` methods are called in a loop by making a call to `changed()`, which is a `helper` method found on a dependency object. Again, `reactive-var` takes care of this for you. You're welcome!

When each computation is invalidated, it reruns the function that it contains. And the entire loop starts over with the newly rerun function calling the getters, which return their values (like the `text` value of our `btnReact` button) and add the computations to the provider's internal list, waiting once again for the setter to be called.

Even though they are extremely oversimplified (any core MDG members reading this are probably spitting coffee right now...), here is what the `ReactiveVar` and `autorun` objects do:

```
function ReactiveVar(value) {
    // create the dependency object (a helper class)
    var _dependency = new Tracker.Dependency;
    //set the default internal value
    var _internalVal = value;

    var getValue = function () {
        // call depend(), which adds the computation
        _dependency.depend();
        // return the internal value
        return _internalVal;
    };

    var setValue = function (newValue) {
        // update the internal value
        _internalVal = newValue;
        // loop through computations and call invalidate()
        _dependency.changed();
    };

    return this;
}


function autorun(func) {
    // creates computation and assigns it to
    // Tracker.currentComputation
    var computation = new Tracker.Computation(func, Tracker.
currentComputation);

    // Calls the onInvalidate method the first time,
    // so that func function will run
    Tracker.onInvalidate({...});

    return computation;
}
```

There are two things that we left out, for clarity, but are important in order to have a complete understanding. First, the `depend()` helper method also sets up an `onInvalidate()` listener, which removes the computation from the reactive provider's internal list. Second, computations are checked to see whether they already exist in an internal list before they are added.

Why are the computations removed when the computation is invalidated, you may ask? The answer, in short, is that it makes the entire computation `add-execute-remove` loop very elegant. It keeps all the computations up to date and the dependent functions only run once each, no matter how many times a getter is called inside the same function. If they weren't removed, the functions would be run multiple times, which is *no bueno*.

So let's review what we did in this recipe:

▶ The `autorun` method creates a computation and passes your function to this computation

▶ The computation has an `onInvalidate` method that, among other things, runs your function

▶ After `autorun` has created a computation, it runs your function once, using the `onInvalidate` method

▶ Your function has reactive variables in it, which have to-do lists

▶ As your function runs, getters are called, which add the computations to the to-do lists

▶ Setters are also called, which execute the to-do lists and clear them

▶ Because your functions in the to-do lists have reactive variables, the process is repeated (the functions are rerun)

▶ Lather, rinse, and repeat

Again, this explanation is drastically simplified, and therefore, pretty inaccurate; however, conceptually, it will hopefully give you a good understanding of what's happening under the hood.

There's more...

Meteor also provides the `ReactiveDict` object, which runs exactly like `ReactiveVar`, but can store collections of reactive variables in key-value pairs. The syntax is exactly the same as for `ReactiveVar`, but you will need to add a key to the `set` and `get` methods, as shown in the following code:

```
btnText.get(); // ReactiveVar
txtFields.get('btnText'); // ReactiveDict
...
btnText.set('Click Me'); // ReactiveVar
txtFields.set('btnText','Click Me') // ReactiveDict
```

To use `ReactiveDict`, simply add the `reactive-dict` package using the following terminal command:

```
$ meteor add reactive-dict
```

Lastly, you don't have to use `ReactiveVar`, or `ReactiveDict`, and can instead *roll your own* reactive providers. Please see the *Making a custom library reactive* recipe found in this chapter as an example.

See also

- ▸ The *Creating dynamic lists* recipe in *Chapter 3, Building Great User Interfaces*
- ▸ The *Making a custom library reactive* recipe in this chapter

Using Ajax query results in ReactiveVar

Whenever we use Ajax, requesting (and even receiving) data is pretty easy. The complications come in when we have to update the UI with new or updated data. With Meteor's reactive programming capabilities, this is no longer an issue. In this recipe, you will see how to update your UI with Ajax results, using Meteor's `ReactiveVar` library.

Getting ready

To get up and run quickly, we will use a default Meteor project with a few packages added. Open a terminal window, navigate to where you would like to create your root project, and execute the following commands:

```
$ meteor create ajaxreactive
$ cd ajaxreactive
$ meteor add reactive-var
$ meteor add http
$ meteor add twbs:bootstrap
$ meteor
```

We are now ready to build a reactive Ajax query!

How to do it...

We will be pulling the weather data from `openweathermap.org`, using their free (but for testing only) API. We will take the results from our `openweathermap.org` queries and put them into a `ReactiveVar` library so that they can then be consumed reactively by our Blaze templates.

Let's start by modifying the UI:

1. Open `ajaxreactive.html` and add a call to our soon-to-be-created `weather` template, just under the call to the existing `hello` template, as shown in the following code:

```
{{> hello}}
{{> weather}}
```

2. We will also want to repurpose the counter in our `hello` template to tell us what the starting longitude will be. Change the description in the `<p>` element inside the `hello` template, as follows:

```
<template name="hello">
    <button>Click Me</button>
    <p>You are starting at {{counter}} longitude.</p>
</template>
```

3. Next, add our `weather` template, which is just a simple table with a bit of prettiness added, thanks to bootstrap! At the bottom of `ajaxreactive.html`, add the following template:

```
<template name="weather">
    {{#if reports}}
    <table class="table">
        <thead>
            <th>name</th>
            <th>weather</th>
            <th>temp</th>
            <th>humidity</th>
        </thead>
        <tbody>
    {{#each reports}}
            <tr class={{severity}}>
                <td>{{name}}</td>
                <td>{{description}}</td>
                <td>{{temp}}</td>
                <td>{{humidity}}</td>
            </tr>
    {{/each}}
        </tbody>
    </table>
    {{/if}}
</template>
```

4. Save your changes and navigate to `http://localhost:3000`. While nothing (except the description of the counter) will change, we will very soon want to view our weather data.

5. Let's open `ajaxreactive.js` and declare our `ReactiveVar` libraries. Just below `Session.setDefault()`, add the following code:

```
Session.setDefault("counter", 0);
weatherlist = new ReactiveVar;
```

6. We will now modify the `'click button'` function to increment the counter and make our Ajax call. Locate the function inside the `Template.hello.events` section and modify the code as follows:

```
// increment the counter when button is clicked
if (Session.get("counter") <= 60)
    Session.set("counter", Session.get("counter") + 4);
else
    Session.set("counter", 0)

getWeather();
```

 Don't forget to update the counter increment to 4; otherwise, your `weather` data won't change much as you click.

7. Next, we need to add `Template.weather.helpers` so that our UI will populate properly. Just after the `Template.hello.events` section, add the following:

```
Template.weather.helpers({
    reports: function () {
        if (!weatherlist) return false;
        return weatherlist.get();
    },
    severity: function () {
        if (this.weather && this.weather[0].main == "Clear")
            return "success";
        else
            return "warning";
    },
    description: function () {
        if (this.weather && this.weather[0])
            return this.weather[0].description;
        else
            return "";
    },
```

```
        temp: function () {
            if (this.main)
                return this.main.temp;
            else
                return "";
        },
        humidity: function () {
            if (this.main)
                return this.main.humidity;
            else
                return "";
        }
});
```

8. Finally, we need to add our Ajax call and the asynchronous callback function once the result comes in. Just after the `Template.weather.helpers` section, add the following two functions:

```
function getWeather() {
    var long1 = +Session.get("counter"),
        long2 = long1+5;
    HTTP.get("http://api.openweathermap.org/data/2.5/
    box/city?bbox=12,"+long1+",15,"+long2+",10&cluster=yes",
    harvestWeather);
}
function harvestWeather(error, data) {
    if (data && data.content) {
        var weather = EJSON.parse(data.content);
        weatherlist.set(weather.list);
    }
}
```

9. Save all your changes and click on the button on the project page in your browser. You should see something similar to the following screenshot:

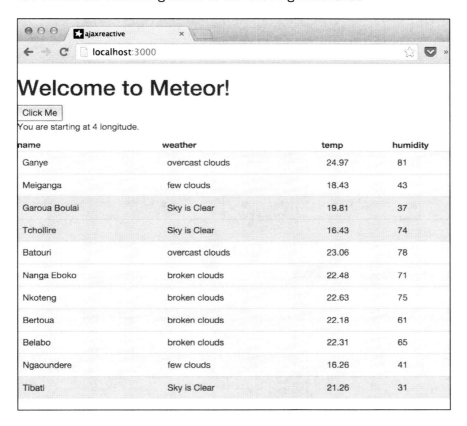

As you click, the weather results for a given area, moving towards north, will be displayed.

How it works...

In this instance, we didn't use a Mongo collection, which is automatically reactive. Instead, we made calls to openweather.org api and updated a ReactiveVar library (in this case, the weatherList variable) using the set method. Because the template helpers rely on a call to the get method of that same ReactiveVar, they are automatically rerun when the ReactiveVar is updated. Let's break it down.

We first created the `weather` template in our HTML:

```
<template name="weather">
  {{#if reports}}
  ...
  {{/if}}
</template>
```

The template iterates over the `reports` helper object using an `{{#each...}}` block, populating an HTML table with the results.

Next, inside our client-side JavaScript, we declared our reactive variable, `weatherlist`, using a new `ReactiveVar` library:

```
weatherlist = new ReactiveVar;
```

We then used `weatherlist.get()` in our `reports` helper object, which is in `Template.weather.helpers`:

```
reports: function () {
  ...
  return weatherlist.get();
}
```

By using it here, we set up a dependency so that anytime `weatherlist.set()` is called, the data for the template is refreshed and the template is updated/rerun.

Finally, we hooked up our button to an Ajax call using `HTTP.get()`, and we passed the `harvestWeather` function as a callback (`HTTP.get(url,arg,callback)`):

```
function getWeather() {
  var long1 = ...
  HTTP.get("...", harvestWeather);
}
```

Once the callback is triggered, it massages the data from the Ajax call and repopulates our reactive variable using `weatherlist.set()`:

```
function harvestWeather(error, data) {
  ...
    weatherlist.set(weather.list);
}
```

As mentioned in the preceding section, when this `set` function is called, it invalidates the template functions and reactively updates our UI.

You can see very clearly in the callback function (`harvestWeather`), and in the weather template helper function (`reports`), that the calls are regular, plain JavaScript. We're literally just calling a `get` or `set` function. Because the object we're calling those functions on is a `ReactiveVar`, all the reactive dependencies and UI updates are handled for us.

You can begin to quickly see how powerful Meteor's reactive programming model is. Instead of messing around with events and handlers or worrying about callback hell, we used a simple, clean `set` command and let Meteor handle all the details for us.

See also

- ▸ The *Creating dynamic lists* recipe in *Chapter 3*, *Building Great User Interfaces*
- ▸ The *Creating and consuming a reactive value* recipe in this chapter

Making a custom library reactive

Because we so often deal with variables and data, it can go unnoticed that Meteor's reactivity doesn't only work with reactive values. Any function from any JavaScript library can be turned into a reactive provider. This recipe will show you how to create your own reactive providers using the `Tracker.depend()` and `Tracker.changed()` commands.

Getting ready

To keep the example simple, we will use a default Meteor project, with a `bootstrap` package, and a random color generator. Open a terminal window, navigate to where you would like to create your root project, and execute the following commands:

```
$ meteor create customreactive
$ cd customreactive
$ meteor add twbs:bootstrap
$ meteor add rzymek:randomcolor
$ meteor
```

How to do it...

Let's pretend you have a (pretty awesome) library called `colorsaurus`. Your `colorsaurus` object likes to roar. A lot. Mostly because "rawr" means "I love you" in dinosaur, but also because the colorsaurus wants to share as many random colors as possible with all his friends. Whenever you ask this motley beast for a color, he instantly gives you a random color. This is obviously the most useful library ever written, so let's get to work building it!

1. Open `customreactive.js` and add the following `colorsaurus` object just below the `Template` declarations, inside the `Meteor.isClient` conditional:

```
colorsaurus = {
    color: function(){
        return randomColor();
    },
    rainbowRoar: function (){
        console.log('rawr');
    }
};
```

2. While we're in `customreactive.js`, let's add the `numcolor` helper function. Locate the `Template.hello.helpers` method and add the following to the top of the method:

```
Template.hello.helpers({
  numcolor: function(){
    return colorsaurus.color();
  },
  counter: ...
});
```

3. Save your changes, navigate to `http://localhost:3000`, and in the console window, type the following commands:

   `> colorsaurus.color()`

   `> colorsaurus.rainbowRoar()`

4. You should get a random color and a nice, short *I love you* from our friend, the `colorsaurus` function:

```
> colorsaurus.color()
< "#4dd666"
> colorsaurus.rainbowRoar()
  rawr
```

5. It's not reactive yet, but we need to prepare our UI first, for all the awesomeness that a reactive `colorsaurus` function can unleash. Open `customreactive.html` and make the following modifications to the `hello` template:

```
<button id='btnColor'>Click Me</button>
<p style="color:{{numcolor}}">You've pressed the button
{{counter}} times.</p>
```

6. We now need to change our `click` event to make `colorsaurus` roar. In `customreactive.js`, modify the `Template.hello.events` section as follows:

```
Template.hello.events({
    'click button': function () {
      // increment the counter when button is clicked
      Session.set("counter", Session.get("counter") + 1);
      colorsaurus.rainbowRoar();
    }
});
```

7. All that's left to do is make `colorsaurus` reactive and set up an `autorun` function. Open `customreactive.js` again and add the following reactive statements, including adding the `Tracker.Depenency` object:

```
var colorDep = new Tracker.Dependency;

colorsaurus = {
    color: function(){
        colorDep.depend();
        return randomColor();
    },
    rainbowRoar: function (){
        console.log('rawr');
        colorDep.changed();
    }
};
```

8. Now, add a `Tracker.autorun` function, immediately after the `colorsaurus` code block, as shown in the following code:

```
Tracker.autorun(function(){
    $('#btnColor').css('background-color' , colorsaurus.color());
    $('body').css('background-color', colorsaurus.color());
});
```

9. Save your changes, go to your browser, and click on the button as many times as your little 'colorsaurus-lovin' heart wishes. You'll get some really great color combinations, as shown in the following screenshot:

How it works...

Notice how the button, text, and the page background change, and they all change to random, separate colors. That's because we used a reactive library function that returns a random color each time it is called instead of returning a set variable.

By having our `color()` function return the result of `randomColor()`, we are ensuring that every time `colorsaurus.color()` is called, we get a different result.

We added `colorDep.depend()` to the returning function, which logs the computations that are created by either `Tracker.autorun` or by a reactive template (see the *Creating and consuming a reactive value* recipe found in this chapter for a full explanation).

Finally, we called `colorDep.changed()`, which runs the logged computations.

Every part of the code is separate from—and therefore not dependent on—the other code parts or libraries. Through the `Tracker.Dependency` object, Meteor keeps track of everything for us so we can add or remove reactive dependencies at will. Try, for example, running the following line in your browser console:

```
> Tracker.autorun(function(){console.log(colorsaurus.color());});
```

Now, every time you click the button on the page, you get yet another random color from the `colorsaurus`, printed to your console:

```
rawr
#5a2ea5
rawr
#bf05a9
rawr
#ffcceb
rawr
#ed9aa3
rawr
#f7ff16
```

This is reactive programming at its very best. Rawr!

See also

▶ The *Using reactivity with HTML attributes* recipe in *Chapter 3, Building Great User Interfaces*

▶ The *Creating and consuming a reactive value* recipe in this chapter

Updating Blaze templates without Mongo

Not everything in our UI has to be dependent on Mongo collections. We can, in fact, use pretty much any reactive object inside our templates, and changes will appear instantly. This recipe will quickly show you how to use custom collections to populate and update UI templates.

Getting ready

Let's start with a base Meteor project and add the `bootstrap` and `reactive-var` packages. In a terminal window, navigate to where you would like your project to reside and enter the following commands:

```
$ meteor create mongoless
$ cd mongoless
$ meteor add twbs:bootstrap
$ meteor add reactive-var
$ meteor
```

Finally, open a browser and navigate to `http://localhost:3000` so that you can see updates in real time.

How to do it...

We will create a simple array of button press snapshots, with a new element being added to the array every time the button on the page is clicked. Subsequently, these buttons will be added to the UI using a `{{#each}}` template block.

1. First, open `mongoless.html` and add the following block to the `hello` template, just after the `<p>` element and just before the closing `</template>` tag, as shown in the following example:

```
{{#each buttonPresses}}
    <div class="btn btn-info pressed">#{{btnRank}}</div>
{{/each}}
</template>
```

2. We now need to add a reactive variable and append some helpers to the `Template.hello.helpers` object. Open `mongoless.js` and add the following highlighted code:

```
if (Meteor.isClient) {
  presses = new ReactiveVar;
  // counter starts at 0
  Session.setDefault("counter", 0);

  Template.hello.helpers({
    counter: function () {
      return Session.get("counter");
    },
    buttonPresses: function(){
        return presses.get();
    },
    btnRank: function(){
        return this.rank;
    }
  });
```

3. All that's left to do is to update the `presses` variable each time the button is pressed. Inside `Template.hello.events`, in the `'click button'` event handler, add the following lines of code immediately after the `Session.set()` call:

```
Session.set("counter", Session.get("counter") + 1);
var _presses = presses.get() || [];
_presses.push({rank:Session.get("counter")});
presses.set(_presses);
```

4. Save all of your changes, go to your browser, and start clicking on the button labeled **Click Me**. You should see a new button created each time you click on the button, similar to the following:

How it works...

When we added the `buttonPresses` helper function to the `Template.hello.helpers` object, we simply replaced what we would usually use a Mongo collection for with a simple array stored inside a `ReactiveVar` element:

```
presses = new ReactiveVar;
```

Collections are reactive providers, which means they track and rerun computations as appropriate. The `presses` object is also a reactive provider, and therefore, does the exact same thing. It reruns any stored computations / reactive functions whenever the value is updated. In this case, it reruns computations when the array is modified, and `presses.set()` is called as a result.

See also

▶ The *Creating dynamic lists* recipe in *Chapter 3, Building Great User Interfaces*

▶ The *Creating and consuming a reactive value* recipe in this chapter

Using inline data to modify UI elements reactively

Typically, when elements in an HTML page are rendered, then that rendering isn't directly linked to any of the data used to create them, for example, if we have an array of objects, we may generate some HTML by iterating over the array and adding <div> elements for each object in the array. Unless we do something to manually link them to the array of objects, these newly created elements aren't associated with the data that created them in any way. This leads to all kinds of development shenanigans, as developers try to shoehorn in associative data, which is used in events and other downstream functions. Long story short, using only existing web technologies, it's difficult to keep all of the data exactly in sync with your HTML DOM elements. Meteor has been designed to help solve this problem gracefully, keeping track of the context of each DOM element and therefore allowing instant access to the data used to create the element in the first place. This recipe will walk you through how to retrieve and use the data associated with individual DOM elements.

Getting ready

We will use the code base from the *Updating Blaze templates without Mongo* recipe, found in this chapter. Please complete that recipe and then add the randomcolor package by running the following terminal command in the root folder of your project:

```
> meteor add rzymek:randomcolor
```

Have your browser open to http://localhost:3000 as well so we can see the changes in real time.

How to do it...

We are going to add some functionality to the existing button creation. First, we'll add a random color to each new button; second, we'll remove this color when the buttons are clicked; and third, we'll restore the color based on the associative inline data.

So let's get started. We need to update the hello template, setting the initial background colors for new buttons. We also need a way to remove those colors at random. We'll do this by adding a new control button.

1. Open your .html file (probably mongoless.html) and modify the hello template to look like the following:

   ```html
   <template name="hello">
     <button id="addBtn">Click Me</button>
     <button id="chgColor">Or Me!</button>
     <p>You've pressed the button {{counter}} times.</p>
     {{#each buttonPresses}}
   ```

```
        <div class="btn btn-info pressed"
            style="background-color:{{btnColor}}">
        #{{btnRank}}</div>
    {{/each}}
</template>
```

2. We now need to add the `btnColor` helper to `Template.hello.helpers` and modify the data object being stored to make room for the new color. We also need to refine the `click` events on the buttons to differentiate between adding a new button and removing a button's color. Open your `.js` file (probably called `mongoless.js`) and make the following changes to the variable declarations and the helpers:

```
if (Meteor.isClient) {
  presses = new ReactiveVar;
  counter = new ReactiveVar(0);


  Template.hello.helpers({
    counter: function () {
      return counter.get();
    },
    buttonPresses: function () {
      return presses.get();
    },
    btnRank: function () {
      return this.rank;
    },
    btnColor: function () {
      return this.color;
    }
  });
  ...
```

3. Now, we need to modify the existing `click` event, add a new event to remove color, and add one final handler to set up all the new buttons to regain their color when clicked. Make the following changes to the `Template.hello.events` section:

```
Template.hello.events({
    'click #addBtn': function () {
        // increment the counter when button is clicked
        counter.set(counter.get() + 1);
        var _presses = presses.get() || [];
        var newBtn = {
          color: randomColor(),
          rank: counter.get()
        };
```

```
      _presses.push(newBtn);
      presses.set(_presses);
    },
    'click #chgColor': function () {
      var rndBtn = ~~(Math.random() * counter.get());
      $('.pressed')[rndBtn].style.backgroundColor = '';

    },
    'click .pressed': function (e, n) {
      e.currentTarget.style.backgroundColor = this.color;
    }
  });
```

4. Save all your changes and click on the **Click Me** Button on your screen 5-10 times. You'll notice that all the new buttons being added have a random color assigned to them, as shown in the following screenshot:

5. Now, click on the **Or Me!** button multiple times. At random, the buttons will lose their random color and change to the default `btn-info` blue color provided by `bootstrap`, as shown in the following screenshot:

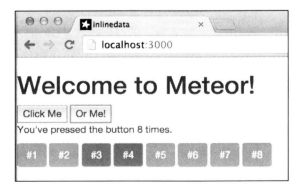

Any of the buttons that have lost their color can regain the color by clicking directly on the button.

How it works...

The crux of this recipe is found inside the `'click .pressed'` event handler. There, we assign the `backgroundColor` attribute of the clicked button to `this.color`:

```
'click .pressed': function (e, n) {
  e.currentTarget.style.backgroundColor = this.color;
}
```

In this case, there is a reference to the associated data object for that DOM element. Meteor keeps track of how each element is created. So when an event is fired inside the template, Meteor provides the data object as the *context* (the `this`) in the event handler. In this way, Meteor can provide instant access to the inline data for each rendered element.

Notice that even after we manually changed the `backgroundColor` using the `'click #chgColor'` event, Meteor still has a reference to the data object used to render the element. This becomes important because we now no longer need to store data as an attribute of the DOM element—no more `data-color` or `data-whatever` attributes that clutter up the UI and potentially expose data. The data objects, though hidden from the UI, are available instantly and inline. So no fancy calculations or DOM manipulation needs to be done in order to access the necessary contextual data.

There's more...

The preceding example uses the default Meteor `Template` event handlers, so of course, the data is available. But, even if you bypass Meteor's `Template` event handlers and use, say, jQuery events instead, the associated data will be available by calling the `Blaze.getData()` function of the element.

Setting up the event handler is a little bit tricky in this case. We have to first move the population of each button to a new template because the jQuery `click` event handler must be run inside of a `rendered()` function callback. To accomplish this, make the following changes to your `.html` file (probably `mongoless.html`):

```
<template name="hello">
  <button id="addBtn">Click Me</button>
  <button id="chgColor">Or Me!</button>
  <p>You've pressed the button {{counter}} times.</p>
  {{#each buttonPresses}}
    {{> helloBtn}}
  {{/each}}
</template>
```

```
<template name="helloBtn">
  <div class="btn btn-info pressed"
    style="background-color:{{btnColor}}">
    #{{btnRank}}</div>
</template>
```

You will also need to remove the `'click .pressed'` event handler from `Template.hello.events`. Once you've removed the event handler, add the `jQuery.click()` event handler inside a `Template.btnRank.rendered` code block, to be run immediately upon the rendering of a new button, as shown in the following code:

```
Template.helloBtn.rendered = function () {
    this.$('.pressed').click(function (e) {
        e.currentTarget.style.backgroundColor = Blaze.getData(this).
color;
    });
};
```

Lastly, because we moved the `div` rendering to the new `helloBtn` template, we need to move the `btnRank` and `btnColor` helpers from `Template.hello.helpers` to a newly created `Template.helloBtn.helpers` block, as shown in the following code:

```
Template.helloBtn.helpers({
  btnRank: function () {
    return this.rank;
  },
  btnColor: function () {
    return this.color;
  }
});
```

That's a lot of work for the same result, but it helps to illustrate the flexibility of the Blaze/Meteor associative data capabilities. We only had to slightly modify the event helper to point to `Blaze.getData(this).color` rather than `this.color`. Although the same keyword exists in each event handler, the `this` inside the jQuery event handler refers to the DOM element, rather than the associated data object inside the original Meteor event handler. `Blaze.getData(element)` takes a DOM element as an argument and retrieves the associated inline data for that element.

In either case, getting to the associated data is very straightforward and allows you to do anything to your UI programmatically, without having to worry about destroying/altering the data associated with each rendered element.

See also

▶ The *Inserting templates with Spacebars* and *Creating dynamic lists* recipes in *Chapter 3, Building Great User Interfaces*

Integrating a jQuery UI

The jQuery library is crazily popular, and for good reason. When used properly, it can speed up the development process and give us reliable ways of doing things that would otherwise take a lot of coding effort.

A complement to jQuery is jQuery UI, which is a set of widgets, themes, and animation effects. With jQuery UI, you can quickly create drag and drop components, sortable lists, and lots of other useful UI niceties.

This recipe will walk you through creating a jQuery UI-sortable widget inside a Meteor template.

Getting ready

For this recipe, we will definitely want client and server folders to keep the code clean and readable. To accomplish this, we will rely on our default template scaffolding. Please create a new project called `swatches` using the *Setting up your project file structure* recipe in *Chapter 1, Optimizing Your Workflow*, as your starting file structure.

Once you've completed the scaffolding, we will need to add the `randomcolor` package to our project. In a terminal window, navigate to the root folder of your project and run the following command:

```
> meteor add rzymek:randomcolor
```

We will also want a nice theme, so let's use the adapted version of Google's Material Design theme, for funzies. Enter the following command in the same terminal window:

```
> meteor add html5cat:bootstrap-material-design
```

Next, we want to get a customized version of jQuery UI directly from `jqueryui.com`. Navigate to `http://jqueryui.com/` in a browser and click on **Custom Download**, placed toward the right:

In the download builder, make the following selections:

- ▶ Select the latest stable version
- ▶ Uncheck the **Toggle All** checkbox under **Components**
- ▶ Check the **Toggle All** checkbox under **UI Core**
- ▶ Check the **Sortable** checkbox under **Interactions**
- ▶ At the bottom, select **No Theme** from the **Theme** dropdown

Your selections will look similar to the following screenshot:

All we need is the sortable interaction and the UI core. Everything else just adds to our file size, so we'll leave it out. Click on **Download**, unzip the downloaded file once complete, locate the `jquery-ui.min.js` file, and copy it to your `[project root]/client/lib/scripts` folder.

We could simply pull in jQuery UI using a community package, but it's a bit bulkier and it doesn't help us see how non-packaged third-party libraries can be used inside Meteor. So, we'll go with this manual installation.

Open a browser to `http://localhost:3000` so we can see the changes in real time. We are now ready to add the jQuery UI-sortable widget to our project.

How to do it...

We will create color swatches, which will display the hexadecimal code they represent, and they will be sortable, which means we can move them around via drag and drop.

1. To accomplish this, we first need to create a `Swatches` collection, accessible on both the client and the server. In your `[project root]/both/` folder, create/edit a file named `model.js` and add the following collection declaration:

   ```
   Swatches = new Mongo.Collection('swatches');
   ```

2. Next, let's create our UI using a template named `swatches`. Open/create the `[project root]/client/main.html` file, remove all the contents, and add the following code:

   ```html
   <head>
     <title>Swatches</title>
   </head>

   <body>
     {{> colors}}
   </body>

   <template name="colors">
     <h1>Yay Colors!</h1>
     <div id="cList">
         {{#each swatches}}
             <div class="swatch"
   style="background-color:{{color}}">
   {{color}}</div>{{color}}</div>
         {{/each}}
     </div>
     <input id="btnNew" type="button" class="btn btn-primary"
   value="New Color" />
   </template>
   ```

3. We will want to style it just a little bit to make the swatches consistently sized. Open/create a file named `[project root]/client/lib/styles/style.css` and add the following CSS declarations:

```css
.swatch {
    min-height: 100px;
    min-width: 100px;
    display:inline-block;
    color:white;
    text-align: center;
}
#cList {
    width: 520px;
}
```

4. Finally, we will create the logic needed to add swatches and be able to drag them around the screen. Open/create the `[project root]/client/scripts/main.js` file, delete anything inside the file, and add the following `Template.helpers` and `Rankings` declarations:

```js
Template.colors.helpers({
    swatches: function(){
        return Swatches.find({},{ sort: { rank:1}});
    }
})


Rankings = {
    beforeFirst: function(first) { return first - 1;},
    middle: function(before,after){ return (before+after)/2;},
    afterLast: function(last){ return last + 1; }
};
```

5. Now, the fun part! We will create the `jQuery.sortable` object with its `stop()` function and hook up our `button.click` event handler using regular jQuery. In order for the `sortable` and `click` event handlers to be added properly, we need to declare them inside a `Template.rendered()` function. In the same `main.js` file, just below the `Rankings` declaration, enter the following code:

```js
Template.colors.rendered = function(){
    this.$('#cList').sortable({
        stop: function (e,ui){
            var el = ui.item.get(0);
            var before = ui.item.prev().get(0);
            var after = ui.item.next().get(0);
            var newRank = null;
            if (!before){
```

```
                newRank = Rankings.beforeFirst(Blaze.
getData(after).rank);
            } else if (!after) {
                newRank = Rankings.afterLast(Blaze.
getData(before).rank);
            } else {
                newRank = Rankings.middle(Blaze.getData(before).
rank,Blaze.getData(after).rank);
            }
            Swatches.update(Blaze.getData(el)._id,
                            {$set: {rank:newRank}});
        }
    });

    this.$('#btnNew').click(function(e){
        var newColor = randomColor({luminosity:'random',
hue:'random'});
        Swatches.insert({color:newColor, rank: Swatches.find().
count()+1});
    });
};
```

Save all of your changes and hop over to your browser. The page should have a nice, stylish blue button labeled **NEW COLOR**. Every time you click on this button, a new swatch will be added with a random color. If you drag and drop any of the swatches from one position to another, the swatches will be reordered appropriately. This reordering is not temporary. If you refresh the page or open another browser window, the reordering you did via drag and drop will remain.

So, for example, let's say you move a swatch from the last element to the first. The change will stick and any other clients/browsers that open to the same page will instantly reflect the change.

When the following purple swatch is dragged and dropped, the changes will be as shown, as displayed on the right-hand side of the following screenshot:

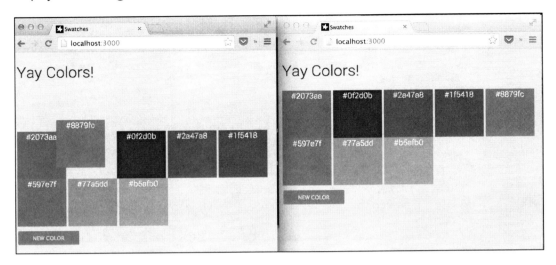

It is instantly updated in every UI, as shown in the following screenshot:

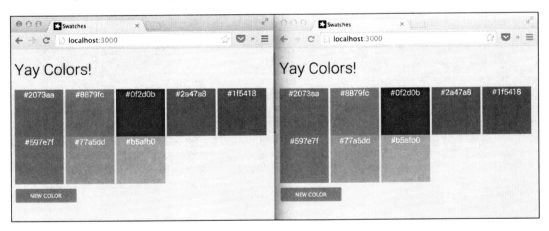

How it works...

Thanks to our `click` event handler, whenever a swatch is added using `Swatches.insert()`, a rank is assigned to that swatch:

```
this.$('#btnNew').click(function(e){
  ...
  Swatches.insert({..., rank: Swatches.find().count()+1});
});
```

If we look at the `swatches` helper inside `Template.colors.helpers`, we can see that the Mongo `Collection.find()` query is sorted by `rank`:

```
swatches: function(){
  return Swatches.find({},{ sort: { rank:1 }});
}
```

This preserves the order of the swatches in the UI and allows us to manipulate their order as a result of drag and drop.

Inside of our `sortable.stop()` function, we were identifying where in the list the swatch had been dragged and dropped to. Once we determine where the swatch is located, we calculate a new rank for that swatch using the `Rankings` helper functions. We then immediately update the `swatches` collection with the new rank, which propagates and makes the position of the UI change permanent.

There's more...

The key takeaway here is that while jQuery (or any other third-party library) may be used to make direct DOM manipulations, these manipulations won't persist beyond a single user's session, or even beyond the next DDP change from the server.

To make the manipulations permanent and to fully utilize the Blaze rendering engine's fantastic reactive programming model, we need to modify the datasource (in this case, the `swatches` collection). The modification is handled immediately, and with no effort on our part, through reactivity.

So, to review, third-party libraries can go right ahead and manipulate DOM elements in a Meteor application, with the third-party code being executed inside a `Template.rendered()` function block.

To make the changes "stick", we simply update the corresponding Mongo collection as well. Using this technique, we can integrate nearly every JavaScript library out there (if someone hasn't already done it for us on `https://atmospherejs.com/`).

See also

- ▶ The *Setting up your project file structure* recipe in *Chapter 1, Optimizing Your Workflow*
- ▶ The *Using inline data to modify UI elements reactively* recipe in this chapter

7
Using Client Methods

In this chapter, you will learn the following topics:

- ▶ Creating dynamic graphs with SVG and Ajax
- ▶ Using the HTML FileReader to upload images
- ▶ Creating a coloring book with the Canvas element

Introduction

Web programming, on the client side, has come a long way since the inception of HTML. Up until recently, it was necessary to write/use third party **polyfill** libraries to do simple things, such as build graphs, read files, and draw on the screen. But that cute lil' bucktoothed kid we all knew and disliked has grown up! With powerful, easy to use scripting and graphics APIs and objects now supported in nearly every browser, web programming is finally ready to be used on its own. The recipes in this chapter will go through some of the most popular Web API objects, and show you how to implement them inside Meteor.

Creating dynamic graphs with SVG and Ajax

While there are a lot of graphing libraries out there (all of which you can use in Meteor, by the way!) it's good to know how to implement fundamental shapes inside an HTML page, using **SVG templates**. Sometimes implementing a full-fledged graphing library is overkill, and having a working knowledge of SVG in your back pocket can be very useful. However, this is a Meteor recipe; we not only want to see an example of SVG, but we want to see it in action! This recipe will teach you how to stream a live data source into MongoDB collections, and then represent that dynamic collection graphically, using SVG tags.

Getting ready

We will be using a default project installation, with `client`, `server`, and `both` folders, to keep the code clean and readable. In a terminal window, navigate to where you would like your project to reside, and execute the following commands:

```
$ meteor create svggraph
$ cd svggraph
$ rm svggraph.*
$ mkdir client
$ mkdir server
$ mkdir both
```

We also want to make use of a few packages, and remove the `autopublish` package, so let's do that now. Run the following commands in the terminal window:

```
$ meteor remove autopublish
$ meteor add http
$ meteor add meteorhacks:aggregate
$ meteor add rzymek:randomcolor
$ meteor
```

We're now ready to start creating our SVG streaming data graph.

How to do it...

Our project is going to read the comments stream from `http://www.meetup.com/`, which is freely available, and very easy to use. We will record the comments from the stream, and display a sum total of comments by state. We will need to create the interface, which will display state totals as a vertical bar chart, and will also show us the last comment made, along with a picture of the Meetup Group it came from.

>
> **Note**
> We are using the data stream collecting code for demonstration purposes only! There is no redundancy checking or hardening built into it. We strongly recommend against using this code as-is in anything even resembling a production application.

Proceed with the following steps to create dynamic graphs with SVG and Ajax:

1. We will first create the SVG element with the `id` of `stateBars`. We will then create a `<rect>` element for each individual state, and adjust the height using the `stateStat` template. Inside the `[project root]/client/` folder, create a `client.html` file, add the following HTML code, and save the file:

```
<body>
  {{> cPic}}
</body>

<template name="cPic">
  <svg id="stateBars" width="800" height="600">
    {{#each stateStats}}
    {{> stateStat}}
    {{/each}}
  </svg>
  <div id="cComment">{{curComment}}</div>
  <img id="cPic" src="{{curPic}}"/>
</template>


<template name="stateStat">
  <rect width="{{width}}" height="{{stackHeight}}"
y="{{stackPosition}}"
       style="fill:{{color}};fill-opacity:0.8;" />
  <text x="5" y="{{textYPos}}" fill="black">{{state}}: {{total}}
</text>
</template>
```

2. We want to provide some basic styling on our page, so let's get that out of the way. In the `[project root]/client` folder, create a `style.css` file, and add the following style declarations:

```
body {
  font-family: 'Helvetica-Neue', sans-serif;
  font-size: 12px;
}
#stateBars {
  border:dashed 3px #ccc;
}
#cComment {
  margin-top: 10px;
}
```

```
#cPic {
  width: 200px;
  margin-top: 10px;
}
```

3. Next, let's set up the `Comments` and `CountryTotals` collections. To keep things cleaner, logic-wise, on the client we will use some server-side logic to aggregate the incoming comments. We first need to declare our collections for use on both the client and the server. In the `[project root]/both/` folder, create a new file called `model.js`, and add the following two declarations to the file:

```
Comments = new Mongo.Collection('comments');
CountryTotals = new Mongo.Collection('countryTotals');
```

4. Next, let's set up monitoring for the `commentsStream` data, and add a code to count the totals. As we removed the `autopublish` package, we need to declare our `Comments` publication, and at the same time, we want to update the totals for a state whenever any new comments come in. We can accomplish this by using the `Meteor.publish()` function and using the `cursor.observeChanges()` method. In your `[project root]/server/` folder, create a new file called `svggraph-server.js`, and add the following method:

```
Meteor.publish("commentsStream", function(country){
  var cursor = Comments.find({country:country});
  var initializing = true;
  cursor.observeChanges({
    added:function(id,doc){
      if (initializing) return;
      var cTots = Meteor.call('totalsByCountry', doc.country);
      var sTots = Meteor.call('totalsByState',doc.country);
      var existingTots = CountryTotals.findOne({country:doc.
country});

      if (!sTots || !cTots) return;
      sTots = _.map(sTots,function(s,i,d){
        s._id.total = s.total;
        if (existingTots){
          var existingState = _.findWhere(existingTots.
states,{state:s._id.state});
          if (existingState) s._id.color = existingState.color ||
randomColor({luminosity: 'light',
hue: 'blue'});
          else s._id.color = randomColor({luminosity:
'light', hue: 'blue'});
        }
        return s._id;
      });
```

```
        var cObj = {country:doc.country, total:cTots[0].total,
    states: sTots};
        CountryTotals.upsert({country:cObj.country},cObj);
      }
    });
    initializing = false;

    return cursor;
});
```

5. We also need to declare the `Meteor.publish()` method for our state totals by country, so let's do that as well. Append the following to the end of the `svggraph-server.js` file:

```
Meteor.publish("graphData", function(country){
  return CountryTotals.find({country:country});
});
```

6. We need to keep track of the country that we are monitoring, and what the last comment and picture from the Meetup Group were. The most straightforward way to do this is through `Session` variables, so let's create a file called `svggraph-client.js` in the `[project root]/client/` folder, and add the following three variables at the top:

```
Session.setDefault("country", "us");
Session.setDefault("msgComment","No comments yet");
Session.setDefault("msgPic",
"https://d14jjfgstdxsoz.cloudfront.net/meteor-logo.png");
```

7. Now that we have specified the country that we will be monitoring, we can add our `Meteor.subscribe` statements, which both take the country as a parameter. In the `svggraph-client.js` file, add the following statements inside a `Tracker.autorun` block:

```
Tracker.autorun(function(){
  Meteor.subscribe("graphData", Session.get('country'));
  Meteor.subscribe("commentsStream",
  Session.get('country'));
});
```

8. We will hook up the data later, but we still need to add the `Template.helpers` method for displaying the latest pictures and comments, based on the `Session` variables declared in the preceding steps. In the `svggraph-client.js` file, add the following code just below the `Tracker.autorun` block:

```
Template.cPic.helpers({
  curPic: function () {
    return Session.get('msgPic');
  },
```

```
      curComment: function() {
        return Session.get('msgComment');
      }
   });
```

9. In anticipation of incoming data from the client, we need a few `helper` methods, to message data and perform *aggregate queries* on our Mongo DB collections. We also want a quick way to reset our collections, because the sheer amount of data we're collecting can get messy for a sample application. As such, we will create the following server-side methods:

    ❏ addMsg: This is used for inserting a message into our `Comments` collection.

    ❏ totalsByState: This is used to aggregate the total number of `Comments`, by state.

    ❏ totalsByCountry: This is used to aggregate totals, by country.

    ❏ resetDB: This is used to reset the `Comments` and `CountryTotals` collections.

Open `svggraph-server.js` and add the following code:

```
Meteor.methods({
  addMsg : function (msg) {
    var upMsg = {};
    try {
    upMsg.country = msg.group.country;
    upMsg.state = msg.group.state;
    upMsg.category = msg.group.category.name;
    upMsg.thumb = (msg.group.group_photo ?
    msg.group.group_photo.thumb_link: "");
    upMsg.createdAt = Date.now();
    }
    catch(e){
      console.log(e.message);
      return null;
    }
    Comments.insert(upMsg);
  },
  totalsByState: function (country){
    return Comments.aggregate([
      {$match:{country:country}},
      {$group:{_id:{state:"$state"},total:{$sum:1}}},
      {$sort:{"total":-1}}
    ]);
  },
  totalsByCountry: function(country){
```

```
        return Comments.aggregate([
          {$match:{country:country}},
          {$group:{_id:{},total:{$sum:1}}}
        ]);
      },
      resetDB: function(){
        Comments.remove({});
        CountryTotals.remove({});
        console.log('Collections have been reset');
      }
    });
```

10. With our server-side helper logic all in place, it's time to read and parse the data stream. In the `svggraph-client.js` file, add the following `connect`, `disconnect`, `onopen`, `onclose`, and `onmessage` websocket functions:

```
function MeetupsStream() {
  var ms = {};
  var ws;
  var sURL = "ws://stream.meetup.com/2/event_comments";
  ms.connect = function (url) {
    sURL = url || sURL;
    ws = new WebSocket(sURL);
    ws.onopen = ms.onopen;
    ws.onmessage = ms.onmessage;
    ws.onclose = ms.onclose;
    return ms;
  };
  ms.disconnect = function () {
    ws && ws.close();
  };
  ms.onopen = function () {
    console.log("Meetup stream started...");
  };
  ms.onmessage = function (e) {
    var rec_msg = EJSON.parse(e.data);
    if (rec_msg.group.group_photo)
      Session.set('msgPic',
      rec_msg.group.group_photo.photo_link);
    Session.set('msgComment', rec_msg.comment);
    Meteor.call('addMsg', rec_msg);
//
  };

  ms.onclose = function () {
```

```
        console.log("Meetup stream closed.");
    };

    return ms;
}
```

11. With the data stream all ready to go, all that's left is to add our display logic, and flip the switch. In the `svggraph-client.js` file, locate the `Template.cPic.helpers` code block, and add the following helper function just below the `curComment` event (don't forget the comma!):

```
curComment: function() {
    return Session.get('msgComment');
},
stateStats: function () {
  var ct = CountryTotals.findOne(
    {country:Session.get('country')});
  if (!ct) return [];
  var stateTotals = ct.states;
  var ctotal = ct.total;
  var SVGWidth = 800;
  var SVGHeight = 600;
  return _.map(stateTotals, function(s,i,l){
    var retObj = {};
    retObj.state = s.state;
    retObj.index = i;
    retObj.total = s.total;
    retObj.width = ~~(SVGWidth * (s.total/ctotal));
    retObj.stackHeight = ~~(SVGHeight/l.length);
    retObj.stackPosition = i*retObj.stackHeight;
    retObj.color = s.color;
    return retObj;
  });
}
});
```

12. We need a few style helpers to properly position our text data, and to let us know where the most recent comment was added (to make the things all fancy!). Append the following `Template.helpers` code block to the bottom of the `svggraph-client.js` file:

```
Template.stateStat.helpers({
    textYPos: function () {
        return this.stackPosition + ~~(this.stackHeight/2);

    },
    textXPos : function(){
        return this.width - ~~(this.width*.2);
    },
    color : function(){
        if (Session.equals('lastState',this.state))
        return '#2ecc71';
        return this.color;
    }
});
```

13. Using the `Template.rendered` method block, we will turn our data stream on and update our `lastState` session variable whenever a new comment is posted, using a simple `autorun` method. Enter the following code at the bottom of your `svggraph-client.js` file:

```
Template.cPic.rendered = function(){
    MStream = new MeetupsStream();
    MStream.connect();
    this.autorun(function(){
        var last = Comments.findOne(
            {country:Session.get('country')},
            {sort:{createdAt:-1}});
        if (last) Session.set('lastState',last.state);
    });
}
```

14. Save all changes, and open a browser (if you haven't already) to `http://localhost:3000`. Wait just a bit, and you should see the new comments coming in, with state totals being updated, as shown in the following screenshot:

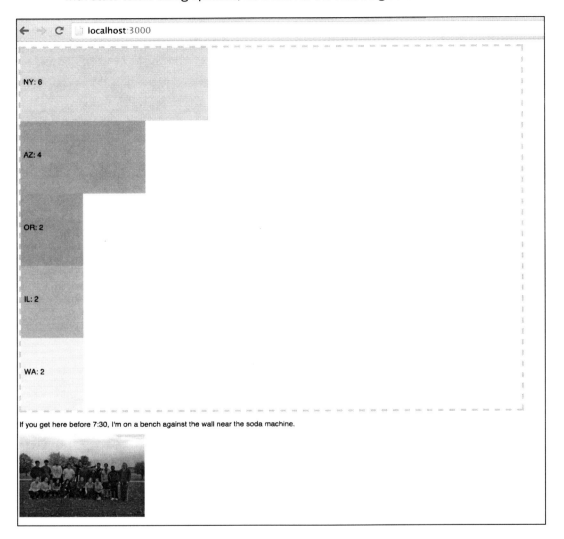

15. Let it run for a bit, so that more states appear. If you let it run long enough, you'll eventually get all 50 states (and maybe even Puerto Rico!). If you would like to reset your collection, open your browser console and enter the following command:

```
> Meteor.call('resetDB')
```

How it works...

As mentioned in the recipe introduction, there are two critical pieces to graphing dynamic data. The first has to do with rendering SVG objects, and can be found mostly in the HTML template code, in the `[project root]/client/client.html` file. We first used the `{{> cPic}}` template inclusion to reference our `cPic` template. The template itself declares our `<svg>` element, then runs a standard `{{#each }}` control structure on the `stateStats` collection:

```
<template name="cPic">
  <svg ...>
    {{#each stateStats}}
    {{> stateStat}}
    {{/each}}
  </svg>
  ...
</template>
```

We set the width and height of the `<svg>` element directly (note that they are *not* CSS style attributes, but are actual element attributes instead), and add a unique `id` attribute for CSS styling as well, as shown in the following example:

```
<svg id="stateBars" width="800" height="600">
```

In the `stateStat` template, we create a `<rect>` element and set pretty much every attribute dynamically:

- ▶ `width`: This is set based on the number of comments.
- ▶ `height`: This is set based on the total number of states.
- ▶ `y`: This is the vertical position and is set based on position in the data collection.
- ▶ `fill`: This is the color value which is set to green if it was the last state updated.

We likewise set the position of the text SVG element to make sure it lines up with the corresponding `<rect>` element:

```
<template name="stateStat">
  <rect width="{{width}}" height="{{stackHeight}}"
y="{{stackPosition}}"
        style="fill:{{color}};fill-opacity:0.8;" />
  <text x="5" y="{{textYPos}}" fill="black">{{state}}: {{total}}
</text>
</template>
```

It's important to understand that SVG elements are not positioned relative to other elements inside the same `<svg>` block. This is why we had to set the position of each element. Also, some attributes (`width` and `height` for example) can be set directly. SVG elements are truly a hybrid between a bonafide DOM element and a graphic element.

 For a great introduction to SVG, you can read the MDN SVG tutorial, found at `https://developer.mozilla.org/en-US/docs/Web/SVG/Tutorial`.

The second critical piece surrounds the use of the `WebSocket` HTML5 Web API object, found in our `MeetupsStream` function of the `svggraph-client.js` file. In this function, we prepare a pretty standard Ajax (actually `WebSocket`) call by setting handlers for `.ondisconnect`, `.onopen`, and `.onmessage`:

```
function MeetupsStream() {
    ms.onopen = ...
    ms.onmessage = ...
    ms.onclose = ...
}
```

The one we are most interested in is the `.onmessage` handler, where we parse the data (which comes in as a string) into an `EJSON` object:

```
var rec_msg = EJSON.parse(e.data);
```

We then (conditionally) set the `msgPic` variable, which immediately changes the image displayed in our `cPic` template. We likewise update `msgComment` to change the displayed comment:

```
if (rec_msg.group.group_photo)
    Session.set('msgPic', ...);
    Session.set('msgComment', rec_msg.comment);
```

Finally, we make a `Meteor.call` method to the server-side `'addMsg'` method, which puts things in motion to update our state totals:

```
Meteor.call('addMsg', rec_msg);
```

 The `WebSocket` object also has a good MDN tutorial, found at `https://developer.mozilla.org/en-US/docs/WebSockets`.

A few more odds and ends can be found in the code we used, such as the `meteorhacks:aggregate` package, which lets us do summations and groupings on the MongoDB collections (official support coming soon!) via the `.aggregate` method, but this recipe was meant to focus on the SVG and Ajax (`WebSocket`) aspects.

See also

▶ The *Creating dynamic lists* recipe in *Chapter 3, Building Great User Interfaces*
▶ The *Handling asynchronous events* recipe in *Chapter 11, Leveraging Advanced Features*

Using the HTML FileReader to upload images

Adding files via a web application is a pretty standard functionality nowadays. That doesn't mean that it's easy to do, programmatically. New browsers support Web APIs to make our job easier, and a lot of quality libraries/packages exist to help us navigate the file reading/uploading forests, but, being the coding lumberjacks that we are, we like to know how to roll our own! In this recipe, you will learn how to read and upload image files to a Meteor server.

Getting ready

We will be using a default project installation, with `client`, `server`, and `both` folders, and with the addition of a special folder for storing images. In a terminal window, navigate to where you would like your project to reside, and execute the following commands:

```
$ meteor create imageupload
$ cd imageupload
$ rm imageupload.*
$ mkdir client
$ mkdir server
$ mkdir both
$ mkdir .images
```

Note the dot in the `.images` folder. This is really important because we don't want the Meteor application to automatically refresh every time we add an image to the server! By creating the images folder as `.images`, we are hiding it from the eye-of-Sauron-like monitoring system built into Meteor, because folders starting with a period are "invisible" to Linux or Unix.

Let's also take care of the additional Atmosphere packages we'll need. In the same terminal window, execute the following commands:

```
$ meteor add twbs:bootstrap
$ meteor add voodoohop:masonrify
```

We're now ready to get started on building our image upload application.

How to do it...

We want to display the images we upload, so we'll be using a layout package (voodoohop:masonrify) for display purposes. We will also initiate uploads via drag and drop, to cut down on UI components. Lastly, we'll be relying on an npm module to make the file upload much easier. Let's break this down into a few steps, starting with the user interface.

1. In the [project root]/client folder, create a file called imageupload.html and add the following templates and template inclusions:

```html
<body>
  <h1>Images!</h1>
  {{> display}}
  {{> dropzone}}
</body>

<template name="display">
  {{#masonryContainer
    columnWidth=50
    transitionDuration="0.2s"
    id="MasonryContainer"
  }}
  {{#each imgs}}
  {{> img}}
  {{/each}}
  {{/masonryContainer}}
</template>

<template name="dropzone">
  <div id="dropzone" class="{{dropcloth}}">Drag images here...
</div>
</template>

<template name="img">
  {{#masonryElement "MasonryContainer"}}
  <img src="{{src}}"
    class="display-image"
    style="width:{{calcWidth}}"/>
  {{/masonryElement}}
</template>
```

2. We want to add just a little bit of styling, including an "active" state for our drop zone, so that we know when we are safe to drop files onto the page. In your `[project root]/client/` folder, create a new `style.css` file and enter the following CSS style directives:

```css
body {
  background-color: #f5f0e5;
  font-size: 2rem;

}

div#dropzone {
  position: fixed;
  bottom:5px;
  left:2%;
  width:96%;
  height:100px;
  margin: auto auto;
  line-height: 100px;
  text-align: center;
  border: 3px dashed #7f898d;
  color: #7f8c8d;
  background-color: rgba(210,200,200,0.5);
}

div#dropzone.active {
  border-color: #27ae60;
  color: #27ae60;
  background-color: rgba(39, 174, 96,0.3);
}

img.display-image {
  max-width: 400px;
}
```

3. We now want to create an `Images` collection to store references to our uploaded image files. To do this, we will be relying on **EJSON**. EJSON is Meteor's extended version of JSON, which allows us to quickly transfer binary files from the client to the server. In your `[project root]/both/` folder, create a file called `imgFile.js` and add the MongoDB collection by adding the following line:

```javascript
Images = new Mongo.Collection('images');
```

4. We will now create the `imgFile` object, and declare an EJSON type of `imgFile` to be used on both the client and the server. After the preceding `Images` declaration, enter the following code:

```
imgFile = function (d) {
  d = d || {};
  this.name = d.name;
  this.type = d.type;
  this.source = d.source;
  this.size = d.size;
};
```

5. To properly initialize `imgFile` as an EJSON type, we need to implement the `fromJSONValue()`, `prototype()`, and `toJSONValue()` methods. We will then declare `imgFile` as an EJSON type using the `EJSON.addType()` method. Add the following code just below the `imgFile` function declaration:

```
imgFile.fromJSONValue = function (d) {
  return new imgFile({
    name: d.name,
    type: d.type,
    source: EJSON.fromJSONValue(d.source),
    size: d.size
  });
};

imgFile.prototype = {
  constructor: imgFile,

  typeName: function () {
    return 'imgFile'
  },
  equals: function (comp) {
    return (this.name == comp.name &&
      this.size == comp.size);
  },
  clone: function () {
    return new imgFile({
      name: this.name,
      type: this.type,
      source: this.source,
      size: this.size
    });
  },
  toJSONValue: function () {
    return {
```

```
        name: this.name,
        type: this.type,
        source: EJSON.toJSONValue(this.source),
        size: this.size
      };
    }
};

EJSON.addType('imgFile', imgFile.fromJSONValue);
```

 The EJSON code used in this recipe is heavily inspired by Chris Mather's Evented Mind file upload tutorials. We recommend checking out his site and learning even more about file uploading at https://www.eventedmind.com.

6. Even though it's usually cleaner to put client-specific and server-specific code in separate files, because the code is related to the `imgFile` code we just entered, we are going to put it all in the same file. Just below the `EJSON.addType()` function call in the preceding step, add the following `Meteor.isClient` and `Meteor.isServer` code:

```
if (Meteor.isClient){
  _.extend(imgFile.prototype, {
    read: function (f, callback) {

      var fReader = new FileReader;
      var self = this;
      callback = callback || function () {};

      fReader.onload = function() {
        self.source = new Uint8Array(fReader.result);
        callback(null,self);
      };

      fReader.onerror = function() {
        callback(fReader.error);
      };

      fReader.readAsArrayBuffer(f);
    }
  });

  _.extend (imgFile, {
    read: function (f, callback){
```

```
          return new imgFile(f).read(f,callback);
      }
    });
};

if (Meteor.isServer){
  var fs = Npm.require('fs');
  var path = Npm.require('path');
  _.extend(imgFile.prototype, {
    save: function(dirPath, options){
      var fPath = path.join(process.env.PWD,dirPath,this.name);
      var imgBuffer = new Buffer(this.source);
      fs.writeFileSync(fPath, imgBuffer, options);
    }
  });
};
```

7. Next, we will add some `Images` collection `insert` helpers. We will provide the ability to add either references (URIs) to images, or to upload files into our `.images` folder on the server. To do this, we need some `Meteor.methods`. In the `[project root]/server/` folder, create an `imageupload-server.js` file, and enter the following code:

```
Meteor.methods({
  addURL : function(uri){
    Images.insert({src:uri});
  },
  uploadIMG : function(iFile){
    iFile.save('.images',{});
    Images.insert({src:'images/'
    +iFile.name});
  }
});
```

8. We now need to establish the code to process/serve images from the `.images` folder. We need to circumvent Meteor's normal asset serving capabilities for anything found in the (hidden) `.images` folder. To do this, we will use the `fs` npm module, and redirect any content requests accessing the `Images/` folder address to the actual `.images` folder found on the server. Just after the `Meteor.methods` block entered in the preceding step, add the following `WebApp.connectHandlers.use()` function code:

```
var fs = Npm.require('fs');
WebApp.connectHandlers.use(function(req, res, next) {
  var re = /^\/images\/(.*)$/.exec(req.url);
  if (re !== null) {
```

```
        var filePath = process.env.PWD
        + '/.images/'+ re[1];
        var data = fs.readFileSync(filePath, data);
        res.writeHead(200, {
          'Content-Type': 'image'
        });
        res.write(data);
        res.end();
      } else {
        next();
      }
    });
```

9. Our images `display` template is entirely dependent on the `Images` collection, so we need to add the appropriate reactive `Template.helpers` function on the client side. In your `[project root]/client/` folder, create an `imageupload-client.js` file, and add the following code:

```
Template.display.helpers({
  imgs: function () {
    return Images.find();
  }
});
```

10. If we add pictures we don't like and want to remove them quickly, the easiest way to do that is by double clicking on a picture. So, let's add the code for doing that just below the `Template.helpers` method in the same file:

```
Template.display.events({
  'dblclick .display-image': function (e) {
    Images.remove({
      _id: this._id
    });
  }
});
```

11. Now for the fun stuff. We're going to add drag and drop visual feedback cues, so that whenever we drag anything over our drop zone, the drop zone will provide visual feedback to the user. Likewise, once we move away from the zone, or actually drop items, the drop zone should return to normal. We will accomplish this through a `Session` variable, which modifies the CSS class in the `div.dropzone` element, whenever it is changed. At the bottom of the `imageupload-client.js` file, add the following `Template.helpers` and `Template.events` code blocks:

```
Template.dropzone.helpers({
  dropcloth: function () {
    return Session.get('dropcloth');
  }
```

```
  });

  Template.dropzone.events({
    'dragover #dropzone': function (e) {
      e.preventDefault();
      Session.set('dropcloth', 'active');
    },
    'dragleave #dropzone': function (e) {
      e.preventDefault();
      Session.set('dropcloth');

    }
  });
```

12. The last task is to evaluate what has been dropped in to our page drop zone. If what's been dropped is simply a URI, we will add it to the `Images` collection as is. If it's a file, we will store it, create a URI to it, and then append it to the `Images` collection. In the `imageupload-client.js` file, just before the final closing curly bracket inside the `Template.dropzone.events` code block, add the following event handler logic:

```
  'dragleave #dropzone': function (e) {
    ...
  },
  'drop #dropzone': function (e) {
    e.preventDefault();
    Session.set('dropcloth');

    var files = e.originalEvent.dataTransfer.files;
    var images =
$(e.originalEvent.dataTransfer.getData('text/html')).find('img');
    var fragment = _.findWhere(e.originalEvent.dataTransfer.items,
{
      type: 'text/html'
    });
    if (files.length) {
      _.each(files, function (e, i, l) {
        imgFile.read(e, function (error, imgfile) {
          Meteor.call('uploadIMG', imgfile, function (e) {
            if (e) {
              console.log(e.message);
            }
          });
        })
      });
    } else if (images.length) {
```

```
      _.each(images, function (e, i, l) {
        Meteor.call('addURL', $(e).attr('src'));
      });
    } else if (fragment) {
      fragment.getAsString(function (e) {
        var frags = $(e);
        var img = _.find(frags, function (e) {
          return e.hasAttribute('src');
        });
        if (img) Meteor.call('addURL', img.src);
      });

    }

  }
});
```

13. Save all your changes and open a browser to `http://localhost:3000`. Find some pictures from any web site, and drag and drop them in to the drop zone. As you drag and drop the images, the images will appear immediately on your web page, as shown in the following screenshot:

As you drag and drop the dinosaur images in to the drop zone, they will be uploaded as shown in the following screenshot:

Similarly, dragging and dropping actual files will just as quickly upload and then display images, as shown in the following screenshot:

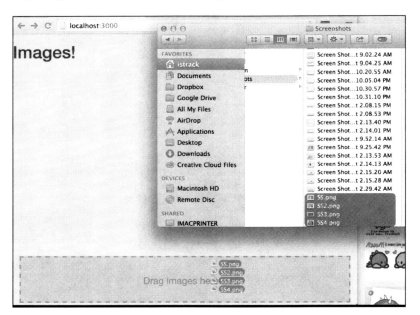

14. As the files are dropped, they are uploaded and saved in the `.images/` folder:

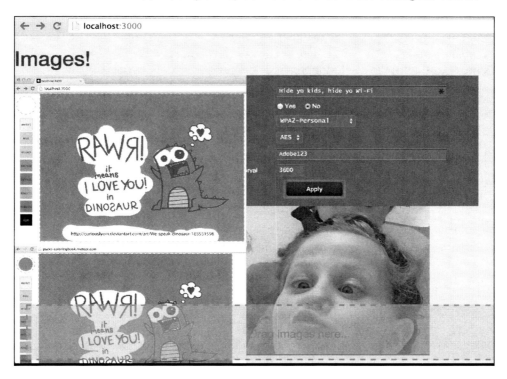

How it works...

There are a lot of moving parts to the code we just created, but we can refine it down to four areas.

First, we created a new `imgFile` object, complete with the internal functions added via the `Object.prototype = {...}` declaration. The functions added here (`typeName`, `equals`, `clone`, `toJSONValue` and `fromJSONValue`) are primarily used to allow the `imgFile` object to be *serialized* and *deserialized* properly on the client and the server. Normally, this isn't needed, as we can just `insert` into Mongo Collections directly, but in this case it is needed because we want to use the `FileReader` and Node `fs` packages on the client and server respectively to directly load and save image files, rather than write them to a collection.

Second, the underscore `_.extend()` method is used on the client side to create the `read()` function, and on the server side to create the `save()` function. `read` takes the file(s) that were dropped, reads the file into an `ArrayBuffer`, and then calls the included `callback`, which uploads the file to the server. The `save` function on the server side reads the `ArrayBuffer`, and writes the subsequent image file to a specified location on the server (in our case, the `.images` folder).

Third, we created an `ondropped` event handler, using the `'drop #dropzone'` event. This handler determines whether an actual file was dragged and dropped, or if it was simply an HTML `<img>` element, which contains a URI link in the `src` property. In the case of a file (determined by `files.length`), we call the `imgFile.read` command, and pass a callback with an immediate `Meteor.call('uploadIMG'...)` method. In the case of an `<img>` tag, we parse the URI from the `src` attribute, and use `Meteor.call('addURL')` to update the `Images` collection.

Fourth, we have our `helper` functions for updating the UI. These include `Template.helpers` functions, `Template.events` functions, and the `WebApp.connectedHandlers.use()` function, used to properly serve uploaded images without having to update the UI each time a file is uploaded. Remember, Meteor will update the UI automatically on any file change. This unfortunately includes static files, such as images. To work around this, we store our images in a file invisible to Meteor (using `.images`). To redirect the traffic to that hidden folder, we implement the `.use()` method to listen for any traffic meant to hit the `'/images/'` folder, and redirect it accordingly.

As with any complex recipe, there are other parts to the code, but this should cover the major aspects of file uploading (the four areas mentioned in the preceding section).

There's more...

The next logical step is to not simply copy the URIs from remote image files, but rather to download, save, and serve local copies of those remote images. This can also be done using the `FileReader` and Node `fs` libraries, and can be done either through the existing client code mentioned in the preceding section, or directly on the server, as a type of *cron* job.

 For more information on `FileReader`, please see the MDN FileReader article, located at `https://developer.mozilla.org/en-US/docs/Web/API/FileReader`.

See also

▶ The *Using npm packages directly* recipe in *Chapter 8, Intergrating Third-party Libraries*

▶ The *Creating custom EJSON objects* recipe in *Chapter 11, Leveraging Advanced Features*

Creating a coloring book with the Canvas element

There are now multiple ways to display graphics on a web page. DOM elements, SVG, WebGL, and, perhaps the most user-friendly, the `Canvas` element. Using JavaScript, the `Canvas` element provides a flexible graphics area where you can paint, erase, color, cut and paste to your heart's content. A good representation of what you can do with the `Canvas` element is found in this recipe, where you will learn how to build a coloring book app from scratch.

Getting ready

Get your crayons! Okay, maybe those won't be needed (don't use them on your monitor!) but what we're about to create is the next best thing, so let's get the app structure and packages out of the way, so we can start coloring!

In addition to the usual suspects, we will need some specialty folders to make the grouping of our code cleaner and more manageable. Open a terminal window, navigate to where you would like to create your root project, and execute the following commands:

```
$ meteor create coloringbook
$ cd coloringbook
$ rm coloringbook.*
$ mkdir -p client/scripts
$ mkdir {both,server,public}
$ meteor
```

How to do it...

It may not seem like it on the surface, but there's actually a lot to developing a coloring book application. You have to worry about user preferences, undo/redo, picking colors, erasing, and so on. We will tackle these steps one at a time, adding packages and functionality as we go along.

1. First, we will add user management packages. Meteor has some fantastic out-of-the-box functionality for user account management, and we will take advantage of that functionality. In a terminal window, navigate to your [project root] folder and add the following two Meteor libraries by entering the following commands:

   ```
   $ meteor add accounts-password
   $ meteor add accounts-ui
   ```

2. We will want to display these on the screen, so let's add the necessary UI elements and style them appropriately. Create a file called `cb-ui.html` in your `[project root]/client/` folder, and add the following code:

```
<body>
  {{> loginButtons}}
</body>
```

Your page will look very spartan at the moment, but just like that, we already have accounts and account creation! In a browser, navigate to `http://localhost:3000` and you should see the accounts dialog dropdown at the top left of your screen, similar to the following screenshot:

3. Let's finish up the visual aspects of our UI by adding a toolbar, where we can see color swatches and adjust the size of our brush; and let's also add our `canvas` element, with a background `<div>` to display the picture we want to color. In the same `cb-ui.html` file, add the following template inclusions in the `body` element block:

```
<body>
  {{> loginButtons}}
  {{> toolbar}}
  <div id="bgpicture"></div>
  {{> picture}}
</body>
```

4. The `picture` template is actually the easiest, so we'll add the code for that first. Add the following template code just below the `</body>` tag:

```
<template name="picture">
  <canvas id="picture" class="no-copy">Images go here...</canvas>
</template>
```

5. Now we add the `toolbar` and the `swatch` templates, which use a bit of SVG and `Masonry.js` to display our brush and color swatches. Just below the template code added in the preceding step, add the following code:

```
<template name="toolbar">
```

```
<div class="brush-size" id="brush-size">
  <svg id="brush-preview"
   height="70" width="70"
   style="display:{{eraseMode}}">
    <circle cx="35" cy="35"
    r="{{preview.size}}"
    fill="{{preview.color}}" />
  </svg>
</div>
{{#masonryContainer columnWidth=50
  transitionDuration="0.2s"
  id="MasonryContainer" }}

  {{#each swatches}}
  {{> swatch}}
  {{/each}}

{{/masonryContainer}}
</template>
<template name="swatch">
  {{#masonryElement "MasonryContainer"}}
    <div class="swatch"
   style="background-color:{{color}};">
{{color}}</div>
  {{/masonryElement}}
</template>
```

6. To get everything all pretty, we need to add some Atmosphere packages, and just a bit of CSS styling. In a terminal window, navigate to your `[project root]` folder and run the following commands:

```
$ meteor add twbs:bootstrap
```

```
$ meteor add voodoohop:masonrify
```

7. Next, create a file named `cb-style.css` in the `[project root]/client/` folder, and add the following style declarations:

```
#picture {
  color: #ccc;
  border: 3px dashed #ccc;
  width:800px;
  height:600px;
  border-radius: 4px;
  line-height: 3em;
  text-align: center;
  left: 100px;
```

```
      position: absolute;

  }

  #bgpicture {
    pointer-events:none;
    touch-events:none;
    position:absolute;
    background: url('Rawr.GIF');
    top:0px;
    left:100px;
    width: 800px;
    height:600px;
    z-index: 999;

  }
  .no-copy {
    -webkit-user-select: none;
  }
  #login-buttons {
    position : absolute;
    min-width: 220px;
    right: 20px;
    top: 10px;
  }
  .login-link-text {
    position:absolute;
    right: 0px;
  }
  .swatch {
    height:50px;
    width:50px;
    border-radius: 4px;
    border: solid #ccc 2px;
    line-height: 50px;
    font-size:0.8em;
    text-align: center;
    margin-bottom: 5px;
  }
  .masonry_container {
    position:absolute;
    top:100px;
    left:23px;
    width: 50px;
```

```
}
.brush-size {
  position:absolute;
  left:10px;
  top:10px;
  border: dashed 3px #ccc;
  border-radius: 40px;
  width:76px;
  height:76px;
}
```

8. Note that the `bgpicture` element has a background image in it, called `'RAWR. GIF'`—You can either obtain this picture from the source files for this recipe, or you can add your own image to be colored. The image *must* have a transparent background, and will look better if it is `800x600` pixels, but in any case, the image you want displayed should go into the `[project root]/public/` folder, and you should change the `background` property in the preceding step, so that it will display properly on the screen.

9. We will need to be able to change brush sizes, change colors, and paint/erase on the canvas, and we want to do that no matter what device we are on, so we will use the official `Hammer.js` package. We also want to include global shortcut keys for undo (*control + Z*) and redo (*shift + control + Z*), so we'll add a handy library that does that! In a terminal window, in your `[project root]` folder, enter the following two commands:

```
$ meteor add hammer:hammer@=2.0.4_1
```

```
$ meteor add gwendall:body-events
```

10. It's cleaner and easier to use `Hammer.js` events in the `Template.events` block, so we want to add the jQuery plugin for the `Hammer.js` file. As Meteor piggybacks on jQuery event handlers, if the plugin is added to jQuery, it's added to Meteor! As of this writing, the most reliable way to add the plugin is to manually copy the `plugin` script file into your `[project root]/client/scripts/` folder. You can either obtain the script by going to `http://hammerjs.github.io/jquery-plugin/` and following the instructions there, or by creating a file in your `scripts` folder called `jquery.hammer.js`, and adding the following code:

```
(function(factory) {
  if (typeof define === 'function' && define.amd) {
    define(['jquery', 'hammerjs'], factory);
  } else if (typeof exports === 'object') {
    factory(require('jquery'), require('hammerjs'));
  } else {
    factory(jQuery, Hammer);
  }
}(function($, Hammer) {
```

```
function hammerify(el, options) {
  var $el = $(el);
  if (!$el.data("hammer")) {
    $el.data("hammer", new Hammer($el[0], options));
  }
}

$.fn.hammer = function(options) {
  return this.each(function() {
    hammerify(this, options);
  });
};

// extend the emit method to also trigger jQuery events
Hammer.Manager.prototype.emit = (function(originalEmit) {
  return function(type, data) {
    originalEmit.call(this, type, data);
    $(this.element).trigger({
      type: type,
      gesture: data
    });
  };
})(Hammer.Manager.prototype.emit);
}));
```

11. We will now add the `Activities`, `Prefs`, and `Swatches` collections. As mentioned previously, we will need to keep track of our undo/redo, through recording activities. We will also need to keep track of color swatches, user preferences for brush size, and so on. To do this, we will declare three MongoDB collections. In your `[project root]/both/` folder, create a file called `cb-model.js` and add the following code:

```
Swatches = new Mongo.Collection('swatches');
Prefs = new Mongo.Collection('prefs');
Activities = new Mongo.Collection('activities');
```

We'll be using these later on, on both the client and on the server, but for now we're all done. You can close the `cb-model.js` file and move on to the next step.

12. Let's add the server-side logic for the preferences and undo/redo history. As unbelievable as this may seem, the server-side code for the coloring book is very light, compared to the client code. So, we're going to get it out of the way. We need to do several things on the server:

   ❑ Initialize swatches and other preferences

   ❑ Allow new swatches to be added, if desired

❑ Track and recall our painting activity (undo/redo)

❑ Clear everything out, so we can start over

In your `[project root]/server/` folder, create a file called `cb-server.js` and add the following `Meteor.methods` declaration:

```
Meteor.methods({

  initSwatches : function(userId){
    // no user = nothing to do. return.
    if (!userId) return;
    // if we already have swatches, return.
    if (Swatches.findOne({user:userId})) return;
    // add initial swatches
    Swatches.insert({color: '#ecf0f1', user:userId});
    Swatches.insert({color: '#ccc', user:userId});
    Swatches.insert({color: '#f1c40f', user:userId});
    Swatches.insert({color: '#e67e22', user:userId});
    Swatches.insert({color: '#e74c3c', user:userId});
    Swatches.insert({color: '#2ecc71', user:userId});
    Swatches.insert({color: '#2980b9', user:userId});
    Swatches.insert({color: '#000', user:userId});
  },

  addSwatch : function (color){
    // no user = nothing to do. return.
    if (!this.userId) return;
    // if it doesn't already exist, add the swatch
    if (!Swatches.findOne({color:color})){
      Swatches.insert({color:color, user:this.userId});
    }
  },

  clearActivity : function(){
    // no user, return.
    if (!this.userId) return;
    // clear the undo history from Activities collection
    Activities.remove({user:this.userId});
  },

  breakHistory : function(snapShot){
    // if we don't have a valid snapshot,
    // or user isn't logged in, return.
    if (!snapShot||!this.userId) return;
    // remove all snapshots after this one in the undo chain
```

```
        Activities.remove({$and: [{createdAt:{$gt:snapShot.
createdAt}},{user:this.userId}]})
    }
});
```

13. Now add the `Accounts.onLogin()` event handler in the same file:

```
Accounts.onLogin(function(login){
  // first, confirm that we have a valid userId
  userId = login.user._id;
  if (!userId) return;
  // if so, and if we don't have preferences, let's initialize
  if (!Prefs.findOne({user:userId})){
    Prefs.insert({user:userId, size:11, color:'#e74c3c'});
  }
  // likewise, let's initialize swatches
  Meteor.call('initSwatches', userId);
});
```

14. It's time to build the main logic that allows us to draw on the screen, using the `canvas` element. Create a file called `cb-client.js` in the `[project root]/client/` folder and add the following initial default values that control what we are drawing, and what our paintbrush color should be:

```
Session.setDefault('drawing', false);
Session.setDefault('color', '#e74c3c');
```

15. Because it's used in multiple places, we want to create a `drawLine` function that will draw/erase parts of the screen as needed. Add the following code just below the `Session.setDefault` declarations:

```
// **drawLine** -- helper function to draw / erase lines
drawLine = function (from, to, color,size) {
  if (size)
    ctx.lineWidth = size;
  if (color)
    ctx.strokeStyle = color;
  if (Session.get('erase')){
    ctx.globalCompositeOperation = 'destination-out';
  } else {
    ctx.globalCompositeOperation = 'source-over';
  }
  ctx.beginPath();
  ctx.moveTo(from.x, from.y);
  ctx.lineTo(to.x, to.y);
  ctx.closePath();
  ctx.stroke();
}
```

16. Now, add some helper functions that help us clean up the screen, or calculate the paint stroke positioning, relative to the page:

```
// **getPosition** -- helper function to calculate cursor position
getPosition = function (event) {
  return {
    x: parseInt(event.gesture.center.x - event.currentTarget.
offsetLeft),
    y: parseInt(event.gesture.center.y - event.currentTarget.
offsetTop)
  };
}
```

```
// **wipe** -- function to clear the painting area
wipe = function (emitAlso) {
  ctx.clearRect(0, 0, canvas.attr('width'),
canvas.attr('height'));
}
```

Whenever the user lifts their mouse/stylus/finger off of the screen, we want to record what they just drew, so let's add a snapshot-taking function just below our helpers:

```
// **addSnapshot** -- helper function to save strokes and update
// undo history
addSnapshot = function(){
  var userId = Meteor.userId();

  if (!userId) return;

  //Convert Canvas into a Picture
  ctx.globalCompositeOperation = 'source-over';
  var canvasPic = canvas[0].toDataURL();
  var timestamp = Date.now();

  //  check current history. if we are in undo-land, need to clean
  // up snapshots
  var curHist = Session.get('history');
  if (curHist){
    var curSnap = Session.get('currentSnapshot');
    Meteor.call('breakHistory',curSnap);
    Session.set('history',0);
  }

  // Save it to our Activities History
  Activities.insert({
    user:userId,
    canvas:canvasPic,
```

```
      createdAt:timestamp
    });
};
```

17. When we first log in, or when we go up and down the undo/redo history chain, we need to repaint the screen. Add the following helper function just below the `addSnapshot` helper:

```
// **paintActivity** -- helper function to redraw screen on undo/
// redo/draw
paintActivity = function(userId,idx){
  var latestActs = Activities.find({user:userId},
{sort:{createdAt:-1}}).fetch();
  if (!latestActs.length) {
    return;
  }
  if(!latestActs[idx]) idx = latestActs.length-1;
  wipe();
  var imageObj = new Image();
  imageObj.onload = function () {
    ctx.drawImage(this, 0, 0);
  };
  Session.set('currentSnapshot',latestActs[idx]);
  imageObj.src = latestActs[idx].canvas;
};
```

18. Okay, we're ready for the final touches, which include enabling our toolbar, and hooking up all the touch/mouse events to adjust brush sizes, change colors, paint and erase. In your `[project root]/client/` folder, create a file named `tmpl-toolbar.js`, and add the following interaction event handler code:

```
Template.toolbar.rendered = function(){
  // we first need to turn on hammer.js touch events...
  var brushSize = this.$('#brush-size').hammer();
  // ...we then change the pan threshold from 10 to 2
  var mgr = brushSize.data('hammer');
  mgr.get('pan').set({ threshold: 2 });
};
```

19. In that same file, add the `Template.helpers` function for displaying brush size, color preference, and so on:

```
Template.toolbar.helpers({
  swatches: function () {
    // Return the swatches for this user
    return Swatches.find({ user: Meteor.userId() });
  },
  preview : function(){
```

```
      // gets preferences for toolbar, with one modification...
      var prefs = Prefs.findOne({user:Meteor.userId()});
      // ...because brush is a circle, we need radius, not diameter
      if (prefs) prefs.size= ~~(prefs.size/2);
      return prefs;
    },
    eraseMode : function(){
      // if we're in erase mode, the brush circle is hidden
      return (Session.get('erase')? 'none':null);
    }
  });
```

20. Let's also add the interactivity logic, via the `Template.events` helper block:

```
Template.toolbar.events({
  'panstart #brush-size' : function(ev){
    // record our offset position, and turn on resizing
    Session.set('brushFrom',ev.gesture.center.x);
    Session.set('brushResize',true);
  },
  'pan  #brush-size': function(ev){
    // if we're not resizing, no need to continue
    if (!Session.equals('brushResize',true)) return;
    // likewise, if there are no prefs, just return
    var prefs = Prefs.findOne({user:Meteor.userId()});
    if (!prefs) return;
    // calculate the delta from last we checked...
    var adjustment = Session.get('brushFrom');
    adjustment = ev.gesture.center.x - adjustment;
    // ...and create a new brush size
    var newbrushSize = prefs.size + adjustment;
    // reset offset position, in case resizing continues
    Session.set('brushFrom', ev.gesture.center.x);
    // new brush size needs to be the 3rd bowl of porridge...
    if (newbrushSize<=70&&newbrushSize>=3){
      // adjust the preferences record and update the collection
      prefs.size = newbrushSize;
      Prefs.update({_id:prefs._id}, prefs);
    }
  },
  'panstop #brush-size': function(ev){
    // job's done. clean up.
    Session.set('brushFrom');
    Session.set('brushResize',false);
  },
```

```
      'doubletap #brush-size': function(ev){
        // turn on 'erase' mode
        Session.set('erase',(!Session.get('erase')));
      }
    });
```

21. We have a little bit of logic/event handling for the `swatch` template as well, so let's create a file called `tmpl-swatch.js` in the `[project root]/client/` folder, and add the following event listener and event interaction logic:

```
// suuuuper simple turning on of touch events
// using hammer.js
Template.swatch.rendered = function () {
  this.$('.swatch').hammer();
};


Template.swatch.events({
    'tap .swatch': function (ev) {
      // if no preference, return;
      var prefs = Prefs.findOne({user:Meteor.userId()});
      if (!prefs) return;
      // change the color to whatever swatch we tapped on
      prefs.color = this.color;
      // update Prefs collection
      Prefs.update({_id:prefs._id},prefs);
    }
});
```

22. Two more files and we're done! We have quite a bit of interaction to handle in the `picture` template (where our `canvas` element is), so let's create a file called `tmpl-picture.js` in the `[project root]/client/` folder, and add our initialization logic, via the `Template.rendered` method block. Add the following code to the `tmpl-picture.js` file:

```
Template.picture.rendered = function () {
  // set the canvas we will be drawing on
  canvas = this.$('#picture');
  // set the context for the canvas
  ctx = canvas[0].getContext('2d');
  // need to properly size the canvas
  canvas.attr({
    width: 800, height: 600
    // ...AND set up tap listeners via hammer.js
  }).hammer();
  // we want to change the default threshold from 10 to 2
  canvas.data('hammer').get('pan').set({threshold:2});
```

```
// we now set the line and line cap style
ctx.lineJoin = ctx.lineCap = 'round';
// Stops iOS from doing that bouncy, janky thing
document.ontouchmove = function (event) {
  event.preventDefault();
};
```

23. On preference changes, or on login/logout of a user, we have to perform some reactive logic to clean up or initialize our canvas. Add two `autorun` method blocks just below `Template.picture.rendered`, as follows:

```
// Reactive function that reruns whenever
  // preference are updated
  this.autorun(function () {
    // if no prefs exist, return
    var prefs = Prefs.findOne({user:Meteor.userId()});
    if (!prefs) return;
    // set stroke color and width
    ctx.strokeStyle = prefs.color;
    ctx.lineWidth = prefs.size;
  });


  // Reactive function that reruns whenever
  // User logs in, or our undo history position changes
  this.autorun(function(){
    // if we're not logged in (no userId), return
    var userId = Meteor.userId();
    if (!userId){
      wipe();
      return;
    }
    // otherwise, paint the proper screen,
    // using the undo chain history position
    paintActivity(userId,Session.get('history')||0);
  });
};
```

24. The last item of business for the `picture` template is to hook up the drawing events themselves. When we start drawing, we need event handlers for `panstart`, `panmove`, `panend`, and we also need one to clean everything up when we `doubletap` on the page. Add the following `Template.events` method block to the bottom of `tmpl-picture.js`:

```
Template.picture.events({
  'panmove #picture': function (ev) {
    // we must be in drawing mode...
```

```
        if (Session.equals('drawing', true)
            && Meteor.userId()) {
          // find our cursor position
          to = getPosition(ev);
          // physically draw the stroke
          drawLine(from,to);
          // update our from position
          from = to;
        }
      },
      'panstart #picture': function (ev) {
        // get our from position, when we start drawing
        from = getPosition(ev);
        // tell everyone that we are in drawing mode
        Session.set('drawing', true);
      },
      'panend #picture': function (ev) {
        // drawing mode is over!
        Session.set('drawing', false);
        // we now record the screen, add to undo chain
        addSnapshot();
      },
      'doubletap #picture': function (ev) {
        // clear the screen
        wipe();
        // wipe out our undo history
        Meteor.call('clearActivity');
      }
    });
```

25. All that's left now is the `keydown` event logic, so that we have proper undo/redo. Quickly make a file called `tmpl-body.js` in your `[project root]/client/` folder and add the following code:

```
Template.body.events({
  'keydown' : function(ev){

      // if there's no undo history, no reason to continue,
  // so return.
      var histLength = Activities.find({user:Meteor.userId()}).
  fetch().length;
      if (!histLength) return;

      // If it's not a CTRL+Z or CMD+Z, we don't care, so
  // return.
```

```
    if ((!ev.metaKey && !ev.ctrlKey)||(ev.keyCode!==90))
return;

    // find the current position in the undo chain, if any.
    var curHist = Session.get('history')||0;

    // if it was SHIFT+CMD+Z, it means redo, so decrement
// the history
    if (ev.shiftKey)
      curHist--;
    // otherwise, increment the history
    else
      curHist++;

    // if we're past the boundaries of TIME and SPACE we
    // certainly don't care about JavaScript anymore, so
let's return.
    if(curHist<0 || curHist> histLength-1 ) return;

    // after all that, set the new undo chain position
    Session.set('history',curHist);
  }
});
```

Whew! We made it through! Save all of your changes and navigate to your project in a browser, via `http://localhost:3000`. After you log in/create an account, you should see a nice color palette, a picture of your choice, and a brush size/preview. The following features are available:

- Double-click on the brush preview to toggle `'eraser'` mode
- Click and drag left and right on the brush preview to resize the brush
- Double-click on the page to erase and clear your undo history
- Press *Ctrl + Z* or *CMD + Z* to undo your strokes
- Press *Shift + Ctrl + Z* or *Shift + CMD + Z* to redo your strokes
- Log out and in with another user, to allow multi-user use

Do note that your undo/redo history chain is preserved, even if you log out. Once you log back in, you can go through your paint creations, stroke by stroke.

If you are a particularly awesome artist like my daughter, and you have properly coded everything, your page will look similar to the following masterpiece:

How it works...

Oh boy! That was a lot of code, just to demonstrate how the `canvas` element works, wasn't it? Instead of going through all of it step by step, let's go through the important pieces, related to the `Canvas` element.

Inside of `tmpl-picture.js`, we initialize our `canvas`. In the `Template.picture.rendered()` helper block, we first find our `canvas` element using `this.$('#picture')`:

```
canvas = this.$('#picture');
```

We then get the context (the handle) using the very appropriately-named `getContext()` function. We only want the 2D representation and not the 3D, so we pass `'2d'` as the argument to `getContext`:

```
ctx = canvas[0].getContext('2d');
```

Moving on to `cb-client.js`, we have several uses for the context, passed around in the global `ctx` variable. In the `drawLine` function, we set the size (`lineWidth`), color (`strokeStyle`) and we set the type of stroke (`globalCompositeOperation`) according to whether we are erasing (`'destination-out'`) or laying down some paint (`'source-over'`):

```
drawLine = function (from, to, color,size) {
  ...
    ctx.lineWidth = size;
  ...
    ctx.strokeStyle = color;
  if (Session.get('erase')){
    ctx.globalCompositeOperation = 'destination-out';
  } else {
    ctx.globalCompositeOperation = 'source-over';
  }
  ...
```

Once all that is set/determined, we tell the canvas that we are starting to draw (`beginPath`); we move our stroke (`moveTo`, `lineTo`) and then we clean up (`closePath`, `stroke`):

```
ctx.beginPath();
ctx.moveTo(from.x, from.y);
ctx.lineTo(to.x, to.y);
ctx.closePath();
ctx.stroke();
```

To save database space/transactions, we don't record every stroke. Instead, we wait for a stroke to be finished (the `'panend #picture'` event) and we add a snapshot of the entire canvas. We did this inside the `addSnapshot` helper function, with a call to the `canvas.toDataURL()` method:

```
var canvasPic = canvas[0].toDataURL();
```

Once we have the `canvas` graphics element represented as data, we simply save it to the `Activities` collection, via `Activities.insert()`:

```
Activities.insert({
  user:userId,
  canvas:canvasPic,
  createdAt:timestamp
});
```

Retrieving and displaying a saved screenshot from the `Activities` Collection is just as easy. The `ctx` handle takes care of the drawing for us. All we have to do to get that monkey to dance is give it the data. So, inside `paintActivity`, we create a new `Image()` object and we add a `.src` to that `imageObj`. We then call `ctx.drawImage()` when the `.onLoad` event callback is triggered:

```
var imageObj = new Image();
imageObj.onload = function () {
  ctx.drawImage(this, 0, 0);
};
```

Lastly, and most simply, if we want to wipe the screen, we simply call `ctx.clearRect()` with the dimensions we want cleared (in this case, the `width` and `height` of the canvas):

```
ctx.clearRect(0, 0, canvas.attr('width'), canvas.attr('height'));
```

There's a lot of Meteor magic going on, in coordination, so that we are using as little functional programming as possible, but that coordination is covered in other recipes.

There's more...

Actually, there's a whole lot more! We could have added custom color swatches (use `Meteor.call('addSwatch', '#yourcolorhere')` to do that from the console, by the way), or enabled drag and drop, and the storing of other pictures. You can use the *Using the HTML FileReader to upload images* recipe found in this chapter to do that, if you would like.

The core functionality, however, will remain the same: reference a `<canvas>` object, grab the context, and draw, baby draw!

 For an informative and thorough tutorial on HTML canvas, please visit: `http://www.html5canvastutorials.com/`.

See also

- ▸ The *Adding Meteor packages* recipe in *Chapter 2, Customizing with Packages*
- ▸ The *Inserting templates with Spacebars* and *Creating customized global helpers* recipes in *Chapter 3, Building Great User Interfaces*
- ▸ The *Creating and consuming a reactive value* recipe in *Chapter 6, Mastering Reactivity*
- ▸ The *Using the HTML FileReader to upload images* recipe in this chapter

8

Integrating Third-party Libraries

In this chapter, you will learn the following topics:

- ▶ Using npm packages directly
- ▶ Building graphs with D3.js
- ▶ Creating cutting-edge UIs with Polymer

Introduction

With so many third-party packages available via Atmosphere it's very easy to build, basically, anything! If you have a specific development need—some type of logic or library—chances are someone else has already packaged it up for you (and if they haven't, what a great opportunity for you!).

That being said, not all packages are created equal. Some will have fantastic documentation, with samples and tutorials on how to implement a library inside Meteor. Others, not so much. In either case, you will at some point need to roll up your sleeves and do a bit of work yourself. In this chapter, we will go over a few of the more popular third-party libraries, and show you how to implement them in Meteor.

Using npm packages directly

We have seen from the *Using npm modules* recipe in *Chapter 2, Customizing with Packages*, how to wrap npm packages inside your own personal package, using the `Npm.depends()` directive. That's all well and good, but what if we want to just use npm directly, without creating a custom package? Arunoda Susiripala — one of the most prolific (and brilliant) Meteor community developers, has written a package that helps us do just that. In this recipe, you will learn how to use the `meteorhacks:npm` package to implement a npm module directly in your code. Specifically, we will use the `Highlight.js` module on the server to properly format JavaScript code, as you might see in markdown or in an online code editor.

Getting ready

We will be using a default project installation, with the `client`, `server`, and `both` folders, to keep the code clean and readable. We will also use the `private` folder for some static content, so let's add that while we're at it. In a terminal window, navigate to where you would like your project to reside, and execute the following commands:

```
$ meteor create npmdirect
$ cd npmdirect
$ rm npmdirect.*
$ mkdir {client,server,private,both}
```

We also want to make use of the `meteorhacks:npm` package, so let's do that now. Run the following commands in the terminal:

```
$ meteor add meteorhacks:npm
$ meteor
```

Lastly, we will want to open a browser to `http://localhost:3000`, so we can watch the fun! We're now ready to start creating our direct npm integrations.

How to do it...

We will be adding the `Highlight.js` Node module and adding some sample code to leverage the module, using an inline template as our work area. Proceed with the following steps to use npm packages directly:

1. We will first add the `Highlight.js` Node module. To add a direct-use npm module, we will make a simple declaration in the `packages.json` file that was automatically added to our project when we added `meteorhacks:npm`. Open `[project root]/packages.json` and add the following declaration:

```
{
  "highlight.js" : "8.4.0"
}
```

If you look in the terminal window where Meteor is running, you will see something similar to the following text:

npm-container: updating npm dependencies -- highlight.js...

=> Meteor server restarted

Our `Highlight.js` module is now ready to use!

2. We will now create the server logic needed to use `Highlight.js`. Create a file named `server.js` in the `[project root]/server/` directory. Open that file for editing and add the following code:

```
Meteor.methods({
  highlight : function(){
    return setC();
  }
});

var setC = function(){
  var hLight = Meteor.npmRequire('highlight.js');
  var code = Assets.getText('code.txt');
  code = hLight.highlight('javascript',code,true);
  return code.value;
};
```

3. Next, let's create a sample code file in the `private` folder. We are going to use a base text file for the code we will highlight to make the syntax much easier (rather than try to do it in a JavaScript `var`, which can be messy with escape sequences). Meteor lets us use the `[project root]/private/` folder to store static files only visible on the server. Create a file in the `private` folder, called `code.txt`, and add some (valid) JavaScript to the file. We will reuse the `var setC = ...` function from the preceding step, but you can put anything you want inside there, provided it's valid JavaScript. Once you've added some code, save your changes.

4. We now need to create a simple code panel template. Create a file in `[project root]/client/` named `main.html`. Open that file for editing, and add the following code:

```html
<body>
{{> code}}
</body>
<template name="code">
  <pre class="hljs">{{{highlighted}}}</pre>
</template>
```

5. With the template in place, we can add `Template.code.helpers`, and use `Meteor.call()`. Create a file in `[project root]/client/` called `tmpl-code.js` and add the following code:

```javascript
Template.code.helpers({
  highlighted : function(){
    return Session.get('code');
  }
});


Meteor.startup(function(){
  Meteor.call('highlight', function(e,d){
    if (e) return;
      Session.set('code',d);
  });
});
```

After saving these changes, your code from the `code.js` file will be visible, albeit with little/no CSS formatting. If you check your browser, you should see something similar to the following screenshot:

```
var setC = function(){
  var hLight = Meteor.npmRequire('highlight.js');
  hLight.configure({
    classPrefix:''
    });
  var code = Assets.getText('code.txt');
  code = hLight.highlight('javascript',code,true);
  return code.value;
};
```

6. Well, that's not all that impressive, is it? Let's really highlight what is happening with some custom CSS. In a browser, navigate to the official list of `Highlights.js` themes, found at `https://github.com/isagalaev/highlight.js/tree/master/src/styles` and pick any theme you like. Simply click on the name of the theme, click on the button labeled **Raw**, and copy the corresponding CSS code. Then, create a file named `style.css` in your `[project root]/client/` folder, paste the code you copied, and save the file. Your formatted text should now have some noticeable formatting and coloring, similar to the following screenshot (this is the `Solarized Light` theme, copied from `solarized_light.css` at the link that we mentioned previously):

```
var setC = function(){
  var hLight = Meteor.npmRequire('highlight.js');
  hLight.configure({
    classPrefix:''
    });
  var code = Assets.getText('code.txt');
  code = hLight.highlight('javascript',code,true);
  return code.value;
};
```

How it works...

Inside of our `server.js` file, we created a simple `Meteor` method, available on (and called by) the client via `Meteor.call()`. We created a separate function that is called inside of the method even though we didn't have to (we could have just put the logic directly in the method call), because we wanted to keep our code clean and illustrative. Inside the `setC()` function, we make direct use of a npm module by using `Meteor.npmRequire()`:

```
var hLight = Meteor.npmRequire('highlight.js');
```

Quickly referencing our text file via `Assets.getText()`, we pipe our sample code into the `Highlights.js` file in the `.highlight()` method, which takes the language (`'javascript'`) as an argument, to let the module know what language highlighting we would like to see in the resultant formatted text:

```
var code = Assets.getText('code.txt');
code = hLight.highlight('javascript',code,true);
return code.value;
```

We return the formatted text, which is subsequently updated in the client UI, through the `Session.get('code')` variable. The template renders the raw HTML string, thanks to the use of `{{{triple moustaches}}}` rather than double, and the CSS file we added takes care of the eye candy for us.

In a nutshell, it really is that simple — by adding the `meteorhacks:npm` package, we can simply declare which npm modules we would like to use in our `packages.json` file, and then use them directly in Meteor, via the `Meteor.npmRequire()` function.

There's more...

As you may be aware, npm runs strictly asynchronously and is non-blocking. This means that a lot of the times when you want to use an npm module in Meteor, and want to do so synchronously, you need to wrap the call in an `Async` wrapper. We will explore how to do this in more depth in *Chapter 11, Leveraging Advanced Features,* but the `meteorhacks:npm` package allows us to do this quickly/easily as well, via the `Async.wrap()` and `Async.runSync()` methods.

 To learn more about `Async.wrap` and other methods available in `meteorhacks:npm`, please see the introduction available at `https://atmospherejs.com/meteorhacks/npm`.

Lastly, even though it's undocumented (and therefore not officially supported/subject to change), there are some npm modules used by the core Meteor server libraries that are exposed and usable on the server side. To use any of these, simply use `Npm.require()` in your server code, and you don't need to implement anything else. You can use them directly. The current list, as of `v1.0.2`, is as follows:

- `child_process`
- `crypto`
- `fibers`
- `fibers/future`
- `fs`
- `http`
- `os`
- `path`
- `semver`
- `source-map-support`
- `underscore`
- `url`

See also

- The *Using npm modules* recipe in *Chapter 2, Customizing with Packages*
- The *Inserting raw HTML using triple braces* recipe in *Chapter 3, Building Great User Interfaces*
- The *Handling asynchronous events* and *Using asynchronous functions* recipes in *Chapter 11, Leveraging Advanced Features*

Building graphs with D3.js

Using third-party libraries to render content inside Meteor is simple and easy to do, and there are a lot of great libraries out there. One of our personal favorites is the `D3.js` library (`http://d3js.org/`). It's well-documented, well-supported, and is a representative example of how to implement other (mostly) self-contained graphics rendering libraries. In this recipe we will create a demo graph application, complete with animations, using `D3.js`.

Getting ready

We will be using a default project installation, with the `client`, `server`, and `both` folders, and we will of course need the official `D3.js` package. In a terminal window, navigate to where you would like your project to reside, and execute the following commands:

```
$ meteor create d3sample
$ cd d3sample
$ rm d3sample.*
$ mkdir {client,server,both}
$ meteor add d3js:d3
$ meteor
```

With that out of the way, let's build us some sample graphs in D3!

How to do it...

Normally, the `D3.js` data sources are updated manually, or as the result of a feed, with an `update` statement of some kind being called. Because Meteor enables reactive computations (see the *Creating and consuming a reactive value* recipe in *Chapter 6, Mastering Reactivity*), we are going to put the `D3.js` rendering logic right into a `Tracker.autorun()` computation instead. Let's set up our reactive data source, throw that rendering logic into an `autorun`, and add some animations for good measure!

1. We first need to create and initialize the `Letters` collection. Create a file named `model.js` in your `[project root]/both/` folder, and add the following code:

   ```
   Letters = new Mongo.Collection('letters');
   ```

   Let's add an initialization of that collection as well. In your `[project root]/server/` folder, create a file named `server.js` and add the following `Meteor.startup` function code:

   ```
   Meteor.startup(function(){
     if (!Letters.find().fetch().length){
       Letters.insert({letter:'A',frequency:.08167});
       Letters.insert({letter:'B',frequency:.01492});
       Letters.insert({letter:'C',frequency:.02782});
       Letters.insert({letter:'D',frequency:.04253});
       Letters.insert({letter:'E',frequency:.12702});
       Letters.insert({letter:'F',frequency:.02288});
       Letters.insert({letter:'G',frequency:.02015});
       Letters.insert({letter:'H',frequency:.06094});
       Letters.insert({letter:'I',frequency:.06966});
   ```

```
        Letters.insert({letter:'J',frequency:.00153});
        Letters.insert({letter:'K',frequency:.00772});
        Letters.insert({letter:'L',frequency:.04025});
        Letters.insert({letter:'M',frequency:.02406});
        Letters.insert({letter:'N',frequency:.06749});
        Letters.insert({letter:'O',frequency:.07507});
        Letters.insert({letter:'P',frequency:.01929});
        Letters.insert({letter:'Q',frequency:.00095});
        Letters.insert({letter:'R',frequency:.05987});
        Letters.insert({letter:'S',frequency:.06327});
        Letters.insert({letter:'T',frequency:.09056});
        Letters.insert({letter:'U',frequency:.02758});
        Letters.insert({letter:'V',frequency:.00978});
        Letters.insert({letter:'W',frequency:.02360});
        Letters.insert({letter:'X',frequency:.00150});
        Letters.insert({letter:'Y',frequency:.01974});
        Letters.insert({letter:'Z',frequency:.00074});
    }
});
```

2. While we have `server.js` open, let's add a quick helper method to update the frequency, which we will use a bit later. Add the following code to `server.js`:

```
Meteor.methods({
    updateFrequency : function(letter,frequency){
        Letters.update({letter:letter},
            {$set:{frequency:frequency}});
    }
});
```

3. Now, we will add some simple scaffolding and styling. Our HTML is extremely simple, because `D3.js` is doing the heavy lifting. That said, we do want to put our `svg` element into a Meteor Template. Navigate to your `[project root]/client/` folder, create a file named `client.html`, and add the following code:

```
<body>
    {{> diagram}}
</body>

<template name="diagram">
    <svg class="chart"></svg>
</template>
```

Let's add some simple styling to adjust fonts and colors, and so on. Create a file named `[project root]/client/style.css` and add the following CSS declarations:

```css
.bar {
  fill: steelblue;
}
.bar:hover {
  fill: brown;
}
.axis {
  font: 10px sans-serif;
}
.axis path,
.axis line {
  fill: none;
  stroke: #000;
  shape-rendering: crispEdges;
}
.x.axis path {
  display: none;
}
```

We are now ready to add the `D3.js` rendering logic, inside `rendered/autorun`. The following code is taken almost line-for-line from Mike Bostock's awesome introductory tutorial on `D3.js`. The easiest thing to do would be to take the existing code base from that tutorial, copy and paste it into a local file, and then modify it. To do this, navigate in a browser to `http://bl.ocks.org/mbostock/3885304` and copy everything inside the `<script>` tag to the ending `</script>` tag. Create a file named `client.js` in your `[project root]/client/` folder, and paste the code into the new file (about 60 lines of code).

We will now modify the code from that page in the following four ways:

- ❑ Wrap all of the code inside a `Template.rendered` callback
- ❑ Wrap and extend the `d3.selectAll` rendering code inside an `autorun` computation
- ❑ Move and modify the axes rendering code outside the `autorun`
- ❑ Change data to point to our `Letters.find()` Mongo query

The completed `Template.diagram.rendered` callback is listed in the following code. It mainly consists of the `D3.js` sample code, with the preceding four modifications highlighted. If it's easier, you can simply copy and paste from below, rather than making the modifications yourself. However, it's worthwhile to at least go over the changes, to see how the code was modified. In your `client.js` file, make the following modifications to the existing code:

```
Template.diagram.rendered = function(){
  //we wrap everything in the Template.rendered() callback,
  // so that we don't interfere with Blaze
  var margin = {top: 20, right: 20, bottom: 30, left: 40},
    width = 960 - margin.left - margin.right,
    height = 500 - margin.top - margin.bottom;

  //We are going to set the domains for x an y immediately
  //(assuming the alphabet isn't going to change)
  x = d3.scale.ordinal()
  .domain('ABCDEFGHIJKLMNOPQRSTUVWXYZ'.split(''))
  .rangeRoundBands([0, width], .1);

  //ALSO: note that we *removed* the 'var' declarations,
  //so that x and y are global / accessible
  y = d3.scale.linear()
  .domain([0,0.15])
  .range([height, 0]);

  var xAxis = d3.svg.axis()
  .scale(x)
  .orient("bottom");

  var yAxis = d3.svg.axis()
  .scale(y)
  .orient("left")
  .ticks(10, "%");

  // We are moving the axes creation (and SVG init)
  // to be *outside* our autorun()
  var svg = d3.select("body").append("svg")
  .attr("width", width + margin.left + margin.right)
  .attr("height", height + margin.top + margin.bottom)
  .append("g")
  .attr("transform", "translate(" + margin.left + "," +
  margin.top + ")");

  svg.append("g")
```

```
.attr("class", "x axis")
.attr("transform", "translate(0," + height + ")")
.call(xAxis);

svg.append("g")
.attr("class", "y axis")
.call(yAxis)
.append("text")
.attr("transform", "rotate(-90)")
.attr("y", 6)
.attr("dy", ".71em")
.style("text-anchor", "end")
.text("Frequency");


//We move D3.js rendering inside Tracker.autorun()
this.autorun(function(){
  // Instead of reading data from a static file,
  // we access the Letters collection
  var data = Letters.find().fetch();
  if (!data.length) return;

  // To use D3.js's built-in update tracking,
  // we need access to our d3.selectAll() object..
  var bars = svg
  .selectAll(".bar")
  .data(data, function(d){return d._id;});

  // On new (when initializing), we append and animate
  bars.enter()
  .append("rect")
  .attr("class", "bar")
  .attr("x", function(d) { return x(d.letter); })
  .attr("width", x.rangeBand())
  .attr("height",0)
  .attr("y", height)
  .transition()
  .attr("y", function(d) { return y(d.frequency); })
  .attr("height", function(d) { return height -
    y(d.frequency); });

  // On change, we just animate to the new position
  bars
  .transition()
```

```
    .duration(200)
    .ease("sin-out")
    .attr("y", function(d) { return y(d.frequency); })
    .attr("height", function(d) { return height -
      y(d.frequency); });

  });
};
```

4. We can now create and call the `randomize` function. Our page should be rendering correctly now (check at `http://localhost:3000` and see for yourself), but it's not moving or doing anything else. Let's change that by changing to random frequency values for our letters. Towards the bottom of `client.js`, just after the `autorun` block, and just before the ending bracket for the rendered `callback` block, add the following timer call:

```
});//<--- end of autorun()

// everything's set! let's randomize 5 times / second...
  Meteor.setInterval(randomize,200);

};//<-- end of rendered()
```

Finally, add the `randomize()` function at the very bottom of the file, after everything else:

```
// Our randomize function
randomize = function(){
  // get a random position between 0-25
  var ranLetter = ~~(Math.random()*26),
  // and a random frequency between 0-15%
    ranFreq = (Math.random()*0.15);

  // get the actual character
  ranLetter = x.domain()[ranLetter];

// update the frequency using a server call,
// because it's easier than tracking down the _id
  Meteor.call('updateFrequency',ranLetter,ranFreq);
};
```

Save all of your changes, and your bar chart should be hopping along happily, similar to the following screenshot:

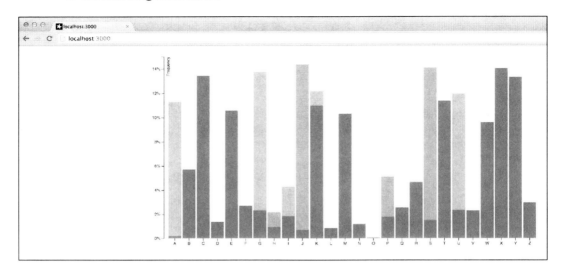

How it works...

There are two key rules to remember when integrating D3.js (and, by extension, any other rendering engine):

1. Put all your DOM/SVG manipulation logic inside Template.rendered()
2. Make the data source reactive, and wrap the rendering logic inside Tracker.autorun()

We followed rule #1 when we added the entire D3.js logic from the tutorial inside of Template.diagram.rendered(). This tells Blaze to keep its (awesome, yet grubby) hands off everything we'll be doing. We're essentially telling Blaze to go have a smoke break, while we implement some good ol' fashioned DOM/SVG manipulation (and animations!).

Then, instead of relying on a non-reactive data source, where we would have to periodically check for updates and/or call an update() function whenever results change, we used Meteor's declarative, reactive programming style by wrapping the D3.js logic inside an autorun function. That autorun function will re-run every time there's a change to the Letters collection, thanks to var data = Letters.find().fetch(); which is a reactive data source.

In other words, we followed rule #2 by creating a D3.js-friendly reactive computation, instead of using a functional (non-reactive) data model, like a hobo. Mike Bostock would be proud of us, as the avoidance of functional programming is one of the core tenets of D3.js.

It seems like we wrote a lot of code because of the `D3.js` sample code, and there are some details we're leaving out, such as moving the `y` and `x` axes rendering logic outside the `autorun` function (because we don't want to re-render it every time), but it really is that simple. Notice how incredibly simple (and loosely-coupled) our update statement is, inside the `randomize()` function: one. single. line.

When it comes to third-party renderers, wrap using `rendered()` and be reactive using `autorun()`.

 Wrap using `rendered()`, be reactive using `autorun()`.

There's more...

We strongly encourage you to look deeper into `D3.js`, which (as mentioned) runs on the same declarative programming principle as Meteor. There's a reason it integrates so cleanly, and for SVG graphs and animations, it really is top notch.

 Tutorials for `D3.js` can be found at `https://github.com/mbostock/d3/wiki/Tutorials`.

See also

▶ The *Creating dynamic lists* recipe in *Chapter 3, Building Great User Interfaces*
▶ The *Creating dynamic graphs with SVG and Ajax* recipe in *Chapter 7, Using Client Methods*

Creating cutting-edge UIs with Polymer

Polymer (`https://www.polymer-project.org/`) is ambitious. It is ambitious in the very best possible way, in that, if it succeeds, it will make our development lives so much better.

One of the largest time-wasting activities we as web developers go through is tweaking CSS, repositioning DOM elements, and trying to manually code animations. It's not that those things are bad (some of us quite enjoy well-designed components); It's that nearly every time, our efforts are thrown away when a new project or design theme is introduced.

Through the use of reusable, reliable components that work the same on every modern browser (or at least that's the goal — ambitious, right?), Polymer intends to abstract the design from the development, allowing developers to focus on development, and designers to focus on design.

This recipe will show you how to use Polymer components inside a Meteor application.

Getting ready

We are going to break down the actual recipe into two parts: configuring Meteor and Polymer and adding Polymer elements to our app. Because of this, we are going to handle the configuration and setup in the *Getting ready* step to keep the code and explanation of the code easier to understand.

Creating your app and folders

We will need several folders and subfolders we don't normally use, so let's get our entire file structure out of the way. Open a terminal window, navigate to where you would like to create your root project, and execute the following commands:

```
$ meteor create polymersample
$ cd polymersample
$ rm polymersample.*
$ mkdir -p client/templates/init
$ mkdir {both,server}
$ mkdir -p public/components
```

Creating your files

To save time creating files one by one later on, let's create them all right now. In the same terminal window, in your [project root] folder, execute the following commands:

```
$ touch .bowerrc
$ touch client/imports.html
$ touch client/main.html
$ touch client/styles.css
$ touch client/templates/tmpl-authors.html
$ touch client/templates/tmpl-authors.js
$ touch client/templates/tmpl-search.html
$ touch client/templates/tmpl-search.js
$ touch client/templates/init/head.html
$ touch both/model.js
$ touch server/server.js
```

Configuring Bower and installing Polymer

Bower is the safest and best way to install the Polymer libraries, as it makes sure we have the latest and greatest. You will want to make sure that you have Bower installed. If you don't, in your terminal window run the following command:

```
$ npm install -g bower
```

 You may need to run npm as `sudo` because you're installing globally. If so, run the following command:

```
sudo npm install -g bower.
```

With Bower installed, we want to tell Bower where we would like the Polymer components installed. In Meteor, that is in the `public/components` folder. In a text editor, open the `[project root]/.bowerrc` file, add the following line and save your changes:

```
{"directory":"public/components/"}
```

We are now ready to initialize our project using Bower. In a terminal window, in your `[project root]/` directory, enter the following command:

```
$ bower init
```

Bower is about to ask you a lot of questions! The good news is the answer to most of them is the *return* key, or a *space* and then the *return* key. Even better news is that most of the answers don't really matter. But, you do need to go through this, so that Bower will generate the `bower.json` file for you, which will keep track of which Polymer libraries we install (more on that in a minute), so answer the questions similar to the following example:

```
? name: Polymer Sample

? version: 0.0.1

? description:

? main file:

? what types of modules does this package expose?:

? keywords:

? authors:

? license: none

? homepage:

? set currently installed components as dependencies?: No

? add commonly ignored files to ignore list?: Yes

? would you like to mark this package as private which prevents it from
being accidentally published to the registry?: Yes
```

You will then get a preview of your `bower.json` file, as shown in the following screenshot:

```
{
  name: 'Polymer Sample',
  version: '0.0.1',
  license: 'none',
  ignore: [
    '**/.*',
    'node_modules',
    'bower_components',
    'public/components/',
    'test',
    'tests'
  ]
}
? Looks good? (Y/n)
```

Provided that `private:true`, and `ignore:` [...] are in place, type *Y* and hit *Enter*. Your Bower configuration is now complete!

We are now ready to install the Polymer libraries. In the same terminal window, enter the following commands, one after another, allowing one to complete before moving on to the next:

```
$ bower install polymer --save
$ bower install polymer/core-elements --save
$ bower install polymer/paper-elements --save
$ bower install polymer-github-card --save
```

On the last install, Bower will ask you what version of `polymer` and `core-components` will be supporting `polymer-github-card`. Select the version that the other components are dependent upon (as of this writing, this is `[library]#^0.5.0`).

Adding helper Meteor packages

There are three third-party packages we need to add. One of them, (`voodoohop:masonrify`), will assist with our layout, and the other two, (`meteorhacks:inject-initial` and `differential:vulcanize`), will allow Polymer elements to be added to our Meteor project with the least amount of pain (we suspect that this will get better in the future, but for now this is the workaround; and honestly it's not really so bad). In a terminal window, in your `[project root]`/ folder, enter the following commands:

```
$ meteor add voodoohop:masonrify
$ meteor add meteorhacks:inject-initial
$ meteor add differential:vulcanize
```

Configuring Meteor

Setup is almost done! Meteor generally gets along with other frameworks, but because Polymer has some pre-rendering DOM manipulations (which are really cool, but mess with Meteor's mojo...) we have to be able to inject an attribute into the `<body>` tag, and we also need to ensure that the base `polymer` and `webcomponents` files are referenced properly.

In an editor, open the `[project root]/server/server.js` file, and add the following HTML injection code:

```
Meteor.startup(function(){
  Inject.rawModHtml('addUnresolved',function(html){
    return html = html.replace('<body>', '<body unresolved>');
  })
});
```

Now we will take care of the baseline file references. Open `[project root]/client/templates/init/head.html` and add the following code:

```
<head>
  <script src="/components/webcomponentsjs/webcomponents.js"></script>
  <title>github authors</title>
</head>
```

One last step (this is for `vulcanize` to be able to consolidate all the component references), open `[project root]/client/imports.html` and add the following lines:

```
<!-- Components -->
<link rel="import" href="/components/polymer/polymer.html">

<!-- Styles -->
<link rel="import" href="/components/font-roboto/roboto.html">
```

Setup is complete! Let's start Meteor (run the `meteor` command in the terminal), open a browser to `http://localhost:3000`, and start using Polymer components!

How to do it...

Two caveats to what we're about to do: first, currently Polymer plays best with the Chrome browser. The samples below will work in other browsers, but there are some idiosyncrasies, such as `click` or `keypress` events, that may cause a little bit of frustration. Second, due to timing issues, as you're making changes to your code, there may be some instances where you will need to manually refresh your browser (which is a very rare thing when using Meteor!).

Keep in mind that Polymer is nowhere near being a 1.0 product — you are on the cutting edge with this recipe — so you'll have to bear with us, as we go through the fundamentals of using Polymer inside Meteor. Optimizing the timing and events and other behaviors across all other browsers would be a book in itself, so let's focus on the foundational part, and as Meteor and Polymer progress, these issues will work themselves out.

1. We will first add our CSS styling. Polymer does the heavy lifting here, so let's get what little CSS we have to contribute out of the way. Open `[project root]/client/styles.css` and add the following CSS declarations:

```css
html,body {
  height: 100%;
  margin: 0;
  font-family: 'RobotoDraft', sans-serif;
}
.container {
  width: 80%;
  margin: 50px auto;
}
div.sText {
  display:inline-block;
  width: 20rem;
}
div.sBtn {
  display: inline-block;
  width: 5rem;
  vertical-align: text-top;
}
paper-button.colored {
  color: white);
}
paper-button[raised].colored {
  background: rgb(66, 133, 244);
  color: white;
}
```

2. Let's take a look at the `polymer-github-card` component, using a static representation, just to see what we're playing around with. Open `[project root]/client/imports.html`, and add the following line just below the "...polymer.html" entry in the `Components` section:

```html
<link rel="import"
href="/components/polymer-github-card/dist/polymer-github-card.
html">
```

Now open `main.html`, found in the same folder, and add the following code:

```
<body>
  <div class="container">
    <polymer-github-card user="meteor"></polymer-github-card>
  </div>
</body>
```

In your browser, after `vulcanize` recompiles your `<header>`, you should see something similar to the following screenshot:

3. Now that we have confirmed that Polymer is working correctly, let's put the `polymer-github-card` component into a Meteor template, and create the ability to add multiple cards, based on a Mongo collection. Open `[project root]/both/model.js` and add the following line:

```
Authors = new Mongo.Collection('authors');
```

4. Now let's create our template. You'll remember that we're using `voodoohop:masonrify` to control the layout, so we will need to wrap our template declarations inside the `{{#masonry...}}` blocks, as appropriate. Open `[project root]/client/templates/tmpl-authors.html` and add the following code:

```
<template name="authors">
  {{#masonryContainer
    columnWidth=265
    gutter=5
    transitionDuration="0.2s"
    id="MasonryContainer"
  }}
```

```
      {{#each authors}}
        {{> authorCard}}
      {{/each}}
    {{/masonryContainer}}
</template>

<template name="authorCard">
  {{#masonryElement "masonryContainer"}}
    <div>
      <polymer-github-card
        user="{{userid}}">
      </polymer-github-card>
    </div>
  {{/masonryElement}}
</template>
```

Again, the majority of the previous code relates to layout. The actual call to dynamically populate `polymer-github-card` components is found in the `authorCard` template, and references `{{userid}}` in the `user` attribute. `userid` comes free, as it will be a property for each record in the `Authors` collection.

5. Let's now create the `Template.helper` function for passing the `Authors` collection, via the `Collection.find()` function. Open `[project root]/client/templates/tmpl-authors.js` and add the following code:

```
Template.authors.helpers({
  authors: function(){
    return Authors.find().fetch();
  }
});
```

6. While we're at it, lets make deleting records very simple. In `tmpl-authors.js`, add the following event handler at the bottom:

```
Template.authors.events({
  'dblclick polymer-github-card': function(e){
    Authors.remove({_id:this._id});
  }
});
```

7. We now need to modify our main template to reference our new dynamic template. Open `main.html` and modify the contents to look like the following:

```
<body>
  <div class="container">
    {{> authors}}
  </div>
</body>
```

8. Save all your changes, look in your browser (give `vulcanize` a second to do its thing), and you should see a completely blank page. Wow! That's only because our `Authors` collection is empty. Let's fix that. In your browser console, execute the following commands:

```
> Authors.insert({userid:'meteor'})
> Authors.insert({userid:'glasser'})
```

As you enter each command, a new card will pop into place, with the Meteor logo, and David Glasser's smiling happy childhood picture, as shown in the following screenshot:

The command line is so 1960's! Let's update our page to use some paper-elements components, and give us an easy way to add more GitHub authors.

9. Open `[project root]/imports.html` and add links for the components we will be using (which are found in our `public/components/` folder, by the way...) just below the "...`polymer.html`" declaration. When finished, your file should look like the following:

```
<!-- Components -->
<link rel="import" href="/components/polymer/polymer.html">
```

```
<link rel="import"
href="/components/paper-ripple/paper-ripple.html">
<link rel="import"
href="/components/paper-shadow/paper-shadow.html">
<link rel="import"
href="/components/paper-input/paper-input.html">
<link rel="import"
href="/components/paper-button/paper-button.html">
<link rel="import"
href="/components/polymer-github-card/dist/polymer-github-
card.html">



<!-- Styles -->
<link rel="import"
href="/components/font-roboto/roboto.html">
```

Let's create our `search` template, which will contain a `paper-input` component, and a `paper-button` component. Open `[project root]/client/templates/tmpl-search.html` and add the following code:

```
<template name="search">
  <div class="sText">
    <paper-input-decorator
      id="searchText"
      floatingLabel
      label="find an author">
      <input is="core-input" id="sInput">
    </paper-input-decorator>
  </div>
  <div class="sBtn">
    <paper-button
      raised
      class="colored"
      role="button"
      tabindex="0">
      search
      </paper-button>
  </div>
</template>
```

There's nothing special about the preceding code, Meteor-wise. It's all just straight up Polymer formatting and configuration.

To learn more about Polymer components, please visit: `https://www.polymer-project.org/docs/polymer/polymer.html`.

10. We will want to add a new card whenever we perform a search, that is, whenever we hit *Enter* inside our `paper-input` component, or click on our `paper-button` component. Open `tmpl-search.js`, found in the same `client/templates/` folder, and add the following code:

```
Template.search.events({
  'keypress #sInput' : function(e){
    if (e.keyCode!=13) return;
    addAuthor();
  },
  'click paper-button': function(e){
    addAuthor();
  }
});

function addAuthor(){
  var sInput = $('#sInput'),
      sVal = sInput.val();
  sInput.blur();
  if (!sVal || (Authors.findOne({userid:sVal}))) return;
  sInput.val('');
  Authors.insert({userid:sVal});
}
```

11. The very last step is to add a template inclusion for our `search` template to `main.html`. Open `[project root]/client/main.html` and add the following highlighted code:

```
<body>
  <div class="container">
    {{> search}}
  </div>
  <div class="container">
    {{> authors}}
  </div>
</body>
```

All done! Check out your app in the browser, allowing for refresh/recompiling, and you should be able to add as many GitHub author cards as you would like. Add some authors (suggestions: `meteorhacks`, `arunoda`, `d3`, `mbostock`, `voodoohop`, `pazguille`, `polymer`, `addyosmani`) and new cards will appear after each entry, as shown in the following screenshot:

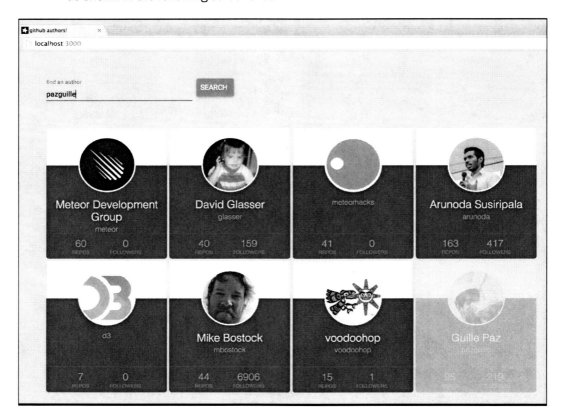

How it works...

Very rarely do we need to refer to the *Getting ready* section to fully understand what's going on, but the context around where and how to place Polymer files is important, so let's start there. We directed Bower to put any and all Polymer files into a subfolder belonging to [project root]/public/. Meteor treats files in the public folder differently than other folders—it treats them as static, and will not process the .js or .html files found inside.

This is to our advantage, because there are currently some pretty nasty conflicts between the Polymer and Meteor renderers. Specifically, both use the `{{double-stache}}` notation and the `<template>` tag, and interpret them differently. To resolve these conflicts (Nobel peace prize incoming!...) we "fence off" each framework, allowing Polymer to link to anything in the `public` folder, and having Meteor ignore everything in the same place. It's almost like the **Meteor Development Group** (**MDG**) planned it that way! Of course they did, anticipating and encouraging the use of other opinionated frameworks. MDG truly does want Meteor to play well with others, and in this case, it allows us to use Polymer in our applications.

A couple of other adjustments had to be made, such as inserting link elements into our `<head>` block, and injecting the unresolved attribute into the `<body>` element, but these are small, one-time issues, and once they're complete, we are free to use Polymer components to our heart's content.

As for the use of the Polymer components themselves, we can either use them directly (as shown in step #2) with no involvement from Meteor, or we can incorporate them into our `{{#each...}}` template or other template inclusions. We then have access to the normal Meteor `Template.helpers` and `Template.events`, which gives us easy, declarative-style access to reactive data.

Specifically, if we look at the `tmpl-authors.html` file, we will see that we are using the `{{#each authors}}` and `{{userid}}` template helpers, to iterate and render `polymer-github-card` components on the fly:

```
<template name="authors">
  ...
  {{#each authors}}
    {{> authorCard}}
  {{/each}}
  ...
</template>

<template name="authorCard">
  ...
    <polymer-github-card
        user="{{userid}}">
    </polymer-github-card>
  ...
</template>
```

In `tmpl-authors.js` and `tmpl-search.js`, we make use of `Template.events` to interpret `keypressed`, `click`, and `dblclick`, and are able to use the in-context (inline) data to modify records, such as when we delete a record, using the `Authors.remove({_id:this._id})` statement:

```
Template.authors.events({
  'dblclick polymer-github-card': function(e){
    Authors.remove({_id:this._id});
  }
});
```

There's more...

There are a very large number of interaction and compatibility/performance nuances between Polymer and Meteor, which are beyond the scope of this recipe (and this book). We recommend perusing Stack Overflow (`http://stackoverflow.com/questions/tagged/meteor`), the Meteor forums (`https://forums.meteor.com/`), or just lifting the hood and experimenting, to gain more experience in properly integrating Polymer and Meteor.

See also

 ▶ The *Adding Meteor packages* recipe in *Chapter 2, Customizing with Packages*
 ▶ The *Creating custom components* recipe in *Chapter 3, Building Great User Interfaces*
 ▶ The *Implementing a simple collection* recipe in *Chapter 4, Creating Models*

9
Securing Your Application

In this chapter, you will learn the following topics:

- ▶ Basic safety – turning off `autopublish`
- ▶ Basic safety – removing `insecure`
- ▶ Securing data transactions with `allow` and `deny`
- ▶ Hiding data with façades
- ▶ Protecting the client with `browser-policy`

Introduction

Meteor makes development and prototyping as fast and easy as possible. To accomplish this, there are some default packages installed that have no business in a production application. As you prepare your app for production, you will want to remove the packages that make prototyping easier, and replace them with some security best practices, to make your application more secure. In this chapter, we will go through the baseline security mechanisms needed to prepare an application for production.

Basic safety – turning off autopublish

Quickly and easily accessing your data saves you an enormous amount of time when you're prototyping! The autopublish package, which is installed by default in every newly-created Meteor app, enables you to quickly manage and access your data collections, so that you can churn out great code. When the time comes, however, broadcasting every field in every data collection is inefficient and unsecure. This recipe will show you the basics of removing the autopublish package, and implementing your own publish/subscribe code to keep your app working as intended.

Getting ready

We will create a very basic application, displaying simple text cards on the screen, and then show the effects of autopublish and subscribe/publish on those cards. To do this, we need to create our folder structure, add some basic templates, and add a bit of styling.

Project setup

In a terminal window, create your root project by entering the following commands:

```
$ meteor create secure-autopublish
$ cd secure-autopublish
$ rm secure-autopublish.*
$ mkdir {client,server,both}
$ meteor
```

Creating a basic template

In a text editor, create a file named collections.js in your [project root]/both/ folder, and add the following line:

```
Cards_open = new Mongo.Collection('open');
```

Next, create a file named [project root]/client/main.html and add the following <template> and <body> declarations:

```
<body>
  <div class="container">
    {{> open}}
  </div>
</body>


<template name="open">
  <h3 id="new-open">open:</h3>
```

```
    {{#each opens}}
    <div class="card {{shared}}">
      <div class="label id">id</div>
      <div class="id">{{_id}}</div>
      <div class="label text">text</div>
      <div class="text">{{text}}</div>
      <div class="label owner">owner</div>
      <div class="owner">{{owner}}</div>
    </div>
    {{/each}}
</template>
```

We need to add just a little bit of logic for display and creation, and we're ready to move on to styles. Create a new file named `[project root]/client/templatehelpers.js`, and add the following `Template.helpers` and `Template.events` functions:

```
Template.open.helpers({
  opens: function(){
    return Cards_open.find({},{sort:{text:1}}).fetch();
  },
  shared: function(){
    return (this.shared? 'shared':null);
  }
});


Template.open.events({
  'dblclick #new-open' : function(e){
    e.preventDefault();
    var txt = 'open card# ' + Cards_open.find({}).count();
    Cards_open.insert({text:txt});
  },
  'click .text' : function(e){
    e.preventDefault();
    var shrd = (!this.shared);
    Cards_open.update({_id:this._id},{$set:{shared:shrd}});
  },
  'dblclick .id' : function(e){
    e.preventDefault();
    Cards_open.remove({_id:this._id});
  }
});
```

Adding CSS styling

We need just a touch of CSS to make things more visually appealing. Create a file named
[project root]/client/styles.css and add the following CSS:

```css
body {
  font-family: 'helvetica neue';
}
.card {
  display: inline-block;
  min-width:10rem;
  height: 10rem;
  border: 2px dashed #ccc;
  border-radius: 0.21rem;
  margin: 0.25rem 0.25rem;
  padding: 0.5rem;
  vertical-align: top;
}

.container {
  width:90%;
  margin: auto;
}

.shared {
  background-color: rgba(25, 121, 36, 0.36);
}

.label {
  font-weight: bold;
  margin: 0.2rem 0;
  padding: 0.1rem;
  padding-left: 0.3rem;
}

.label:hover {
  background-color: rgba(7, 180, 21, 0.76);
  border-radius: 0.2rem;
}
```

Your app should now be up and running. Navigate to `http://localhost:3000` in a browser, and double click on the **open:** label to create some new cards. Click on the **text** tag in a card to modify the sharing property (the card will turn green) and double click on the **id** tag to delete a card. Your screen, after playing with it a bit, will look simlar to the following screenshot:

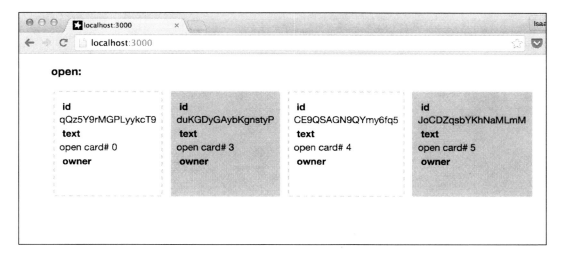

If everything is copacetic, we're ready to remove the `autopublish` package.

How to do it...

Proceed with the following steps to turn off `autopublish`:

1. In a new terminal window (keep Meteor running!), navigate to your `[project root]` and enter the following command:

   ```
   $ meteor remove autopublish
   ```

The screen on your web page will now show no results, and if you do a count on the `Cards_open` collection, even if you have many records created, the count will come back as **0**:

2. We will now add `publish` and `subscribe`. The `Cards_open` collection still exists. Because we removed the `autopublish` package, however, the communication between the client and the server has been severed. To restore it, we need to add a `publish` method on the server, and a `subscribe` method on the client. Create a file named `[project root]/server/collections-server.js` and add the following `publish` function call:

```
Meteor.publish('open',function(){
  return Cards_open.find({});
});
```

3. Now, create a file named `[project root]/client/collections-client.js` and add the following `subscribe()` function call:

```
Meteor.subscribe('open');
```

All done! You have successfully removed the `autopublish` package, and re-created the `publish/subscribe` calls necessary to allow the client to still see the `Cards_open` collection. Your browser should now display results properly when you create, modify, and delete using the clicks and double clicks mentioned previously.

How it works...

In a nutshell, `autopublish` checks to see what collections exist, and automatically writes your `publish` and `subscribe` function calls for you. It does this for every collection it can find, and is therefore neither performant nor secure.

By removing `autopublish`, we stopped the `publish` and `subscribe` functions from automatically being called. Because of this, we had to re-create those calls, creating a simple `publish()` call (on channel `'open'`) on the server, and a `subscribe()` call (on the same `'open'` channel) on the client.

Our `find()` statement in the `publish` function retrieves everything, which is inherently not secure or performant, but we will be fixing that in other recipes. The focus of this recipe was on how to remove the `autopublish` package, without affecting the functionality of our application.

See also

▶ The *Removing Meteor packages* recipe in *Chapter 2, Customizing with Packages*

Basic safety – removing insecure

Right after removing `autopublish`, we will want to control how data is added, removed, and updated, and put in some security measures, as appropriate. To enable this level of control, we need to remove the appropriately-named `insecure` package. To restore functionality after removing the `insecure` package, we will need to utilize a basic `collection.allow` declaration. This recipe shows you how to do exactly that.

Getting ready

We will use the *Basic safety – turning off autopublish* recipe found in this chapter as our baseline. Once you have completed that recipe, make a copy of the `secure-autopublish` folder (note: you will need all subfolders, including the hidden `.meteor` folder), rename it to `secure-rm-insecure`, start your app using the `meteor` command in the terminal, and you will be ready to proceed.

How to do it...

Just like the previous recipe for `autopublish`, we simply need to remove the `insecure` package, and then restore functionality.

1. In a new terminal window (keep Meteor running!), navigate to the root of your project and enter the following command:

    ```
    $ meteor remove insecure
    ```

    Your application now disallows any client changes to the `Cards_open` collection. Try to add a new card, share a card, or delete a card, and you will be unable to do so. Whether through the UI using clicks and double clicks, or even programmatically through the web console, you will be unable to make any changes, as shown in the following screenshot:

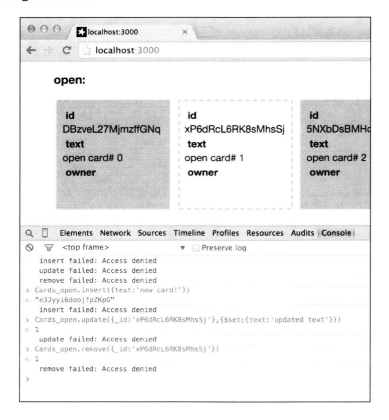

2. Okay, now we need to get our super powers back! Open the `[project root]/` `server/collections-server.js` file, and add the following code to the bottom of the file:

```
Cards_open.allow({
  insert : function(userId,doc){
    return true;
  },
  update : function(userId,doc,fieldNames,modifier){
    return true;
  },
  remove : function(userId,doc){
    return true;
  }
});
```

After saving these changes, our `insert`, `update`, and `remove` capabilities have been restored. You can now add, modify, and delete as many cards as you would like, either through the UI or programmatically through the web console.

How it works...

The `insecure` package does almost exactly the same thing for data collection security that `autopublish` does for publish security – it finds every collection it can and automatically creates a `collection.allow` function for all functions (`insert`, `update`, and `remove`). By removing the `insecure` package, we prevented our `Cards_open` collection from allowing any client-side changes.

To remedy this, and to prepare for more granular security (see later recipes in this chapter for details), we called `Cards_open.allow()` and enabled all collection modifications by returning `true` for every checking function.

So, although the net security of our application hasn't changed, we are now prepared to modify our publishing and security settings to make our application production-ready.

See also

▶ The *Removing Meteor packages* recipe in *Chapter 2, Customizing with Packages*

Securing data transactions with allow and deny

Properly configured, Meteor collections are quite secure. The granular control we have over what is allowed and what is not allowed enables us to secure our applications appropriately. In this recipe, you will learn how to use `allow` and `deny` to secure your collections and control access.

Getting ready

Using the *Basic safety – removing insecure* recipe found in this chapter, we already have an application with both the `autopublish` and `insecure` packages removed. Once we add and configure the appropriate user `accounts` packages, we will be ready to proceed.

Using a copy of the *Basic safety – removing insecure* recipe as a baseline, open a terminal window, navigate to your project root, and execute the following commands:

```
$ meteor add accounts-ui
$ meteor add accounts-password
```

If your app isn't already running, make sure to start it using the `meteor` command.

We now need to add the `loginButtons` template, and modify our `insert` statement, to add an `owner` property to each record.

Open your `[project root]/client/main.html` file and add the `loginButtons` template inclusion just below the `<body>` tag, as shown in the following example:

```
<body>
  {{> loginButtons}}
  <div class="container">
    . . .
```

Next, open your `[project root]/client/templatehelpers.js` file and modify the `Template.open.events` insert logic to add `owner`, and only fire if there is a logged-in user. Your code changes should look as follows:

```
Template.open.events({
  'dblclick #new-open' : function(e){
    e.preventDefault();
    if (!Meteor.userId()) return;
    var txt = 'open card# ' + Cards_open.find({}).count();
    Cards_open.insert({text:txt , owner: Meteor.userId()});
  },
```

Finally, in your browser, create a new user, and make sure you are logged in as that user (the name of the user doesn't matter – we suggest using a fake one such as `user1@test.com`).

Now, whenever you create new cards, the **owner** section will be filled in with the logged-in user's unique ID, as shown in the following screenshot:

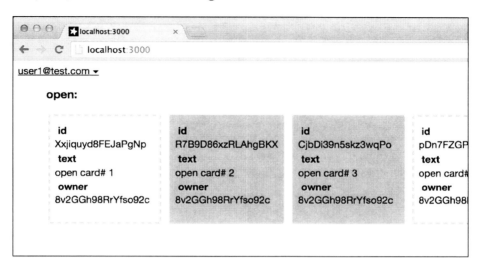

The current state of the application is not secure. Anybody can `insert`, `remove` and `update` any of the cards, even if they belong to another user! We are going to fix this situation by using the `collection.allow()` and `collection.deny()` declarations.

1. First, we will require a logged-in user for `insert`. Open your [project root]/`server/collections-server.js` file, locate the `Cards_open.allow()` function call, and make the following modification to the `insert` function declaration:

```
Cards_open.allow({
  insert : function(userId,doc){
    return(userId!=null);
  },
```

   You will now no longer be able to create new cards while being logged out (you can test this if you would like).

2. Next, we will allow only the owner of a record to `update` or `remove` cards. In the same `collections-server.js` file, modify the `update` and `remove` function declarations as follows:

```
update : function(userId,doc,fieldNames,modifier){
  return (doc.owner==userId);
```

```
  },
  remove : function(userId,doc){
    return (doc.owner==userId);
  }
```

3. Save your changes, and test your new rules by logging in as a new user (create one if needed), trying to change results, trying to add new cards without being logged in, and so on. With these rules in place, only a logged-in user will be able to create new cards, and only the owner of a card can modify the card or delete it.

How it works...

All client-side attempts to alter collections in any way flow through two callbacks: `allow` and `deny`. In order for a collection change to be accepted by the server, the incoming change must receive one `true` response from one of the `allow` functions (for example, we return `true` on the `insert` function if the `userId!=null`), and must receive zero `true` responses from any of the `deny` functions.

In this particular case, we are doing a simple check on `insert`, under the `allow` callback, to make sure the user is logged in, which translates to `userId!=null`. For `update` and `remove`, the check is to see if the logged-in user is the owner/creator of the card, through `return (doc.owner==userId)`.

There is no limit to the number of `allow` or `deny` callbacks you can declare, although it's usually best to consolidate them when possible, using a "pessimistic" security model (only allow what is needed, rather than allowing everything and only denying what is needed).

There's more...

The preceding `allow` rules work just fine, if only the UI is being used. However, it's possible for someone to open the console window and make direct collection manipulation calls, which could cause some problems.

First, our check for `insert` is only `userId!=null`. Any additional fields, or even a malicious `insert`, can be added via the command line, for example, let's say that I am in possession of the `userId` for another user (not hard to get, it's found in the `owner` field of each card). I could easily `insert` a card with something nasty in the text, or `update` the text and owner of an existing cart, so as to make it appear that another user was the one that created the note.

For example, If I am logged in as `user2@test.com`, and I know that the `userId` value for `user1@test.com` is `'8v2GGh98RrYfso92c'`, I can run the following command in the browser console, and potentially get `user1` in trouble:

```
> Cards_open.insert({text:'NSFW !@##%!!!',owner:'8v2GGh98RrYfso92c'})
```

We can handle this in several ways. We can either make our `allow` callback functions more complex, with multiple `if...else` statements, or we can use the `deny` callback to prohibit certain behavior. In `[project root]/server/collections-server.js`, create a new `deny` callback with the following code:

```
Cards_open.deny({
  insert : function(userId,doc){
   return (doc.owner!=userId);
  },
  update : function(userId,doc,fieldNames,modifier){
    return (fieldNames.length!=1 || !(~fieldNames.indexOf('shared')));
  }
});
```

For `insert`, if `doc.owner!=userId`, the deny callback will return `true`. For `update`, if an attempt is made to modify any field except shared, the `deny` callback will return `true` as well. Using these two callback functions, we have further tightened security, and taken away any console line shenanigans.

See also

For a breakdown of what's possible with `allow` and `deny`, consult the official Meteor documentation available at `http://docs.meteor.com/#/full/allow`.

Hiding data with façades

Some of our security (and performance) problems can be resolved through limiting access to certain fields and records in our data collections, for example, if the `owner` field of a record isn't sent to the client, a potential hacker will never be able to get the `userId` value of another user. Likewise, if only records belonging to a certain `userId`, or ones marked for sharing, are passed to the client, private records can stay private and visible only to the user that created them. This recipe will show you how to create a façade to limit fields and records being sent to the client.

Getting ready

Please complete the *Securing data transactions with allow and deny* recipe found in this chapter, including the additional `deny` callback functions found in the *There's more...* section. Once completed, and your Meteor app is running, you are ready to use this recipe.

How to do it...

We are going to modify the `publish` function on the server so that it only returns records that are owned by or shared with the logged-in user, and we will stop broadcasting the `owner` field.

1. Open the `[project root]/server/collections-server.js` file, locate the `Cards_open.publish` section, and make the following changes to the `Cards_open.find()` method:

```
Meteor.publish('open',function(){
   return Cards_open.find({$or:
          [ {shared:true},
            {owner:this.userId}
          ]
        },
        {fields:{owner:0}});
});
```

2. Now that the `owner` field is no longer visible on the client, we can remove the following two lines from our open template in the `[project root]/client/main.html` file:

```
<div class="label owner">owner</div>
<div class="owner">{{owner}}</div>
```

3. With those changes saved, any given logged-in user will only be able to see cards that have been created by that same user, or cards that have been shared. If you log in to two different browsers, with two different users, you will be able to see how sharing makes records visible to the other user, and vice versa. The following screenshot shows an example of two users sharing some records, and not sharing others:

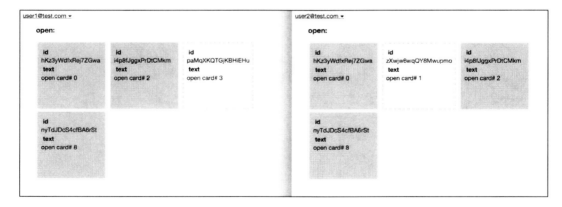

How it works...

By modifying the selector and the `fields` option, we were able to limit the recordset being published to the client. The client, try as it might, will never be able to see any of the records excluded by the selector, nor any of the excluded `fields`, because the server simply isn't sending them when it is publishing.

Specifically, we used a `{$or: [...]}` selector to limit which records are published, by including only records created by the current user (`owner:this.userId`), or records that have been shared (`shared:true`). We used the `{fields:{owner:0}}` option, to return all `fields` except `owner`. This *blacklist* approach is less secure than a *whitelist* approach, but to keep this recipe simpler, we decided to tell the query what fields to exclude (optimistic) rather than what fields to include (pessimistic).

To whitelist, rather than blacklist, enumerate the fields you would like displayed, and pass a value of 1 with them (for example: `{text:1 , _id:1 , shared:1}`). All fields not specified will automatically not return with the query.

See also

  ▸ The *Filtering with MongoDB queries* recipe in *Chapter 4*, *Creating Models*

Protecting the client with browser-policy

Securing your database is pretty straightforward in Meteor, but what about client-side security? Meteor has you covered there as well, using standard `Content-Security-Policy` and `X-Frame-Options` safeguards. This recipe will walk you through adding the `browser-policy` package, and configuring basic client-side security.

Getting ready

We will create a brand new project as usual, but we will be keeping the default files, creating some *unsafe* scripting functionality along the way.

Scaffolding setup

In a terminal window, navigate to where your project root will be, and execute the following commands:

```
$ meteor create secure-client
$ cd secure-client
$ mkdir {client,server,both}
$ mv secure-client.* client/
$ meteor
```

Add CDN-hosted bootstrap

Visit the official Bootstrap `Getting Started` page, located at `http://getbootstrap.com/getting-started/` and scroll to the section marked as **Bootstrap CDN**. Copy the contents from that section, and insert them into the `<head>` block of your `[project root]/client/secure-client.html` file. When finished, your changes should look similar to the following code:

```
<head>
  <title>secure-client</title>
  <!-- Latest compiled and minified CSS -->
  <link rel="stylesheet" href="https://maxcdn.bootstrapcdn.com/
bootstrap/3.3.2/css/bootstrap.min.css">

  <!-- Optional theme -->
  <link rel="stylesheet" href="https://maxcdn.bootstrapcdn.com/
bootstrap/3.3.2/css/bootstrap-theme.min.css">

  <!-- Latest compiled and minified JavaScript -->
  <script src="https://maxcdn.bootstrapcdn.com/bootstrap/3.3.2/js/
bootstrap.min.js"></script>
</head>
```

Add inline and eval() scripts

While we have `secure-client.html` open, let's modify the template, adding some indicators, an inline script in an `href` attribute, and a new section for displaying `eval()` results. Modify your `hello` template so that it looks like the following code:

```
<template name="hello">
  <button>Click Me</button>
  <p>You've pressed the button
    <div class="badge">{{counter}}</div>
  times.</p>
  <p>Which is 1/2 of our eval value: {{dblCounter}}</p>
  <a href="javascript:alert('hax0rz!'); Meteor.call('dropTable');">
      <div class="btn btn-info">Bootstrap!</div>
  </a>
</template>
```

We have a bit of logic to add, so that the template will be displayed properly. First, we will create a simple collection called `Test`. Create a file named `[project root]/both/model.js` and add the following line:

```
Test = new Mongo.Collection('test');
```

Now, configure the server method `dropTable` to simulate someone erasing the database. Create a file named `[project root]/server/methods.js` and add the following code:

```
Meteor.methods({
  dropTable: function(){
   Test.remove({});
  }
});
```

Next, we need to modify the `hello` template helpers and events to be "vulnerable" to our clever hacks! Open `[project root]/client/secure-client.js`, modify the `Template.hello.helpers` section to the following:

```
Template.hello.helpers({
  counter: function () {
    try {
      var x = Test.find().count();
      Session.set('counter', eval("x*2"));
    } catch (err) {
      console.log('ERROR: ', err);
    }
    return x;
  },
  dblCounter: function () {
    return Session.get('counter');
  }
});
```

Finally, modify `Template.hello.events` to add a record to the `Test` collection, rather than updating the `counter` variable. Your code should look similar to the following:

```
Template.hello.events({
  'click button': function () {
    // increment the counter when button is clicked
    Test.insert({action:'click'});
  }
});
```

Once all of these changes are saved, our application is thoroughly "hacked" with an `eval()` being used to double the normal click counter, an inline script that will remove all records from our `Test` collection, and with scripts and styles being used from an alternate site (the Bootstrap CDN).

Navigate to `http://localhost:3000/` and play around with the buttons for a bit. After a few clicks, your screen will look similar to the following screenshot:

To activate the inline "hack", click the button labelled **Bootstrap!** – a notice will come up that you've been hacked, and after you click on **OK,** the `Test` collection will be cleaned out. The notice will look something like the following screenshot:

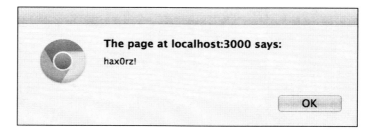

You're now ready to shut down all these expert hacking techniques!

How to do it...

To secure our application, we will add the `browser-policy` package, and then configure it appropriately for our environment.

1. In a new terminal window, navigate to the root folder of your project (keep your app running!) and execute the following command:

    ```
    $ meteor add browser-policy
    ```

Your application will now have lost all Bootstrap formatting, and the `eval()` function which was doubling your counter and the eval() function, which was doubling your counter, will no longer work. When you click the **Click Me** button, your counter will increment but the double counter will not. Your screen should look similar to the following screenshot, with a lot of errors in the web console explaining that the unsafe "hacks" from before are no longer allowed:

2. We will now fine-tune our security settings with `BrowserPolicy.content`. The inline scripting vulnerability still exists (click on **Bootstrap!** if you would like to test it), and our formatting, which we don't consider a hack, is no longer working. So, we are currently not strict enough in one area (inline scripts) and too strict in another (refusing all content from the Bootstrap CDN, a trusted source). Let's rectify that. Create a new file named `policy.js` in the `[project root]/server/` folder. Add the following two lines, and save your changes:

```
BrowserPolicy.content.allowStyleOrigin(
'https://maxcdn.bootstrapcdn.com/');
BrowserPolicy.content.allowScriptOrigin(
'https://maxcdn.bootstrapcdn.com/');
```

3. Our Bootstrap formatting has been restored! Now, let's disallow inline scripts, as well as prevent connections to any servers. Add the following two lines to the `policy.js` file and save your changes:

    ```
    BrowserPolicy.content.disallowInlineScripts();
    BrowserPolicy.content.disallowConnect();
    ```

    The inline script that was erasing our `Test` collection will now no longer run. However, by disallowing all connections, we have inadvertently destroyed the `DDP` connection to our server. We need to rectify that by whitelisting our `//:localhost:3000` address for HTTP and for websockets (for `DDP`).

4. Add the following three lines to the end of the `policy.js` file and save your changes:

    ```
    var rootUrl = __meteor_runtime_config__.ROOT_URL;
    BrowserPolicy.content.allowConnectOrigin(rootUrl);
    BrowserPolicy.content.allowConnectOrigin
    (rootUrl.replace('http', 'ws'));
    ```

 As we are dealing with your browser's security policy, a manual refresh is required each time you make a change to `policy.js`.

Refresh your browser one final time, and now everything that should be allowed is working, and everything that shouldn't (inline scripts, `eval()`, etc.) is prohibited. Your screen, after a few clicks, should look like the following screenshot:

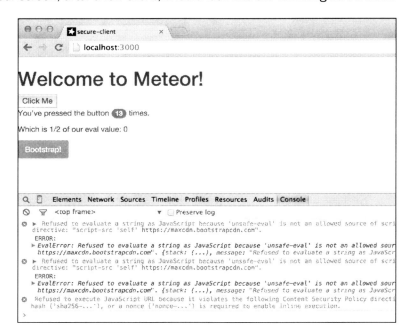

How it works...

By default, installing the `browser-policy` package will disable the `eval()` scripts, and only allow resources (images, etc) from your site. This is why just adding `browser-policy` disabled the double counter `eval()` script, and stripped away all the Bootstrap files.

To allow Bootstrap resources, we whitelisted the styles and scripts of the Bootstrap CDN, using the two `BrowserPolicy.content` functions – `allowStyleOrigin()` and `.allowScriptOrigin()`.

Next, we shut off inline scripts with the `disallowInlineScripts()` function. We also prevented any and all AJAX / remote server calls, using the `disallowConnect()` function.

Being this strict also broke our server's DDP connection, which we restored using the `allowConnectOrigin()` function, for both HTTP and `ws`.

See also

There are many other options available to us (this is just a primer), so if you would like to really fine-tune your security settings, we recommend the most excellent article from Arunoda Susiripala, located at `https://meteorhacks.com/xss-and-meteor.html`, and the `browser-policy` documentation, found on Atmosphere: `https://atmospherejs.com/meteor/browser-policy`.

10
Working with Accounts

In this chapter, you will learn the following topics:

- ▶ Implementing OAuth accounts packages
- ▶ Customizing the accounts login
- ▶ Performing two-factor authentication

Introduction

Critical to nearly every application we build is some type of authentication and user identification. Usually, we will spend days and weeks developing an accounts system, when we could spend that time programming our app. Meteor solves this problem, and solves it well. From integrations with major OAuth providers (Twitter, Google, Facebook, etc.) to a simple, secure password-based system, adding accounts and authentication inside of your Meteor app is quick and painless. The recipes in this chapter will cover the most important aspects of Meteor's `accounts` packages, enabling you to easily take care of user accounts and move on to other things.

Implementing OAuth accounts packages

Today, there are so many popular authentication services available, with such large user bases, that it's kind of silly not to take advantage of those services. If you use the accounts system of a major service, like Twitter or GitHub, you instantly tap into an enormous user base which can increase the use of your app. This recipe will show you how to implement an OAuth accounts system in a Meteor app, using the Twitter accounts service as an example.

We are going to focus almost exclusively on the accounts and authentication piece of our application, and as such, we only need a very simple, baseline application.

In a terminal window, create your root project by entering the following commands:

```
$ meteor create twitter-login
$ cd twitter-login
$ mkdir {client,server,both}
$ mv twitter-login.* client/
$ meteor add twbs:bootstrap
$ meteor
```

That's all it takes. Everything else will be done inside our recipe, so let's get going!

How to do it...

We will add the appropriate `accounts` packages, and configure our Twitter login service. Proceed with the following steps:

1. In a new terminal window (keep your application running), navigate to the root folder of your project, and enter the following two commands:

   ```
   $ meteor add accounts-twitter
   $ meteor add accounts-ui
   ```

   This will add several dependent packages, so you don't have to. How thoughtful and gentlemanly of Meteor to do that for us!

   > You can just as easily use another authentication service by replacing `accounts-twitter` used in this step with any of the following: `accounts-facebook`, `accounts-github`, `accounts-google`, `accounts-meetup`, `account-weibo`, or `accounts-meteor-developer`.

2. Open `[project root]/client/twitter-login.html` and add the following template inclusion just after the starting `<body>` tag:

   ```
   <body>
     {{> loginButtons}}
   ```

3. Save this change, and navigate to your app in a browser (usually `http://localhost:3000/`). At the top-left of your screen you will see a red button that says **Configure Twitter Login**, as shown in the following screenshot:

4. Click on **Configure Twitter Login** button, and a set of instructions for configuring your Twitter app will appear. Follow those instructions *exactly*, entering your `consumerkey` (API key) and consumer `secret` key(API secret) where appropriate.

 For this recipe, the value you enter in the website field is going to be `http://127.0.0.1:3000` rather than `http://localhost:3000`. Twitter doesn't allow the use of `localhost`.

5. With your service configured, you are ready to log in. Click on the blue (formerly red) button labeled **Sign In** with Twitter, and a new window should pop up, asking you to authorize your app, as shown in the following screenshot:

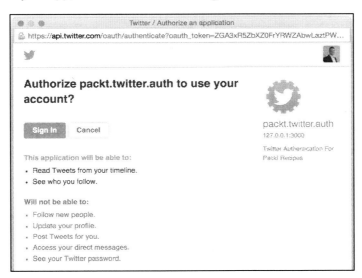

6. Once you authorize the app, you should be logged in, indicated by a status change in the login button, as shown in the following screenshot:

How it works...

This recipe is pretty packaged up, so there's not a lot of code involved. That said, we can dissect what's going on, so that we can understand where to tweak this recipe when needed.

Let's do a deep dive into how the authentication piece is working. `accounts-twitter` relies on the `accounts-base`, `accounts-oauth` and `twitter` packages. If we crack open each of those packages, we can see just how much legwork has been done for us:

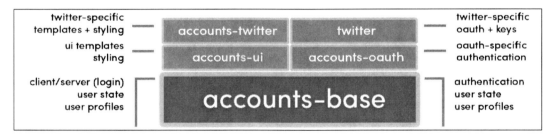

Put as simply as possible, `accounts-ui` and `accounts-twitter` give you a responsive UI, and make calls to `accounts-base`, which handles all of the account administration. `accounts-oauth` helps `accounts-base` by handling the OAuth-specific events and calls. `accounts-oauth` is configured by the `twitter` package, which provides specific URLs and parameters needed to use Twitter's OAuth service.

Here's a more detailed explanation:

The `accounts-base` package is a generic accounts package that accepts different types of login methods, provides helper methods for account administration, and helps maintain the `users` collection. The `users` collection is where we store logged-in state, preferences, and profile information.

One of the exposed methods in `accounts-base` is `Accounts.registerLoginHandler()`, which can be used by more specific login packages (such as `accounts-oauth` or `accounts-password`) to register handlers for login information:

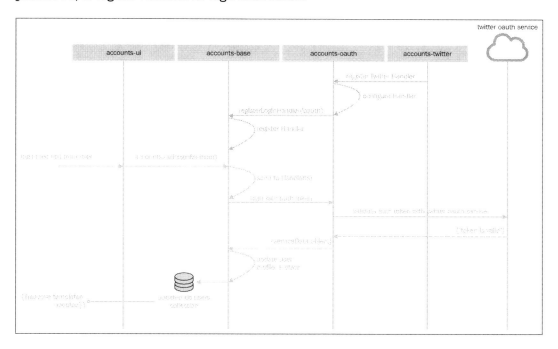

When `accounts-base` gets a request for a login, that request has a certain `type`, and has certain `service` parameters. `accounts-base` runs the information through all the login handlers that were registered, and lets each of those handlers respond with either `undefined` ("this is not my login method"), `error` ("the credentials were wrong"), or `serviceData` object ("login was accepted"), including a token for reconnecting easily.

The `accounts-oauth` package builds off of the `accounts-base` by registering a login handler of type: `'oauth'`, and exposing some helpers of its own. The `accounts-oauth` helpers allow us to configure a specific OAuth service. Each OAuth service requires customized URLs and parameters. We chose the Twitter OAuth service, and therefore used the `twitter` and `accounts-twitter` packages to configure those URLs and parameters.

The `accounts-oauth` packages is also responsible for handling the message/callback from the OAuth service, via the popup authentication form. That is, when the popup authentication from Twitter was complete, it redirected to `http://localhost:3000/_oauth/twitter` and had an OAuth token to pass to our app. The `accounts-oauth` package evaluates that particular URL (because we configured it with the `twitter` package), snatches up the token, and then attempts a login, using the `Accounts.callLoginMethod()` with some JSON that looks similar to the following:

```
{
methodArguments: [{oauth: {
credentialToken: "m3OHQUrRWU34anuq40Bx3q7JBoEmVgwKGICU1jY4H7_"
credentialSecret: "2qPoqew8m-AXiC2OVfrkWem0_M_APcdMpnz-cGsl6-k"
}},
...
]}
```

The login handler that `accounts-oauth` registered receives this JSON, and confirms with the (Twitter) OAuth service that the token is valid. If it is valid, a `user` profile is created/updated in the `users` collection, and `serviceData` (containing a login token, among other things) is passed to the client via a callback function. Because of the callback, and because the client is subscribing to the `users` collection, the client sees that there is a logged-in user, and acts accordingly.

The `twitter` and `accounts-twitter` packages contain convenience methods that work on top of `accounts-base` and `accounts-oauth`. For example, the `twitter` package has a server file (`twitter_server.js`) that declares the specific Twitter URLs, registers the `twitter` service through the `OAuth.registerService()` method, and even creates a Twitter-specific credential call, as shown in the following code:

```
Twitter.retrieveCredential =
  function(credentialToken, credentialSecret) {
    return OAuth.retrieveCredential(
      credentialToken, credentialSecret);
};
```

The `accounts-twitter` packages creates the `Meteor.loginWithTwitter()` method, and declares which profile fields are visible on the client, using `Accounts.addAutoPublishFields()`.

There's more...

Sometimes, seeing how the user and configuration information is stored can be helpful in understanding what's going on under the hood. We can do this using the `meteor mongo` command in a terminal window. Open a new terminal window (keep your application running), navigate to your project root, and enter the following command:

```
$ meteor mongo
```

You will now have command line access to the collections that store user information and login service configurations.

To view the Twitter configuration settings, enter the following command:

```
> db.meteor_accounts_loginServiceConfiguration.find()
```

You will see the configuration for your Twitter login service, as shown in the following code:

```
{ "service" : "twitter",
  "consumerKey" : "th2is2i2safa333kecon442sume24r433key",
  "secret" : "th9isi9sa9fa87kesecr666e3t",
  "loginStyle" : "popup", "_id" : "DBfakeYnnFbmidbC"
}
```

If you would like to reconfigure your Twitter login service, you can remove the entry using the following command:

```
> db.meteor_accounts_loginServiceConfiguration.remove({})
```

Once you do this, you can follow the instructions on the screen and re-enter your Twitter credentials as you did in the preceding recipe.

To view the different states of a logged in user, run and re-run the following command:

```
> db.users.findOne()
```

Go ahead and experiment with this, running it when the user is logged out, when the user is logged in, and when the user doesn't exist yet. Pay special attention to the `services` section and you'll be able to see how logins are handled by both the `twitter` and `resume` login services.

See also

► The *Customizing the accounts login* recipe in this chapter
► The *Building custom server methods* and *Handling asynchronous events* recipes in *Chapter 11, Leveraging Advanced Features*

Customizing the accounts login

Packaged accounts logins are great and all, but they don't always go with the design of the rest of our page, or they provide too much functionality when all we need is a little functionality. This recipe will show you how to customize Meteor's accounts packages using the Twitter OAuth service as an example.

Getting ready

We will essentially be using the *Implementing OAuth accounts packages* recipe found in this chapter as our baseline, but we aren't going to add the `accounts-ui` package, and therefore will not be configuring the Twitter service through the UI, so we need to roll our own.

In a terminal window, create your root project by entering the following commands:

```
$ meteor create twitter-custom
$ cd twitter-custom
$ mkdir {client,server,both}
$ mv twitter-custom.* client/
$ meteor add twbs:bootstrap
$ meteor
```

Open a new terminal window (keep your app running) and add the `accounts-twitter` and the `service-configuration` packages:

```
$ meteor add service-configuration
$ meteor add accounts-twitter
```

We now need to configure our login service manually, using the API key and API secret from our existing Twitter service (the one we created with the *Implementing OAuth accounts packages* recipe). Create a file named `[project root]/server/auth-init.js` and add the following code, replacing the appropriate sections with your key and secret:

```
ServiceConfiguration.configurations.upsert({
  service:"twitter" },
  {
    $set: {
      "consumerKey" : "[your API Key from apps.twitter.com]",
      "secret" : "[your API secret from apps.twitter.com]"
    }
  }
);
```

When you copy your keys from the Twitter Apps page, there's usually an extra space character on the end. Make sure you remove that character (e.g. "key123 " needs to be "key123") or your authentication will fail!

We are now ready to build our own customized login.

How to do it...

To build our own login, we'll need a couple of buttons, and some type of indicator that we're logged in. Easy peasy.

1. Open [project root]/client/twitter-custom.html and add the following template:

```
<template name="customLogin">
  {{#if currentUser}}
    <div id="logout" class="btn btn-info">Log out</div>
    <img src="{{profPic}}" alt="">
  {{else}}
    <div id="login" class="btn btn-default">Log in</div>
  {{/if}}
</template>
```

2. We now want to call our template. Make the following changes inside the `<body>` tag, and save the file:

```
<body>
  <div class="container">
    {{>customLogin}}

    <h1>Welcome to Meteor!</h1>

    {{> hello}}
  </div>
</body>
```

3. Create a new file named [project root]/client/templatehelpers.js, and add the following customLogin template helpers:

```
Template.customLogin.helpers({
  profPic: function(){
    var loggedin = Meteor.user();
    return loggedin &&
loggedin.services...url;
  }
});
```

4. Now, let's hook up our login and logout buttons. In the same `templatehelpers.js` file, add the following events declarations:

```
Template.customLogin.events({
  'click #login' : function(e){
    Meteor.loginWithTwitter();
  },
  'click #logout': function(e){
    Meteor.logout();
  }
});
```

5. Save your changes, and navigate to your app in a browser (usually `http://localhost:3000`). You should see a login button, as shown in following screenshot:

6. If you click the **Log in** button and authorize the Twitter app when prompted by the popup window, you will be authenticated and your Twitter avatar will appear, next to a **Log out** button, as shown in the following screenshot:

How it works...

Starting in the `customLogin` template, we make use of the `{{#if currentUser}}` helper, which checks to see whether `Meteor.user()` is `null` or not. In other words, if a user is logged in, `currentUser` returns `true`.

If `currentUser` is `true`, we add a **Log out** button, and an `<img>` tag, with the `src` attribute set to a property found on the user profile. Specifically, `profPic` returns the `services.twitter.profile_image_url` property if a user is logged in.

For the login and logout events, we simply call the `Meteor.loginWithTwitter()` (provided by the `accounts-twitter` package) and the `Meteor.logout()` methods. Meteor takes care of the rest for us.

There's more...

The accounts interface itself is quite customizable, with many packages available at `https://atmospherejs.com/?q=accounts-ui`.

We suggest installing the `accounts-ui-unstyled` package and experimenting with CSS/styling. You can get a great overview of what options and DOM elements are available by checking out the raw repository available at `https://github.com/meteor/meteor/tree/devel/packages/accounts-ui-unstyled`.

Pay particular attention to the `login_buttons.html` and `login_buttons.js` files, as they'll give you some pointers on what's possible.

See also

▸ The *Implementing OAuth accounts packages* recipe in this chapter

Performing two-factor authentication

We can make any application more secure (and safer from bots or hack attempts) by providing two-factor authentication. Two-factor authentication requires an individual to verify their identity using two separate methods. One such method, SMS text verification, has become quite popular, due to its convenience and difficulty in mimicking. This recipe will show you how to create two-factor authentication in a Meteor app, using the Twitter OAuth and Twilio SMS services.

Getting ready

Using the *Customizing the accounts login* recipe found in this chapter, we already have an application that authenticates against Twitter. We will expand that recipe, and add the Twilio SMS service to send a 6-digit verification code for our second authentication challenge. So that we can focus on the authentication part of the recipe, we will set up the Twilio service here rather than in the main recipe.

Creating our baseline application

Please follow the *Customizing the accounts login* recipe found in this chapter, and recreate that project, changing the name from `twitter-custom` to `two-factor`.

Signing up for the Twilio SMS service

Navigate to `https://www.twilio.com/try-twilio` in a browser, or visit the home page at `https://www.twilio.com/`, and click on the **SIGN UP** link on the top right.

Enter the necessary information to create an account, and click **Get Started**.

Verify that you're human by entering your phone number and clicking on **Text Me**. Shortly thereafter, you will receive a text message (if not, you can retry). Enter the code from that message into the verify section, and click on the **Verify** button.

You will now have a phone number generated for you. Accept the default number, or choose one for yourself (the default one is free), and click on the **Go To Your Account** button.

 Make a note of your assigned phone number, as you will need it later in this recipe.

Congratulations, you're all set up with a trial account from Twilio!

Creating an SMS service on Twilio

While logged in to Twilio, click on your name in the top right corner of the page. Select the **Account** option to go to the **Account Settings** page. There you will be presented with two sets of API keys. You can use either of those for testing, but would obviously want to use the Live credentials for a production application. Your screen should look like the following screenshot:

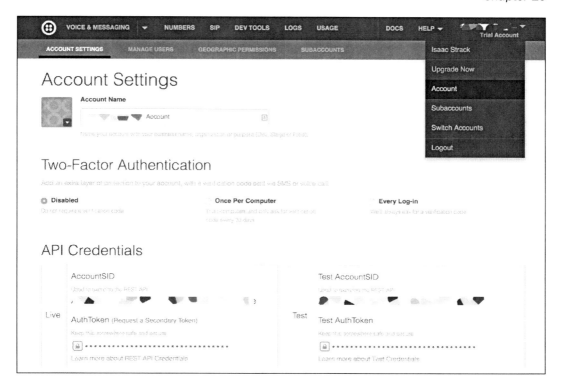

Decide which credentials you'll be using, and make note of both the **AccountSID** and the **AuthToken**.

Installing the twilio-node npm package

Stop your application (*Ctrl + C*) in the terminal, and enter the following command:

```
$ meteor add meteorhacks:npm
```

Run your application again by entering the following command:

```
$ meteor
```

You will receive a message letting you know that meteorhacks:npm has been initialized, as shown in the following example:

```
-> npm support has been initialized.
-> please start your app again.
```

Before starting our app again, we will need to declare that we are going to use the `twilio-node` npm package. Open the newly-created `[project root]/packages.json` file, and add the following declaration:

```
{
   "twilio":"1.10.0"
}
```

Now, start your application back up again in the terminal, using the `meteor` command, as shown in the preceding examples.

With the `twilio-node` npm package installed, all that's left to do is create a Twilio messaging method and test it.

Creating and testing the sendTwilio() method

Create a new file named `[project root]/server/twilio.js` and add the following code, replacing the `AccountSID`, `AuthToken`, and `Twilio Phone Number` as appropriate:

```
sendTwilio = function (phone, message) {
  return Meteor.wrapAsync(function (phone, message, callback) {
    var Twilio = Meteor.npmRequire('twilio')
      ('[YOUR AccountSID GOES HERE]',
        '[YOUR AuthToken GOES HERE]');
    var phoneNum = '+1' + phone;
    var twilioPhone = '[TWILIO NUMBER PATTERN: +1NUMBER]';

    Twilio.sendMessage({
      to: phoneNum,
      from: twilioPhone,
      body: message
    }, function (err, msg) {
      if (err) {
        callback && callback(err);
      } else {
        callback && callback(null, msg);
      }
    });
  })(phone, message);
};
```

A good chunk of time could be spent explaining what all the preceding code does, but sufficeth to say, the `Twilio.sendMessage()` method gets called using `Meteor.wrapAsync()` with a callback, because Twilio is an npm module and therefore requires the wrapper. You should now be able to send messages to your phone, which you can test by opening a new terminal window (keep your app running), navigating to your root folder, and using the `meteor shell` command to test.

If your mobile number were `555.867.5309`, you would enter the following:

```
$ meteor shell
> sendTwilio('5558675309','test',function(e,d){console.log(e,d);})
```

If everything is set up properly, you will get a text message on your phone, similar to the following screenshot:

If something went wrong, the console will spit out an error message, and you can trace down the source of your error.

Hopefully everything went right, and we are now ready to complete our two-factor authentication recipe!

How to do it...

We'll start by getting everything running smoothly on the server side, incorporating a new login state called `verified`. Once the server side is complete, we'll then build out the different user states in our UI.

We will need to generate a 6-digit code to be sent to the user, and we can leverage an existing Meteor package to do so.

1. In a new terminal window (keep your app running), in the project root, enter the following command:

    ```
    $ meteor add random
    ```

2. Now, create a file named `[project root]/both/helpers.js` and add the following code:

```
Random.digits = function(len){
  var numArr = [0,1,2,3,4,5,6,7,8,9];
  var ret = '';
  while(ret.length<len){
    ret+=Random.choice(numArr);
  }
  return ret;
};
```

3. We've just extended the random package to spit out simple codes of any length we choose. You can test this if you would like by entering `Random.digits(6)` in the web console.

4. Open `[project root]/server/auth-init.js` and append the following declaration:

```
var verifiedField = ['services.twofactor.verified',
                     'services.twofactor.phone'];
Accounts.addAutopublishFields({
  forLoggedInUser: verifiedField,
  forOtherUsers: []
});
```

5. Now, to make sure that the `services.twofactor.verified` property exists on each account, we will initialize it both when an account is created, and when a user logs in successfully. Append the following code to `auth-init.js`:

```
Accounts.onCreateUser(function(options,user) {
  check(options, Object);
  check(user, Object);
  user.services.twofactor = {};
  user.services.twofactor.code = Random.digits(6);
  user.services.twofactor.verified = false;
  user.profile = options.profile;
  return user;
});

Accounts.onLogin(function(options){
  if (options.type!=='resume'){
    Meteor.users.update(
      options.user._id,
      {$set:
        {"services.twofactor.verified":false,
         "services.twofactor.code":Random.digits(6)
        }
```

```
        }
      );
    }
});
```

6. Everything is in place for us to now create the SMS authentication challenge. Create a new file named `[project root]/server/auth-methods.js` and add the following `Meteor.methods` declarations:

```
Meteor.methods({
  sendChallenge : function (phone){
    if (!this.userId) return;
    var newCode = Random.digits(6);
    if (phone!=null){
      Meteor.users.update(
        this.userId,
        {$set:
          {"services.twofactor.phone":phone,
           "services.twofactor.code":newCode}});
    } else {
      Meteor.users.update(
        this.userId,
        {$set:
          {"services.twofactor.code":newCode}});

    }
    var curUser = Meteor.users.findOne(this.userId);
    return sendTwilio(curUser.services.twofactor.phone, curUser.
services.twofactor.code);
  },
  verifyCode : function(code){
    if (!this.userId) return;
    var curUser = Meteor.users.findOne(this.userId);
    if (!curUser) return;
    if (curUser.services.twofactor.code == code){
      Meteor.users.update(
        this.userId,
        {$set:
          {"services.twofactor.verified":true}});
    }
  }
});
```

7. With everything on the server set, we now need to update our templates and events on the client side. Let's first create some kind of visual sign that we've successfully authenticated. Open [project root]/client/two-factor.html and modify the <button> element as follows:

```
<button class="btn {{btnState}}">Click Me</button>
```

8. Now open two-factor.js in the same folder and make the following addition to the Template.hello.helpers declaration:

```
counter: function () {
    return Session.get('counter');
},
btnState: function(){
  var curUser =Meteor.user();
  if (curUser && curUser.services.twofactor.verified)
    return 'btn-success';
  return 'btn-danger';
}
```

9. Finally, make the following changes to the 'click button' event handler:

```
'click button': function () {
    // increment the counter when button is clicked
    var curUser =Meteor.user();
    if (curUser && curUser.services.twofactor.verified) {
      Session.set('counter', Session.get('counter') + 1);
    } else {
      alert ('not authorized!');
    }
}
```

10. Everything else is done. We now only need to provide a way to make our server calls. Open [project root]/client/two-factor.html and make the following changes to the customLogin template:

```
<template name="customLogin">
  <div class="btn-toolbar">
    <div class="btn-group" role="group">
      {{#if currentUser}}
      <div type="button" id="logout"
      class="btn btn-info btn-lg">Log out</div>
      <div id="profile" class="btn btn-default btn-lg">
       <img src="{{profPic}}" alt="">
      </div>
      {{else}}
      <div type="button" id="login"
      class="btn btn-default btn-lg">Log in</div>
      {{/if}}
```

```
    </div>
    {{#if currentUser}}
    {{>secondLogin}}
    {{/if}}
  </div>
</template>
```

11. We now need to create the `secondLogin` template, with conditionals based on whether the user is verified or not. Append the following template to the bottom of `two-factor.html`:

```
<template name="secondLogin">
  {{#if verified}}
  <div class="btn btn-success btn-lg">
    <span class="glyphicon glyphicon-ok"></span>
  </div>
  {{else}}
  <div class="btn-group" role="group">
    <div class="btn btn-primary btn-lg" id="btnChallenge">
      <span class="glyphicon glyphicon-phone"></span>
    </div>
    <input type="text" id="phoneNum"
    class="btn btn-default btn-lg"
    placeholder="{{defaultPhone}}">
  </div>
  <div class="btn-group" role="group">
    <input type="text" id="verCode"
    class="btn btn-default btn-lg"
    placeholder="code...">
    <div class="btn btn-primary btn-lg" id="btnVerify">
      <span class="glyphicon glyphicon-check"></span>
    </div>
  </div>
  {{/if}}
</template>
```

12. We have the tiniest bit of CSS to add to make our profile pic behave. Open the file named `[project root]/client/two-factor.css` and add the following CSS declarations:

```
#profile img {
  max-height: 44px;
  margin: 0 0;
}

#profile {
  padding: 0 0;
}
```

13. Open [project root]/client/templatehelpers.js and add the following helpers:

```
Template.secondLogin.helpers({
  verified: function(){
    var curUser = Meteor.user();
    return (curUser&&curUser.services.twofactor.verified);
  },
  defaultPhone: function(){
    var curUser = Meteor.user();
    return curUser && curUser.services.twofactor.phone;
  }
});
```

14. Last of all, we need to add the event handlers for the buttons to send SMS texts and to verify the code found in the SMS messages. Append the following code to templatehelpers.js:

```
Template.secondLogin.events({
  'click #btnChallenge' : function (e){
    var phoneNum = $('#phoneNum').val();
    if (!phoneNum.length)
      phoneNum = $('#phoneNum').attr('placeholder');
    if (!phoneNum.length==10) return;
    Meteor.call('sendChallenge',phoneNum);
  },
  'click #btnVerify' : function(e){
    var verCode = $('#verCode').val();
    if (!verCode.length==6) return;
    Meteor.call('verifyCode',verCode);
  }
});
```

15. Save all your changes, and go ahead and test your new UI. Upon authenticating via Twitter, you will receive two text prompts and two buttons, as shown in the following screenshots:

The button on the left will send a randomized code to the phone number you specify (or the saved phone number, if one exists). The button on the right will submit a verification code. If you entered the correct code (found in the text message sent to your phone), you will be verified, and your screen will look similar to the following screenshot:

Congratulations, you've just implemented two-factor authentication in your Meteor app!

How it works...

Several things had to be accomplished in order for two-factor authentication to work. First, we had to extend the users collection with a new service named `twofactor`. Some of the `services.twofactor` properties needed to be exposed for use on the client, and we had to set `services.twofactor.verified` to `false` whenever a new user was created, or when a user logs in using Twitter OAuth. Inside of our `auth-init.js` file, we accomplished both of these tasks, first by calling the `Accounts.addAutopublishFields()` method, and then by listening and updating via the `Accounts.onCreateUser()` and the `Accounts.onLogin()` event handlers:

```
Accounts.addAutopublishFields({
  forLoggedInUser: verifiedField,
  forOtherUsers: []
});
Accounts.onCreateUser(function(options,user) {
  ...
  user.services.twofactor.code = Random.digits(6);
  user.services.twofactor.verified = false;
  ...
});
  Accounts.onLogin(function(options){
  ...
      {$set:
      {"services.twofactor.verified":false,
       "services.twofactor.code":Random.digits(6)
      }
  ...
  });
```

We added two server methods to helps us with verifying the user. The first, `sendChallenge()`, generates a new 6 digit random code, updates the `services.twofactor.code` property, and then sends the code to the specified phone number via the Twilio service. The second, `verifyCode()`, receives manual input from the user, checks the manually entered code against the `services.twofactor.code` property, and updates `services.twofactor.verified` to `true` if they match:

```
Meteor.methods({
  sendChallenge : function (phone){
    if (!this.userId) return;
    var newCode = Random.digits(6);
    ...
    return sendTwilio(...);
  },
  verifyCode : function(code){
    ...
    if (curUser.services.twofactor.code == code){
      Meteor.users.update(
        this.userId,
        {$set:
          {"services.twofactor.verified":true}});
    }
  }
});
```

With the addition of the `verified` property, and the server methods used to change the `verified` property from `false` to `true`, we can now use `verified` in our UI. We created a helper method, `Template.secondLogin.verified`, that checks to see if the `services.twofactor.verified` property is set to `true`. We then use this helper in our `secondLogin` template to show that the user is logged in and verified:

```
<template name="secondLogin">
  {{#if verified}}
  <div class="btn btn-success btn-lg">
    <span class="glyphicon glyphicon-ok"></span>
  </div>
  {{else}}
  ...
  {{/if}}
</template>
```

The rest of the event handlers and helpers on the UI are used for convenience, or to make calls to the server methods previously outlined.

The simplified version is this: we extended the `users` collection, adding a `verified` property. We used the SMS text and verification to change the value of the `verified` property. We disallow any activity in the client UI unless `verified==true`. This check, as a complement to checking if there is a logged in user, allows us to require two-factor authentication in our UI.

There's more...

This model of extending the `users` collection with new `services` properties can be used for pretty much anything, and is not just limited to SMS text challenges. By adding and exposing new `services` properties, you can control what features are available, depending on the user status. Imagine being able to limit some features of the UI, based on the subscription plan a user has purchased. Or imagine remembering layout and view preferences based on the saved preferences of the user. All of this, and more, is possible by extending the `users` collection.

See also

- ► The *Building a smooth interface with Bootstrap* recipe in *Chapter 3, Building Great User Interfaces*
- ► The *Using npm packages directly* recipe in *Chapter 8, Integrating Third-party Libraries*
- ► The *Customizing the accounts login* recipe in this chapter
- ► The *Using asynchronous functions* recipe in *Chapter 11, Leveraging Advanced Features*

11
Leveraging Advanced Features

In this chapter, we will cover the following topics:

- ▸ Building custom server methods
- ▸ Creating custom EJSON objects
- ▸ Handling asynchronous events
- ▸ Using asynchronous functions

Introduction

There are some unique functions Meteor offers that make our lives in a full-stack development environment even easier. This chapter will go into these lesser-advertised areas of functionality, providing you with even more under the hood knowledge to make your applications elegant and powerful.

Building custom server methods

The majority of communications we perform between the client and server in Meteor is done via DDP. There are times, however, where direct server calls can come in very handy. For example, while you're testing, or as an admin, you may create some `'hidden'` helper methods to make debugging easier. In other instances, you may want to make very secure or very simple methods available to reduce the vulnerability or complexity of your code. In any case, server methods are a staple of development, and this recipe will walk you through creating and using server-side methods, using the `Meteor.methods()` function.

To create server methods, we first need a basic application. We'll quickly create a color swatch app. Nothing fancy, but once we're done, we will be able to create server methods with good visual feedback.

Project setup

You will need Meteor installed, and have a project created. In a terminal window, create your root project by entering the following commands:

```
$ meteor create server-calls
$ cd server-calls
$ rm server-calls.*
$ mkdir {client,server,both}
$ meteor add twbs:bootstrap
$ meteor
```

Creating a simple app

Create a file named [project root]/both/helpers.js and add the following code:

```
Swatches = new Mongo.Collection('swatches');

randomColor = function(){
  var retCol = '#';
  while (retCol.length<4) {
    retCol += Random.choice('06F');
  }
  return retCol;
}
```

Next, create a file named [project root]/client/client.js and add the following code:

```
Template.colors.helpers({
  swatches: function(){
    return Swatches.find().fetch();
  }
})

Template.body.events({
  'click #newColor' : function(e){
    Swatches.insert({color:randomColor()});
  }
})
```

Create some simple styling by creating a file named `[project root]/client/styles.css` with the following style declarations:

```css
.swatch{
  display:inline-block;
  height:8rem;
  width:8rem;
  border-radius: 0.5rem;
  margin-top: 1rem;
}

#newColor{
  display:block;
  margin-top: 0.5rem;
}
```

Finally, create your templates by creating `[project root]/client/main.html` and adding the following templates:

```html
<body>
  <div class="container">
    <div id="newColor" class="btn btn-info btn-lg">
      <span class="glyphicon glyphicon-plus"></span>
    </div>
    {{> colors}}
  </div>
</body>


<template name="colors">
  {{#each swatches}}
  <div class="swatch" style="background-color:{{color}}"></div>
  {{/each}}
</template>
```

Save all your changes, navigate to `http://localhost:3000` in a browser, and click the button with the plus sign on it repeatedly to add random color swatches. You should see something similar to the following screenshot:

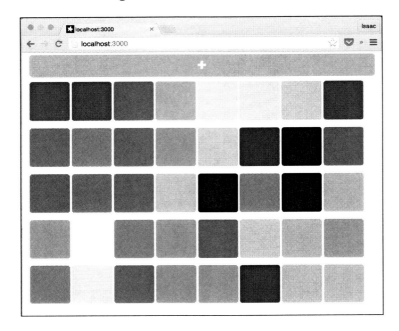

You are now ready to create some helper server methods.

How to do it...

We will create two server methods. One to clear the `Swatches` collection, and one that adds only unique colors.

1. First, let's build the `clearSwatches()` function. Create a file named `[project root]/server/methods.js` and add the following `Meteor.methods` declaration:

```
Meteor.methods({
  clearSwatches: function(){
    Swatches.remove({});
  }
});
```

In your browser console, enter the following command:

```
> Meteor.call('clearSwatches')
```

All your color swatches should disappear. Don't fret, friend, you can always create more swatches by clicking the button on the screen.

2. Next, let's create the `addUniqueSwatches()` function. Open `methods.js` from the preceding step and add the following declaration just after the `clearSwatches` declaration:

```
clearSwatches: function(){
    Swatches.remove({});
},
addUniqueSwatch: function(newColor){
    if (Swatches.findOne({color:newColor})) return null;
    Swatches.insert({color:newColor});
}
```

3. Now, open `[project root]/client/client.js`, and make the following change to the `Template.body.events` declaration:

```
Template.body.events({
    'click #newColor' : function(e){
        Meteor.call('addUniqueSwatch' , randomColor());
    }
})
```

Now, as you click on the button to add colors, you will find that, eventually, no new swatches will be added. This is because the total number of unique colors is 27. If you start with no swatches, your screen will eventually look similar to the following screenshot:

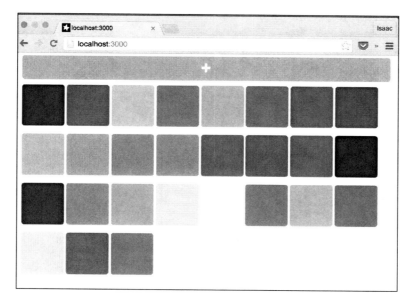

You won't be able to add more than the 27 colors, no matter how many times you click the button.

How it works...

We created two calls on the server by creating code inside the `server` folder. These calls are exposed to the client because we declared them using the `Meteor.methods()` function.

The `clearSwatches()` method we created in the `methods.js` file is *hidden*, in that, unless you know it's there, there's no easy way to know that it exists. The `addUniqueSwatch()` method is used inside of the `onclick` event for our button, so someone could discover it by looking at our client code.

In both cases, the methods are not called through an Ajax/traditional server call, but are instead automatically exposed by Meteor, and , very easy to invoke via the `Meteor.call()` method, which accepts the name of the method as the first parameter, and any additional parameters, as method arguments.

There's more...

If you pass a callback function as the last argument in `Meteor.call()`, the callback will be automatically invoked when the server method has completed execution. You can use this to perform actions after the call is complete. The following is an example.

Open `[project root]/server/methods.js` and make the following changes to `addUniqueSwatch()` function:

```
addUniqueSwatch: function(newColor){
    if (Swatches.findOne({color:newColor})) return null;
    Swatches.insert({color:newColor});
    return Swatches.find().count();
}
```

Now, in your browser console, quickly reset the `Swatches` collection:

```
> Meteor.call('clearSwatches')
```

Finally, make the following manual call to `addUniqueSwatch()` multiple times:

```
> Meteor.call('addUniqueSwatch',randomColor(),
function(err,data){console.log(data);})
```

Each time you run that command, the console will print out the total number of swatches. Meteor is auto-running the callback you passed, populating the data parameter with the results from the `addUniqueSwitch()` method.

▸ The *Using the web console* recipe in *Chapter 1, Optimizing Your Workflow*

▸ The *Adding Meteor packages* recipe in *Chapter 2, Customizing with Packages*

Creating custom EJSON objects

It's pretty easy to pass simple objects between the client and the server using DDP. But did you know that you can pass custom, named objects complete with methods? The folks at Meteor have extended JSON to allow customized, complete objects to be passed over DDP, without you having to worry about serialization/deserialization. This recipe will teach you how to create and use custom EJSON objects, and pass those custom objects between the client and the server.

Getting ready

We will be using the previous recipe found in this chapter, *Building custom server methods*, as a baseline. Please complete that recipe, and then make the following modifications.

Declaring the Swatch object

Create a new file named `[project root]/both/swatch.js` and add the following code to the file:

```
Swatch = function (color){
  this.color = color;
}

Swatch.prototype = {
  constructor: Swatch,

  switch: function(){
    this.color = randomColor();
  },
  toString: function(){
    return "My color is: " + this.color;
  }
}
```

Modifying Swatches.insert()

In preparation for using EJSON objects, which are not the normal, plain objects MongoDB expects, we need to layer our objects by one level when inserting. In the web console, execute the following line to clear out the `Swatches` collection:

```
> Meteor.call('clearSwatches')
```

Now, open `[project root]/server/methods.js` and modify the `Swatches.insert()` method as follows:

```
addUniqueSwatch: function(newColor){
  ...
  Swatches.insert({swatch:new Swatch(newColor)});
}
```

Changing Swatch colors

The layering on insert will break our UI a bit, but that's okay, we can recover because we're awesome. Inside the `[project root]/client/client.js` file, in the `Template.colors.helpers` section, and just below the `swatches` helper, add the following helper:

```
  },
color: function(){
    return this.swatch.color;
}
```

Lastly, let's add the following `events` declaration, so that we can change the color of our swatches:

```
Template.colors.events({
  'click .swatch' : function(e){
    this.swatch.color = randomColor();
    Swatches.update(this._id,this);
  }
})
```

Save your changes, and test in a browser by clicking on any of the added swatches. The corresponding swatch should change to a random color each time you click. You are now ready to proceed with creating custom EJSON objects.

How to do it...

As mentioned, Meteor takes care of the serialization and deserialization for us. We just need to declare our object as an EJSON object. Proceed with the following steps to create a custom EJSON object:

1. Let's add the `typeName` and `toJSONValue` functions. Open the `[project root]/both/swatch.js` file, and add the following two functions to the `Swatch.prototype` declaration, just below the `toString()` function:

```
},
typeName: function(){
  return 'Swatch';
},
toJSONValue: function(){
  return {
    color:this.color
  };
}
```

2. Next we need to declare our object with `EJSON.addType`. In the same `swatch.js` file, at the very bottom, add the following function call:

```
EJSON.addType("Swatch", function fromJSONValue(value){
  return new Swatch(value.color);
});
```

3. We're now ready to use our EJSON object methods. Open the `[project root]/client/client.js` file, and make the following changes to `Template.colors.events`:

```
'click .swatch': function (e) {
    this.swatch.switch();
    Swatches.update(this._id, this);
    console.log(this.swatch.toString());
  }
```

In the browser, add some new swatches and click on them with your browser console window open. The swatches will change colors, and they will tell you what their new colors are in the console. Your screen should look similar to the following screenshot:

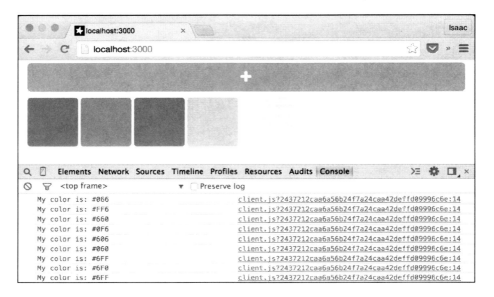

How it works...

When known EJSON objects are inserted into, or retrieved from MongoDB, Meteor automatically serializes and deserializes the objects using the EJSON library.

To do this properly, the objects themselves have to have at least two methods. First, the object must have the typeName function, which aids in mapping the object to the declared EJSON object. Second, the object must have the toJSONValue() function, so that Meteor can properly serialize the object to a string/standard JSON value. Without the toJSONValue() function, MongoDB would choke on the object, and refuse to insert it. Transporting the object over DDP would be equally unfeasible.

The other action needed is to declare the EJSON object, which we did in swatch.js with the EJSON.addType() function. This function takes a fromJSONValue() function as an argument, which (exactly as it sounds) takes the JSON value passed over the wire and instantiates an actual object of the appropriate type. In our case, this was a Swatch object, and the only property needing to be created was the color property, which was passed in through the constructor.

Once the previous methods are declared, and the `addType` function called, Meteor takes care of the rest for us, and stores our objects rather cleverly in MongoDB. As an example, here is what the raw JSON looks like for one of our serialized `Swatch` objects:

```json
{
  "_id" : "tktEzxMGTGNZ8oB4R",
    "swatch" : {
      "EJSON$type" : "Swatch",
        "EJSON$value" : {
          "EJSONcolor" : "#66F"
        }
    }
}
```

There's more...

The `EJSON` object has other helper functions that you can declare in an object to aid in the development and use of `EJSON` objects.

The `.clone()` method can be implemented on an `EJSON` object to perform a deep copy with logic. If you don't declare the `.clone()` function, Meteor uses `toJSONValue()` instead.

The `.equals()` method takes another object as a parameter and performs a custom comparison of your choosing. If you don't declare the `.equals()` function, Meteor simply takes both objects, performs a `toJSONValue()` transformation on each, and compares the result.

 Learn more about the EJSON library by viewing the Meteor documentation, found here: `https://www.meteor.com/ejson`.

See also

▶ The *Building custom server methods* recipe in this chapter

Handling asynchronous events

Meteor is a reactive framework. As you've probably noticed, it's built on top of `Node.js`, but when writing or using packages, it somehow magically avoids all of the callback and event loop drama you'd normally face with `Node.js`. Meteor lets you code in a declarative, synchronous-like style. This recipe will show you one of the ways Meteor does this, and how you can handle asynchronous events coming in from a third-party package. In this case, we will read an incoming Twitter stream from the npm `twit` package.

Getting ready

We need to quickly set up a test application on Twitter and load the npm `twit` module, so we'll do that here, so as not to distract from the recipe itself. Note that you can use any asynchronous event stream you would like for this recipe, including the standard `setInterval()` method, which could be used to mimic an asynchronous event stream.

Creating a baseline Meteor app

Open a terminal window, navigate to where you would like your project to reside, and enter the following commands:

```
$ meteor create thirdpartyevents
$ cd thirdpartyevents
$ rm thirdpartyevents.*
$ mkdir {client,server,both}
$ meteor add meteorhacks:npm
$ meteor
```

Instead of starting Meteor like usual, this will instead create a file called `[project root]/packages.json`. Open that file in an editor and add the following declaration:

```
{
   "twit" : "1.1.20"
}
```

Save your changes, and in the terminal, run the `meteor` command again:

```
$ meteor
```

Obtaining your Twitter Access Tokens

Use a browser to log in to `http://twitter.com`, and then navigate to `https://apps.twitter.com`. Create a new app, following the instructions, and click on the **Keys and Access Tokens** tab to obtain your Consumer Key + Secret and a valid Access Token + Secret found on that page. *Keep this page open*, as we will need to reference it a bit later.

For Meteor-specific instructions on setting up a Twitter App, please see the *Implementing OAuth accounts packages* recipe, found in *Chapter 10, Working with Accounts*.

Initializing twit

Create a file named [project root]/server/config-twit.js and add the
following code, replacing the consumer_key, consumer_secret, access_token,
and access_token_secret with the information you obtained previously. When
completed, your file should look similar to the following code:

```
Twitter = Meteor.npmRequire('twit');

Twit = new Twitter({
  consumer_key: 'egrdttfakeconsumerkeyFMx42339eMR8',
  consumer_secret: 'fR2r02CthisnJCDtVisMij2WjNiafakeo6QPqsecretnxztb',
  access_token: 'q8thisnEkn3xMiscUhafake9I5EOAtoken3DvDZM',
  access_token_secret: '7mel7Kr8fakeaccesstokensecretdzpiDuaqtRaij914'
});

simplifyTweet = function(tweet){
  var retObj = {};
  if (!tweet) return retObj;
  retObj.created_at = tweet.created_at;
  retObj.text = tweet.text;
  retObj.user = '@' + tweet.user.screen_name;

  return retObj;
}
```

Creating the Tweets collection, and building a stream reader

Create a file named [project root]/both/model.js and add the following line:

```
Tweets = new Mongo.Collection('tweets');
```

Now, create a file named [project root]/server/twitter-stream.js and add the
following code:

```
stream = {};
Meteor.methods({
  TwitterStream: function (query) {
    if (query == 'off') {
      if (stream.stop != null) stream.stop();
      Tweets.remove({});
      return;
    }
    stream = Twit.stream('statuses/filter', {
      track: query
    });
    stream.on('tweet', function (tweet) {
```

```
        var simpleT = simplifyTweet(tweet);
        console.log(simpleT);
    });
  }
})
```

Tracking and testing changes

Create a file named `[project root]/client/consoleTracking.js` and add the following code:

```
Tracker.autorun(function(){
    console.table(Tweets.find().fetch());
  });
```

Now, navigate in a browser to `http://localhost:3000`, open the console window, and enter the following command:

```
> Meteor.call('TwitterStream','JavaScript')
```

In your terminal window where you started Meteor with the `meteor` command, you should periodically see some JSON-formatted tweets. If tweets aren't showing up, it may be that the query you used isn't popular enough (this is a live Twitter feed!), so you can select something else, like *lmao* or *lebron*, if you want to see a steady stream.

Lastly, you will want to test the `Tweets` collection tracking. In the browser console, enter the following command, and run it multiple times:

```
> Tweets.insert({a:Tweets.find().count()})
```

If everything is set up properly, you will see a growing table of entries in your console.

To turn off the Twitter feed and to clear out the `Tweets` collection, enter the following in the browser console:

```
> Meteor.call('TwitterStream','off')
```

With everything all cleaned up, let's proceed to the recipe.

How to do it...

This recipe concentrates on only one thing: handling asynchronous events synchronously. As such, there are one two very simple steps as follows:

1. Open `[project root]/server/twitter-stream.js`, and add the following `insert` statement to the `stream.on` handler, as follows:

```
stream.on('tweet', function (tweet) {
      var simpleT = simplifyTweet(tweet);
```

```
    console.log(simpleT);
    Tweets.insert(simpleT);
});
```

Because the event handler is an asynchronous event, if you try turning the stream on as-is, you will get a very nasty error stating the following:

Meteor code must always run within a Fiber.

2. Modify the `stream.on` handler as follows:

```
stream.on('tweet', Meteor.bindEnvironment(
    function (tweet) {
    var simpleT = simplifyTweet(tweet);
    console.log(simpleT);
    Tweets.insert(simpleT);
}));
```

You can now turn on the stream in the browser console, as follows:

```
> Meteor.call('TwitterStream','JavaScript')
```

As entries come in from the stream, they will populate in the Tweets collection, and you will see the results in your browser console, similar to the following:

(index)	_id	created_at	text	user
0	"GgdRdaGJeCXrwXGTL"	"Sun Mar 01 03:35:48 +0000 2015"	"UI resource, Other – India, 0 – 10 Yea...	"@tech_career"
1	"tu7FGqC5xkX4nxKYp"	"Sun Mar 01 03:35:48 +0000 2015"	"RT @leopixeli9: Best Ways to Learn Pro...	"@jonDevBot"
2	"tnDAQhSXxuBfokbiN"	"Sun Mar 01 03:36:07 +0000 2015"	"PHP Developer, Other – India, 0 – 10 Y...	"@tech_career"
3	"pBFhr6R93pRRu3rWa"	"Sun Mar 01 03:36:09 +0000 2015"	"RT @WebInDev: Nothing to say.. just th...	"@AK_Nisha"
4	"aXpdwk75dp9hvBe2f"	"Sun Mar 01 03:36:12 +0000 2015"	"Angular JavaScript Developer Contract ...	"@p2pWebMobileIt"
5	"JHaKXdz5NSwG3hprS"	"Sun Mar 01 03:36:21 +0000 2015"	"光ポ・シーンは未だにjavascriptすら使用しない し...	"@taiyounomatecha"

How it works...

To accomplish the declarative, reactive environment we've come to know and love, the Meteor server intentionally runs on a single thread per request. Therefore, when you create some type of asynchronous action, such as listening to a `Node.js` event stream, the callback (handler) for that asynchronous action operates on a different thread. When the callback is fired, if you try to call Meteor functions (like `Tweets.insert()` for example), Meteor will throw an error, because the callback and the main Meteor server are on different threads. In addition, if you used any global variables with values, you can't guarantee that those values have remained the same while the asynchronous call was waiting. Some other operation could have changed the environment!

Meteor has an elegant way of dealing with this situation, using `Meteor.bindEnvironment()`.

By wrapping the callback function with `Meteor.bindEnvironment()`, a *Fiber* is created. The Fiber keeps track of the variables and their values (the environment), and knows that sooner or later the callback is going to be called.

In the meantime, the Fiber removes the operation from the event loop, so that the operation isn't blocking any other operations. Once the callback is ready, the Fiber puts the operation back into the event loop, restores the environment, and the operation completes.

In this particular case, when we use `Meteor.call('TwitterStream',…)` we are sending a request to the Meteor server on a single thread. The `Twit.stream` service is started on that thread but the events (the incoming stream) are asynchronous. By wrapping the handler for `stream.on()` with `Meteor.bindEnvironment()`, we are instructing Meteor to "take a snapshot" of the current environment. Meteor then takes the current operation out of the event loop so that other things can get through. Then, we wait.

When the stream has new data, the event fires, which triggers the callback. Meteor (or more accurately, the Fiber) sees that the callback is ready, restores the environment from the snapshot created using `Meteor.bindEnvironment()`, and puts the operation back on the event loop. This process happens again and again, as many times as needed, whenever a new Tweet comes in and triggers the callback function.

At the risk of oversimplifying, `Meteor.bindEnvironment()` wraps some code into the Fiber and then waits, without blocking any other code operations. Once the wrapped code is ready/activated, the Fiber makes sure that the code is executed on the correct thread with the correct data.

There's more...

We can be very granular about what code is wrapped, and we can separate out wrapped code, to make the overall code easier to read.

Add the following function to the top of the `twitter-stream.js` file:

```
wrappedInsert = Meteor.bindEnvironment(function(simpleT){
  Tweets.insert(simpleT);
});
```

Now, revert `stream.on` by removing the `Meteor.bindEnvironment()` wrapping, and call `wrappedInsert()` instead of `Tweets.insert()`, as follows:

```
stream.on('tweet', function (tweet) {
    var simpleT = simplifyTweet(tweet);
    console.log(simpleT);
    wrappedInsert(simpleT);
  });
```

This will operate exactly the same as wrapping the entire callback function.

One last alternative, we could take the entire callback out, wrap it with a user-friendly name, and use that name in the callback section, as shown in the following example:

```
wrappedCallback = Meteor.bindEnvironment(
  function (tweet) {
    var simpleT = simplifyTweet(tweet);
    console.log(simpleT);
    Tweets.insert(simpleT);
  }
);
...
stream.on('tweet', wrappedCallback);
```

 The most concise explanation of Fibers, Futures, and `Meteor.bindEnvironment()` can be found here: `http://bit.ly/meteor-fibers-explained`. Make sure to thoroughly review all the links from that page!

See also

▶ The *Implementing OAuth accounts packages* recipe in *Chapter 10, Working with Accounts*

Using asynchronous functions

`Node.js`, for all its awesomeness, has a flaw: callbacks. Being asynchronous and non-blocking has a ton of advantages, and we can't imagine life without it. But, wouldn't it be great if there were a way to avoid the "callback hell" by writing our code in a synchronous style but still reaping the benefits of asynchronous code? As you might have guessed, Meteor has a way of doing just that. This recipe will show you how to write and handle asynchronous functions in a synchronous style using `Meteor.wrapAsync()`.

Getting ready

Because brevity breeds clarity, we will keep this recipe as simple as possible.

Open a terminal window, navigate to where you would like your project to reside, and enter the following commands:

```
$ meteor create wrap-sample
$ cd wrap-sample
$ mkdir server
$ meteor
```

How to do it...

We are going to simulate a delayed call to an asynchronous method, using the standard JavaScript `setTimeout()` function.

1. First, let's prep for the server call. Open `[project root]/wrap-sample.js` and modify the `Template.hello.events` function, as follows:

```
'click button': function () {
    var x = 0;
    while (x < 5) {
      x++;
      var q = "" + x + ". do work";
      Meteor.call('someCall', q, function (e, d) {
        console.log(d);
      });
    }
}
```

2. Create a file named `[project root]/server/method.js` and add the following asynchronous function:

```
asyncCall = function(query,cb){
  var ranLen = ~~(Math.random()*3000);
  setTimeout(function(){
    cb && cb(null,query + " complete!");
  },ranLen);
};
```

3. Now, add a simple `Meteor.methods` declaration, using `Meteor.wrapAsync()` to write synchronous-style code, as follows:

```
Meteor.methods({
  someCall: function (query) {
    console.log('performing: '+query);
    this.unblock();
    var syncCall = Meteor.wrapAsync(asyncCall);
    var result = syncCall(query);
    return result;
  }
});
```

4. Open a browser to `http://localhost:3000`, open the browser console, and click the button on the screen. As you look at the server terminal, you will immediately see five log entries, printed in consecutive order, similar to the following:

performing: 1. do work

performing: 2. do work

```
performing: 3. do work
performing: 4. do work
performing: 5. do work
```

In the Browser window, you will see five log entries. These entries, however, will not be immediate, and will likely be out of order, similar to the following example:

```
1. do work complete!
4. do work complete!
2. do work complete!
5. do work complete!
3. do work complete!
```

5. Click the button again, and notice the random order and time of completion for each of the five server calls.

How it works...

`Meteor.wrapAsync()` is a bit of syntactic sugar for running asynchronous calls as if they were synchronous. As discussed in the *Handling asynchronous events* recipe from this chapter, Fibers and Futures are the way that Meteor handles asynchronous logic. In this case, we are dealing with what would be considered a *standard asynchronous function* in `Node.js`.

Meteor defines a standard asynchronous function as a function as follows:

▶   Takes a callback as the last argument

▶   Is non-blocking

▶   Executes the callback upon completion

The signature of the callback passed in is always the same. There are two arguments, the first of which is an `error` object. If there is an `error`, this object will have a value, otherwise, the `error` argument will be `null`.

The second argument is a `data` object. If the call does not return an `error` object as its first parameter, this data argument will have data in it that can be used by the callback function.

In our case, we declared a standard asynchronous function named `asyncCall()`. The signature of `asyncCall()` looks as shown in the following example:

```
function(query,cb)...
```

Nothing in `asyncCall()` will block the event loop, even though we're making a call to `setInterval()`. The `setInterval()` call is asynchronous, and is therefore non-blocking (very much like an ajax call, or a file i/o operation, etc). Once `setInterval()` is complete, it invokes our callback, `cb(null , query + '...')`.

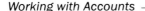

In the `Meteor.methods` declaration, we created a method named `someCall`. Inside of `someCall`, we first make sure it won't clog up the event loop by calling `this.unblock()`.

We then take our standard asynchronous function (as defined previously) and we wrap it with the `Meteor.wrapAsync(asyncCall)` command.

Once wrapped, we can use the wrapped call as if it were synchronous. It's not. There will be a delay in the result, but our operation will wait until the asynchronous call is complete, which allows us to better understand what is happening. If we look at the lines of code after `Meteor.wrapAsync()`, we can easily wrap our heads around what is happening:

```
var result = syncCall(query);
return result;
```

The `result` variable is being assigned to the result of the call. We then return `result` like we would in a synchronous function. Easy peasy.

There's more...

The rule for using `Meteor.wrapAsync()` can be stated this way: any time you have a standard asynchronous function, where you would normally have to nest your logic in the callback, you can instead wrap the function and use the result as if it were a synchronous call.

Under the hood, Meteor is wrapping a Fiber/Future and automatically implementing the `.current`, `.yield()`, `.run()`, and `.wait()` pieces for you. But don't worry about that. If you just stick with the idea that `.wrapAsync()` is turning asynchronous functions with callbacks into standard functions without callbacks, you'll be well on your way to writing elegant, declarative code.

See also

- ▸ The *Handling asynchronous events* recipe in this chapter

12
Creating Useful Projects

In this chapter, we will cover the following topics:

- ► Creating RESTful web services
- ► Creating a complete app with Iron Router
- ► Deploying apps to mobile devices
- ► Adding social sharing

Introduction

Somewhere along your journey towards learning Meteor, you'll reach a point where you will have mastered the fundamentals. At that point, you will want to start putting all the fundamentals together into the applications or packages that are actually useful. It's a big development world out there, with many opportunities. The Meteor landscape is still in its infancy, and if you've followed all (or most) of the recipes in this book, you're probably ready to start defining that landscape. This last chapter will walk you through four of the most useful recipes that apply to most projects. It will give you an even more solid foundation for going out on your own to define, discover, and build!

Creating RESTful web services

Alas, alas, the entire development world hasn't caught on to how amazing the DDP protocol is (yet!). Data-over-the-wire is an amazing concept, and we believe that it (or something like it) is the future of how applications will communicate. In the meantime, we have some very useful and well-established protocols that, if implemented in our applications, increase the reach and accessibility of our apps for other platforms.

The granddaddy of all of these protocols is REST. REST is mature, well-defined, and has been implemented in nearly every programming language imaginable. It wouldn't surprise us to discover that, if/when we contact an alien race, the first signal will be a POST request. Given its current status (and our most likely option for peaceful interstellar negotiations), we will want to add REST capabilities to some of our applications. This recipe will walk you through implementing a server-side REST implementation using Iron Router.

Getting ready

Since we're only dealing with the REST part of an app in this recipe, we don't need anything fancy. A simple, standard Meteor app will do, with just a couple of server-side files.

Creating the baseline application

Open a terminal window, navigate to where you would like your project root to be, and enter the following:

```
$ meteor create RESTSample
$ cd RESTSample
$ rm RESTSample.*
$ mkdir -p server/api
$ mkdir server/model
$ meteor add iron:router
$ meteor
```

Installing and configuring Postman

We need a way to manually call our REST service, and the Postman plugin/app for Chrome is as good as any. If you have your own way of manually calling REST services, feel free to use it. If not, here's how to install Postman:

1. In a browser, navigate to http://getpostman.com and click on the **Get it now** link towards the bottom. A preview of the Postman app will pop up, and towards the top-right corner will be a button to install Postman. Click on that button, follow the directions, and open Postman.

2. In the request window in Postman, under the **Normal** tab, enter the following URL:

   ```
   http://localhost:3000/api/
   ```

3. Next, click on the **Headers** button, and enter the following under the **Header | Value** sections:

   ```
   Content-Type | application/json
   ```

4. When complete, your screen should look like the following screenshot:

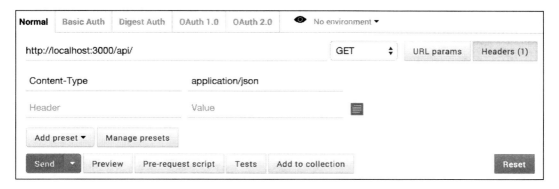

We're now ready to build our REST service and test it using Postman.

How to do it...

Proceed with the following steps to create RESTful web services:

1. First, we will declare the `Quotes` collection. Create a file named `[project root]/server/model/quotes.js` and add the following code:

    ```
    Quotes = new Mongo.Collection('quotes');
    ```

2. Next, we will add the `writeHeaders` function. Create a file named `[project root]/server/api/REST.js` and add the following function to the bottom:

    ```
    function writeHeaders(self) {
      self.response.statusCode = 200;
      self.response.setHeader('Content-type',
    'application/json');
      self.response.setHeader('Access-Control-Allow-Origin',
    '*');
      self.response.setHeader('Access-Control-Allow-Headers',
        'Origin, X-Requested-With, Content-Type, Accept');
    }
    ```

3. We will now write the code to handle `GET` requests. At the very top of the `REST.js` file, create the following `Router.route()` method call:

    ```
    Router.route('/api', {
        where: 'server'
    })
    .get(function () {
      //write headers
      writeHeaders(this);
    ```

```
    //send our response...
    this.response.end('GET not supported\n');
});
```

Save all of your changes, make sure your app is running, and click on the **Send** button in Postman. In the results section, click on the **Body** tab and the **Raw** button. You should see the following message:

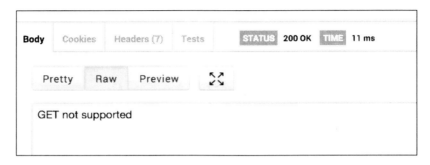

Congratulations, you've just created your first REST service!

4. Now, let's move on to `post` calls. We are going to assume that a POST query is asking to see any quotes in our `Quotes` collection that are owned by a particular user. In `REST.js`, remove the last semicolon from the `.get()` function call (we are chaining commands, so it's important that you do this) and add the following code where you removed the semicolon:

```
.post(function () {
    writeHeaders(this);
    var user = this.request.body.owner;
    if (!user) {
        this.response.end('No user specified...\n');
        return;
    }
    var quotes = Quotes.find({
        owner: user
    }).fetch();
    this.response.end(JSON.stringify(quotes));
})
```

5. It doesn't make much sense to test a POST query until we have some data in our collection, does it? Let's take care of that right now by adding support for PUT. Immediately after the code you just entered (as a continuation of the function chain), add the following code:

```
.put(function () {
    writeHeaders(this)
```

```
var upQuote = this.request.body.update;
if (!upQuote) {
  this.response.end('nothing to update');
}
var update = Quotes.upsert({
  _id: upQuote.id
}, {
  $set: upQuote.changes

});
this.response.end('Quote accepted!...\n');

});
```

 Note that we have a semicolon at the end, which means we're done and can start using our fully functional service!

6. In Postman, change the service type from GET to PUT. In the input field, click on the button labeled **raw**, and enter the following JSON code:

```
{"update":{
"changes":{"author":"Jerry Pournelle and Larry Niven",
"text":"Second guessing God is an old, old game.",
"owner":"me"
}
}}
```

Your screen should look like the following screenshot:

7. Click on the **Send** button, and in just a few milliseconds, the response area will display the following message:

    Quote accepted!...

8. Repeat the preceding steps as many times as you would like, varying the quote/ author and owner as desired.

9. We can now test the POST query. Change the service type from PUT to POST, and enter the following JSON in the input field:

    `{"owner":"me"}`

10. Click on the **Send** button, and on the output window, click on the **Pretty** button. The output will be some well-formatted JSON with at least one entry, similar to that in the following screenshot:

```
[
  — {
        "_id": "b8PiXZxX4cHeCsd7Z",
        "author": "Jerry Pournelle and Larry Niven",
        "owner": "me",
        "text": "Second guessing God is an old, old game."
    }
]
```

You have just written a simple yet fully functional REST service in Meteor!

How it works...

The heavy lifting for this recipe is done by Iron Router. When we add the `iron:router` package, that package listens for all incoming requests on the server side. We configured Iron Router to listen on the `http://[yourapp.url]/api/` route for the GET, POST, and PUT requests. To get Iron Router to listen on that particular route, we used the `Router.route('/api'...)` method call. Importantly, we declared that, that route is to be handled on the server side using the `{where: 'server'}` parameter.

Chaining each type of request to the `.route()` call, we used the `.get()`, `.post()`, and `.put()` method calls. In each of these, we can read the JSON data passed in with the request by referencing `this.request.body.[key]`.

Finally, we are able to send a response by using Iron Router's `response` object, which we used to form the headers and to send messages back to the calling client.

There's more...

As usual, we've tried to keep the functionality to a minimum, to reduce the signal-to-noise of what this recipe is about. There's enough here, however, to give you a good taste of what is possible with REST services using Iron Router. If you would like more information and specifics on what the RESTful functions in Iron Router can do, please visit the Iron Router guide at: `https://github.com/iron-meteor/iron-router/blob/devel/Guide.md#server-routing`.

See also

> ▸ The *Creating a multipage application with Iron Router* recipe in *Chapter 2, Customizing with Packages*
> ▸ The *Creating a complete app with Iron Router* recipe in this chapter

Creating a complete app with Iron Router

From nearly the beginning of Meteor, the development emphasis has been on "smart" client-based applications. We left the server-dominated world behind a long time ago, and as a result, the single-page model is extremely well-supported inside the Meteor development stack.

Essential to this type of application is the `iron:router` package (`https://atmospherejs.com/iron/router`). Yes, you technically could build a multi-functional, mobile-first app without Iron Router, but it would be much more time consuming and complex by comparison. Think of Iron Router as the equivalent of using a microwave versus cooking outdoors on a campfire. With no utensils. In a rainstorm. With rabies-carrying raccoons all up in your business. Okay, okay, maybe it's not that bad, but you get the point—you should use Iron Router.

This recipe will walk you through the building of a fully functional, quote tracking service with a single-page app frontend built using Iron Router.

Getting ready

We would usually add a lot of preparation steps to a recipe, but in this one, we need to build everything in one go as part of the recipe. As such, we are only going to add the bare minimum here.

Open a terminal window, navigate to where you would like your application root to be, and enter the following commands:

```
$ meteor create QuotesApp
$ cd QuotesApp
```

```
$ rm QuotesApp.*
$ mkdir {client,both}
$ meteor add twbs:bootstrap
$ meteor
```

We've got a lot of work to do, so let's get started!

How to do it...

The major sections of this recipe are as follows:

- ▸ Creating the top `navbar`
- ▸ Adding user authentication
- ▸ Adding the `Quotes` collection
- ▸ Adding Iron Router routes
- ▸ Creating page transition animations
- ▸ Displaying the `Quotes` collection
- ▸ Adding and editing `Quotes`
- ▸ Deploying the App

There will be a little crossover from section to section, but we should be able to keep things fairly clean, so if you would like to switch out some functionality or add some features, feel free to do so as we move along.

1. First up, we need to create the top `navbar`.

   We will be using the standard Bootstrap `navbar` elements because we don't want to spend a large chunk of time with CSS styling. Once you're more comfortable with CSS, you can extend or replace the Bootstrap styling and make it your own.

   First, since this is a mobile-oriented app, let's set our headers, and use a Google font. Create a new file named `[project root]/client/header.html` and add the following declarations:

   ```html
   <head>
     <meta name="viewport"
     content="width=device-width,
     initial-scale=1.0,
     maximum-scale=1.0,
     user-scalable=0">
     <link
   href='http://fonts.googleapis.com/css?family=Raleway'
     rel='stylesheet'
     type='text/css'>
   </head>
   ```

Create a new file named `[project root]/client/layout.html` and add the following template, which will act as the foundation for our navigation toolbar:

```html
<template name="layout">
  <div class="navbar navbar-default navbar-fixed-top"
role="navigation">
    <div class="navbar-header">
      <a class="navbar-brand" id="btn-home" href="/">
        <span class="glyphicon glyphicon-book"></span></a>
      <button type="button"
              class="navbar-toggle collapsed"
              data-toggle="collapse"
              data-target=".navbar-collapse">
        <span class="sr-only">Toggle navigation</span>
        <span class="icon-bar"></span>
        <span class="icon-bar"></span>
        <span class="icon-bar"></span>
      </button>
    </div>
    <div class="navbar-collapse collapse">
      <ul class="nav navbar-nav navbar-right">
        <!-- Login buttons will go here -->
      </ul>
    </div>
  </div>
  <!-- App panels will go here-->
</template>
```

We will want to temporarily add a `body` element afterwards, just so we can check the display (we will remove it when we implement `iron:router`):

```html
<body>
  {{> layout}}
</body>
```

Lastly, we have some minor CSS to add, to make sure everything upcoming runs smoothly. Create a file named `[project root]/client/styles.css` and add the following CSS declarations:

```css
body {font-family: 'Raleway', sans-serif;}
.page {vertical-align: top;position: absolute;width: 100%;height: 100%;background-color: #eee;top: 50px;}
.page-detail {background-color: #fff;color: #555;}
.glyphicon-book {font-size: 3rem;line-height: 2rem;}
.toggle-edit{margin-top: 1.4rem;font-size: 2rem;
background-color: #777;border-radius: 50%;
border: none;padding:
1.5rem;width: 5rem;height: 5rem;}
```

```
.input-group {margin-top: 1.4rem;}
.quote {font-size:2rem;}
.title {font-size:3rem;}
.author {margin-bottom:2rem;margin-top:1rem;}
.tag {margin:0.25rem;}
.tags {margin-top:1rem;}
.add-quote {height:9rem;}
.add-quote .btn{color:#5bc0de;font-size:4rem;}
```

2. Next, we need to add user authentication.

   Because we've had experience with it in the past, we will enable authentication using Twitter. We will also use some stylized login buttons that fit in with our Bootstrap toolbar. Open a terminal window, navigate to your project root, and enter the following commands:

   ```
   $ meteor add accounts-twitter
   ```

   ```
   $ meteor add ian:accounts-ui-bootstrap-3
   ```

   We now need to add the `loginButtons` template to our toolbar. Open `[project root]/client/layout.html` and locate the comment that reads as follows:

   ```
   <!-- Login buttons will go here -->
   ```

   Replace this comment with the following code:

   ```
   {{> loginButtons}}
   ```

   Save your changes and navigate to your app in a browser. The top-right corner will contain a **Configure Twitter** button. Click on this button and configure Twitter according to the instructions, just as we did in the *Implementing OAuth accounts packages* recipe in *Chapter 10, Working with Accounts*.

   After configuration, you may want test the login with your Twitter account. If everything is satisfactory, we can move on to the meat of our application.

3. Let's add the `Quotes` collection.

   We're definitely ready to add our `Quotes` collection, but we want to have some control over what records will be sent to the client, based on whether the user is logged in or not. To accomplish this, we need to remove `autopublish`. In a terminal window, in our project root directory, enter the following command:

   ```
   $ meteor remove autopublish
   ```

   Next, create a file named `[project root]/both/model.js` and add the following line to that file:

   ```
   Quotes = new Mongo.Collection('quotes');
   ```

Ordinarily, we would add a `subscribe` command in a client-only file and a `publish` command in a server-only file, but the logic is so simple that we'll just add them directly to the `model.js` file in this case. Add the following code to `model.js` and save your changes:

```
if (Meteor.isClient) {
  Meteor.subscribe('quotes');
} else {
  Meteor.publish('quotes', function () {
    return Quotes.find({
      owner: this.userId
    });
  })
}
```

4. Up next, we need to add our Iron Router routes.

   When you add Iron Router, the changes needed in the running Meteor instance are pretty major. Technically, you could add Iron Router without stopping your app, but we recommend stopping your Meteor app while installing and configuring Iron Router.

   Once you've stopped your app, enter the following command in the terminal window:

   $ meteor add iron:router

   Let's now declare our default layout template. Create a file named `[project root]/both/router.js` and add the following line:

   ```
   Router.configure({ layoutTemplate: 'layout' });
   ```

   Now that our layout template is being called by Iron Router, we no longer need the body element we temporarily put in the `layout.html` file. Open `[project root]/client/layout.html` and remove the entire `<body>...</body>` segment.

   We also have a placeholder in `layout.html` for our application pages, which we need to fill in with the customary Iron Router yield directive. In `layout.html`, locate the following line:

   ```
   <!-- App panels will go here-->
   ```

   Replace that line with the following code:

   ```
   {{> yield}}
   ```

   We have two routes to create, so let's do that now. Open `[project root]/both/router.js` and add the following `Router.map` declaration:

   ```
   Router.map(function(){
     this.route('main', {
       path: '/',
       template:'main'
     });
   ```

```
    this.route('detail', {
      path: '/quote/:_id',
      template:'detail',
      data: function () {
        return Quotes.findOne({_id: this.params._id});
      }
    });
  });
});
```

We've created our routes, and now we need to create placeholder templates for those routes. Create a file named `[project root]/client/main.html` and add the following template:

```html
<template name="main">
  <div class="page">
    <h1>this is the main page</h1>
  </div>
</template>
```

Create a file named `[project root]/client/detail.html` and add the following template:

```html
<template name="detail">
  <div class="page page-detail">
    <h1>this is the detail page</h1>
  </div>
</template>
```

You can now start your app back up (enter the `meteor` command in your terminal) and test the routes. As you navigate to `http://localhost:3000` and to `http://localhost:3000/quote/1234`, you should see pages similar to those in the following screenshot:

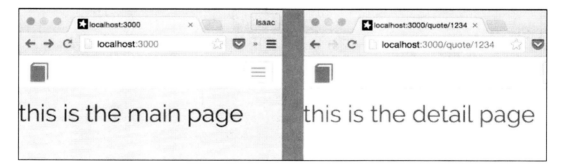

5. We will now create page transition animations.

There's an excellent Atmosphere package out there called `momentum`. With an Iron Router-specific package created by Percolate Studios, we can extend `momentum` to do Iron Router route transitions with very little fuss. In a terminal window, enter the following command:

```
$ meteor add percolate:momentum-iron-router
```

Create a file named `[project root]/client/transitions.js` and add the following transition declaration as a `Template` helper:

```
Template.layout.helpers({
  transition: function () {
    return function (from, to, element) {
      if (to.template=="main") return 'left-to-right';
      return 'right-to-left';
    }
  }
});
```

We also need to surround our `{{> yield}}` inclusion with the `momentum` template helper. Open `layout.html` and add the following wrapper around the inclusion:

```
{{#momentum plugin='iron-router' options=transition}}
    {{> yield}}
{{/momentum}}
```

Save your changes and navigate again to `http://localhost:3000/page/1234`. Once the page loads, click on the book icon in the top-left corner of the page. The main page should slide into place. The reverse animation will occur if you click the back button in your browser.

6. We are now ready to display the `Quotes` collection.

We will display some light summary information for each quote in our main template and then expand that into a lot more detail for the detail template. Let's start with the main template.

Open `[project root]/client/main.html`, remove the `<h1>` placeholder tag, and add the following code, which iterates over the `Quotes` collection and creates group items for each one:

```
<template name="main">
 <div class="page">
   <div class="list-group">
     {{#each quotes}}
     <a class="list-group-item quote-title">
       <span class="glyphicon glyphicon-menu-right
       pull-right"></span>
       <h4 class="list-group-item-heading">{{title}}</h4>
```

```
      {{#each tagsFormatted}}
      <div class="btn btn-xs btn-primary">{{tag}}</div>
      {{/each}}
    </a>
    {{/each}}
  </div>
 </div>
</template>
```

We need to add a couple of helpers to support the previously created template, so create a file named `[project root]/client/main.js` and add the following code:

```
Template.main.helpers({
  quotes: function(){
    return Quotes.find().fetch();
  },
  tagsFormatted: function(){
    var tags = this.tags;
    if (!tags) return [];
    return _.map(tags.split(','),function(d){
      var retTag = '#' + d;
      return {tag:retTag};
    });
  }
});
```

We will also need a `click` event handler, which will get us to the `detail` page template whenever we click on a quote group item. Add the following code to the bottom of the `main.js` file:

```
Template.main.events({
  'click .quote-title' : function(e){
    Router.go('/quote/'+this._id);
  }
});
```

Save your changes. Now let's programmatically add a couple of entries to the `Quotes` collection. Navigate in a browser to `http://localhost:3000/`. Make sure that you are logged in with your Twitter account, open the browser console, and execute the following command two or so times:

```
Quotes.insert({owner:Meteor.userId(),
title:'quote title',
quote:'quote body',
author:'quote author',
tags:'test,tags,field'})
```

After doing so, your screen should look similar to the following screenshot:

If you click on one of the items, the generic detail page should slide into view. Let's now take care of the detail page template, so that it will display the details of our quotes. Open the [project root]/client/detail.html file and replace the template contents with the following:

```
<template name="detail">
  <div class="page page-detail">
    <div class="container">
      {{#if editing}}
      {{else}}
      <h3 class="title">{{title}}</h3>
      <div class="container quote">{{quote}}</div>
      <div class="row container author">
        <div class="pull-right">-{{author}}</div>
      </div>
      <div class="row container tags">
        {{#each tagsFormatted}}
        <div class="btn btn-xs btn-primary
tag">{{tag}}</div>
        {{/each}}
      </div>
      {{/if}}
    </div>
  </div>
</template>
```

Save your changes and click on one of the placeholder quotes. You should see a screen come into view that looks similar to the following screenshot:

The tags aren't showing up because we haven't added the necessary helpers yet. Create a file named `[project root]/client/detail.js` and add the following helpers declaration:

```
Template.detail.helpers({
  tagsFormatted: function () {
    var tags = this.tags;
    if (!tags) return [];
    return _.map(tags.split(','), function (d) {
      var retTag = '#' + d;
      return {
        tag: retTag
      };
    });
  }
});
```

Look back in your browser; the tags should now appear on the detail page template.

7. Now that we've got our display taken care of, let's add the ability to edit and insert new `quote` objects.

    First, let's adjust the `detail.html` file and add an editing toggle button. Open `detail.html` and add the following `div` element just before the last `</div>` tag:

    ```
    </div>
    <div class="container">
      <div class="btn btn-danger toggle-edit pull-right">
        <span class="glyphicon {{editbuttonstate}}"></span>
    ```

```
      </div>
    </div>
  </div>
</template>
```

Next, let's add the input fields for editing/inserting. In the same `detail.html` file, in the `{{#if editing}}` section, add the title input field. Do this using the Bootstrap `input-group` styling, like so:

```
{{#if editing}}
        <div class="input-group input-group-lg">
          <span class="input-group-addon"
           id="addon-title">Title</span>
          <input type="text"
                 id="input-title"
                 class="form-control"
                 placeholder="title..."
                 value="{{title}}">
        </div>
{{else}}
```

Next is the `input-group` element for the `quote` body. Add the following just after the `title` group in the preceding code snippet:

```
        </div>
        <div class="input-group">
          <span class="input-group-addon"
          id="addon-quote">Quote</span>
          <textarea name="input-quote"
                    id="input-quote" rows="4"
                    class="form-control">{{quote}}
          </textarea>
        </div>
{{else}}
```

We need an `input-group` element for the author. Add that just below the `quote` group, as follows:

```
        </div>
        <div class="input-group">
          <input type="text"
            id="input-author"
            class="form-control"
            placeholder="author..."
            value="{{author}}">
          <span class="input-group-addon"
          id="addon-author">Author</span>
        </div>
{{else}}
```

Last but not least for the template are the tags. Just below the `author` group, add the following code:

```
</div>
<div class="form tags">
  <textarea name="input-tags"
    id="input-tags"
    class="form-control"
    rows="5">{{tags}}</textarea>
</div>
{{else}}
```

We have a couple of extra helpers to add. Open `detail.js` and add the following two helpers immediately after the `tagsFormatted` helper block, in the `Template. detail.helpers()` method (don't forget the extra comma at the top!):

```
  },
  editbuttonstate: function () {
    return (Session.get('editing')) ?
      'glyphicon-ok' : 'glyphicon-pencil';
  },
  editing: function () {
    return (Session.equals('editing', true));
  }
});
```

We now need to add the event handler for toggling between editing and display. We also need to add a submit button. So, let's kill two birds with one stone and give our toggle button the ability to turn into a submit button depending on the state. At the bottom of `detail.js`, add the following Template `events` declaration:

```
Template.detail.events({
  'click .toggle-edit': function (e) {
    e.preventDefault();
    var editflag = Session.equals('editing', true);
    if (editflag && Meteor.userId()) {
      var upQuote = {};
      upQuote.title = $('#input-title').val();
      upQuote.quote = $('#input-quote').val();
      upQuote.author = $('#input-author').val();
      upQuote.tags = $('#input-tags').val();
      upQuote.owner = Meteor.userId();
      Quotes.upsert({
        _id: this._id
      }, {
        $set: upQuote
      });
```

```
      }
      if (!editflag && !Meteor.userId()) return;
      Session.set('editing', (!editflag));
    }
});
```

Save your changes, navigate to display a single quote, and click on the pencil icon at the bottom right. You can change the generic quote into a specific quote, as shown in the following screenshot:

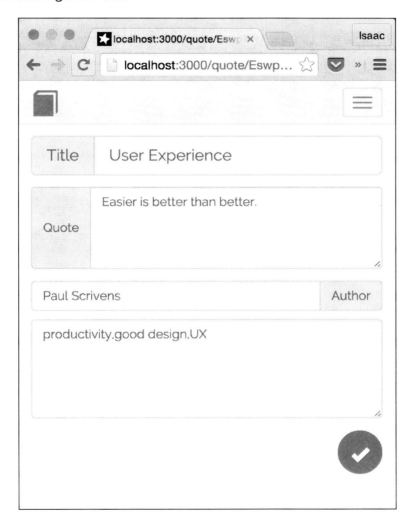

Click on the checkmark and your changes should be saved, as shown in the following screenshot:

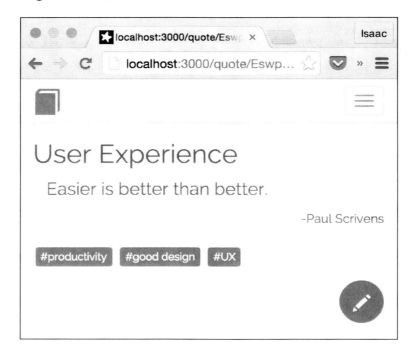

We've taken care of editing; now we need to allow the user to add new quotes. The logic we're going to use will piggyback on our editing. When the "new qoute" button is clicked, we will instantly create a new `quote` object in the `Quotes` collection and then navigate to the editing screen. Open `[project root]/client/main.html` and add the following button group just after the last `{{/each}}` tag, but still inside the `list-group </div>` tag:

```
    {{/each}}
    <a href="#" class="list-group-item add-quote">
      <div class="btn btn-lg center-block">
        <span class="glyphicon glyphicon-plus"></span>
      </div>
    </a>
  </div>
  </div>
</template>
```

When this button is clicked, we want to insert a new object into the `Quotes` collection and then navigate to the editing screen. Open `main.js` and add the following event handler inside the `Template.main.events()` method call, just after the `.quote-title` event handler (again, don't forget the comma!):

```
  },
  'click .add-quote' : function(e){
    if (!Meteor.userId()) return;
    Quotes.insert({owner:Meteor.userId()},
      function(e,d){
        if (!e){
          Session.set('editing',true);
          Router.go('/quote/'+d);
        }
    });
  }
});
```

Save all of your changes, navigate to `http://localhost:3000` in a browser, and you should see a big blue plus sign at the bottom of the quote group. Click on the button and you'll be taken to a fresh, clean editing screen similar to the following sceenshot. Here, you can enter a new quote:

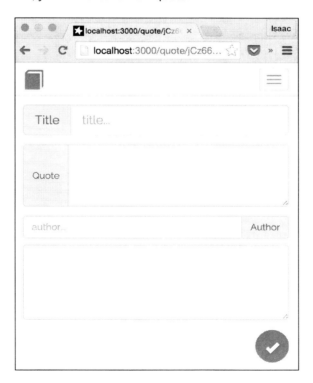

8. With all functionality in place, we are ready to deploy our app.

We can deploy our app wherever we would like to (please refer to one of the many deployment recipes in *Chapter 1*, *Optimizing Your Workflow* for details), but for this recipe we'll pick the easiest/quickest way to deploy, which is directly to the Meteor servers.

Stop your application from running in the terminal using *Ctrl + C* and execute the following command, replacing [your-test-url] with whatever you would like:

```
$ meteor deploy [your-test-url].meteor.com
```

In our case, we used the following command:

```
$ meteor deploy packt-quotes.meteor.com
```

Wait for your app to build and then upload, and you should get a familiar message, similar to the following:

```
Deploying to packt-quotes.meteor.com.

Now serving at http://packt-quotes.meteor.com
```

Navigate to your newly-deployed app, configure Twitter if needed (you will need a new Twitter app ID, one that points to your new deployment URL), log in, and add some quotes. When you're finished, your app should look similar to the following screenshot:

Congratulations! You've just created and deployed a complete application in eight steps. You should be proud of yourself. Go get a soda or a celebratory slice of pizza. You deserve it!

How it works...

Since each of the preceding steps involves recipes from other chapters, we won't focus too much on the code specifics. Instead, we'll have a general overview of what each step does and add detail where needed.

We first added our top menu/navbar. Using the `navbar` and `navbar-fixed-top` CSS classes built in to Bootstrap, we were able to position our `navbar` at the top of our screen with very little effort. We added a web font (thank you, Google!) and set the parameters for use on mobile devices in our header file.

For user authentication, we relied on the default Meteor packages for accounts (specifically the `accounts-twitter` package). For formatting, we used the excellently designed `Bootstrap` package created by Ian Martorell. He did the heavy lifting for us, so all we had to do was add the package and place our `{{> loginButtons}}` inclusion in the correct place.

We declared the `Quotes` collection in a file visible to the client and the server, as usual, and added a `publish` function that will only send those results to the client which were created by the logged in user.

We added the Iron Router package and took advantage of the `Router.map()` and the `layoutTemplate` helpers of that package to implement a baseline layout template, a main template, and a details template.

We next leveraged a bit of wizardry from Percolate Studios, called `momentum`. They've created a plugin for `momentum` that allows you to wrap the `{{>yield}}` directive and point it to a template helper, where we perform some quick logic to say, "If we're going to the main page, go left to right. If not, go right to left." It's a well-designed package and is very easy to implement!

Our next steps (displaying, editing, and creating quotes) could be considered the meat of the recipe, but because all the scaffolding was already in place, and because this type of functionality is so easy to implement in Meteor, we simply used an `{{#each...}}` directive, some reactive data bindings, and a few `click` event handlers to display and edit the records from the `Quotes` collection.

In fact, the most complicated bit in the entire project was taking the `tags` property and parsing it into an array using `_.map()`. Think about that for a second. The most technically "challenging" part of our entire app was parsing a string. Meteor is pretty awesome, isn't it?

Our last step was deployment, which is also pretty straightforward, since we have already done it a few times in *Chapter 1, Optimizing Your Workflow*.

Taken as a whole, the building of an entire app from scratch seems daunting. Breaking it down into discreet steps made it not only straightforward, but actually pretty fun as well. We hope that you enjoyed it, and we hope that you will take this recipe, modify it and expand on it, and create some quick, useful apps of your own!

There's more...

If you examined the finished product of this recipe closely, you probably noticed that there is some missing functionality and some refinement that still needs to happen. For example, there's currently no way to delete a quote, we can't sort by tags/subject/author, and we actually deployed without removing the insecure package.

In other words, there are a lot of other recipes from previous chapters we could apply to improve the app. We will leave you to that, as you build and expand your own applications, and we can't wait to see what you come up with!

See also

- The *Deploying a test app to Meteor* recipe in *Chapter 1, Optimizing Your Workflow*
- The *Adding Meteor packages* recipe in *Chapter 2, Customizing with Packages*
- The *Building a smooth interface with Bootstrap* recipe in *Chapter 3, Building Great User Interfaces*
- The *Implementing OAuth accounts packages* recipe in *Chapter 10, Working with Accounts*

Deploying apps to mobile devices

What good is building single-page apps with all kinds of cool functionality if you're only going to make it available as a web page? This recipe will take you through all the steps necessary to test and deploy your app to an iOS device.

Getting ready

You need an app to complete this recipe. We will be using the app created in the *Creating a complete app with Iron Router* recipe found earlier in this chapter. If you don't have your own app you would like to deploy, please complete that recipe first and then come back to this one to learn how to deploy your app.

How to do it...

There are two parts to deploying your application. The first is testing it on a device while using the server-side code that has already been deployed to a production URL. The second is to prepare an app build for deployment to the App Store.

1. First, let's set up our mobile app building environment. To deploy to an iOS device, you will need an Apple developer license, a machine running Mac OS X, and Xcode installed on that machine.

    To obtain an Apple Developer license, visit `https://developer.apple.com/programs/` and follow the links/instructions to join the iOS Developer program.

    Once you have joined the program, download and install Xcode from `https://developer.apple.com/xcode/downloads/`. You will need to properly configure Xcode, including adding certificates and mobile provisions as needed. There is a learning curve involved, and we strongly recommend that you take some time to learn the development, certification, and the App Store submission processes before proceeding.

    Open a terminal window, navigate to your app directory, and enter the following command:

    ```
    $ meteor install-sdk ios
    ```

    This can take a while, but make sure that the SDK is installed properly and fix any errors or outstanding installation items as directed.

    Once completed, enter the following command:

    ```
    $ meteor add-platform ios
    ```

    You're now properly configured, and can test/deploy your app on an iOS device.

2. Let's now test our app on an iOS device.

    Connect your iOS device to your machine via a USB cable. Enter the following command in the command line:

    ```
    $ meteor run ios-device --mobile-server [your-app-url.com]
    ```

    Here, `[you-app-url.com]` is replaced by the URL for your deployed server instance. In our case, we used the following command (all on one line, of course):

    ```
    $ meteor run ios-device --mobile-server
    packt-quotes.meteor.com
    ```

The application will be built and bundled, and then Xcode will open. Once the app has been compiled in Xcode, you will see the following message at the top-middle of the Xcode app:

QuotesApp | Build QuotesApp: **Succeeded** | Yesterday at 12:37 AM

Select your iOS device from the dropdown menu and click the play button, as displayed in this screenshot:

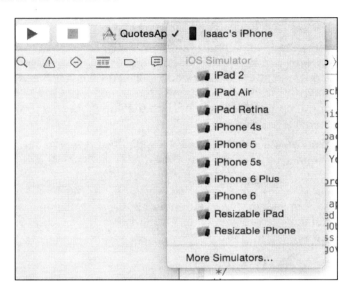

Make sure that your device is unlocked, and after some download and code push activity, an icon with the Meteor logo will appear on your device. The app will quickly open; then, after a short delay, your app will run just as if you pulled it up in a browser, but it is running as a full-fledged application on your device! Here's a screenshot of the Quotes app running on an iPhone:

3. The next step is to build a standalone mobile app file.

Once you've tested everything and it's working as it should be, you will want to create an actual app file that you can submit to the Apple App Store. When you installed a test app on your mobile device, Meteor auto-created several assets for your app. You can view these assets by navigating to the `[project root]/.meteor/local/cordova-build/resources` folder, as shown in the following screenshot:

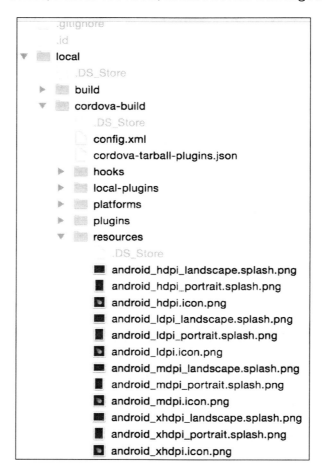

You can use these resources or swap them out as needed. Once you've got your correct icons and splash screens in place, you will need to create a file named `[project root]/mobile-config.js` and add the following parameters, at a bare minimum:

```
App.info({
name: '[yourappname]',
description: 'Description of my app',
```

```
version: '0.0.1'
});

App.icons({
'iphone': 'resources/icons/icon-60.png',
'iphone_2x': 'resources/icons/icon-60@2x.png'
});

App.launchScreens({
'iphone': 'resources/splash/Default~iphone.png',
'iphone_2x': 'resources/splash/Default@2x~iphone.png',
'iphone5': 'resources/splash/Default-568h@2x~iphone.png'
});
```

You can, of course, change anything you would like in this file, and there are several other parameters you can add to further tweak the installation. See the `[project root]/.meteor/local/cordova-build/config.xml` file for a good solid list of options.

Once you're satisfied with your configuration, navigate to the root app directory and enter the following command in the terminal (all on one line, of course):

```
$ meteor build [your-output-directory]
--server=[your-app-url]
```

For example, our command for the `Quotes` application would look like this (all on one line, of course):

```
$ meteor build ~/builds/
--server=packt-quotes.meteor.com
```

Once completed, you can open the project directory in `Xcode` (in our case, the project directory would be `~/builds/ios/project`) and configure to your heart's content. Once everything is correct and running how you would like it, you can sign the app and submit it to the Apple App Store.

How it works...

Meteor leverages the `cordova` library, `Xcode`, and your Mac's operating system to bundle, compile, and package your application. The emphasis is to get it into `Xcode`, where you can then manipulate the app as you would any native app, testing or deploying or submitting to the App Store.

The specifics on what to do inside `Xcode` and while submitting to the Apple App Store are beyond the scope of this book. If you would like more Meteor-specific app building information, please visit `https://github.com/meteor/meteor/wiki/How-to-submit-your-iOS-app-to-App-Store`.

There's more...

Everything is brain surgery the first time. Building and deploying a mobile app is no exception. Here are some tips to help you troubleshoot, should things go wrong:

- **Do a "dial tone" test**: If your app is being built but is taking forever to "boot up" on the device, or if you just get a blank screen, first try making sure all of your network and Xcode configurations are correct. You can do this by building a brand new Meteor project using `meteor create my-test-app` and deploying that barebones app to your mobile device. If it comes up properly, you've successfully gotten a "dial tone" and you can start finding out which package or piece of code is the source of your slow-loading woes.

- **The Iron Router configuration must be on point**: If you are using Iron Router and you don't have your Iron Router routes configured properly, the app will usually refuse to load. If you are running into problems, implement the bare minimum routes, with no fancy code, and see if you can get the routes to come up on the device. Again, start simple.

- **Use the simulator**: You don't have to always push to the actual device. Using the `meteor run ios` or `meteor run android` commands will boot up a simulator in almost no time, where you can test and debug much more quickly than you could on an actual device.

- **Use Xcode's logs**: If there's a problem, check the logs, found in the bottom-right panel of Xcode. You can also set breakpoints using Xcode while the app is running on your device, which can help you isolate potential problems.

Above all else, stick with it. We can assure you that deploying to mobile devices, once you're properly configured, is extremely straightforward, with very high rates of success. Don't give up! Have faith that very soon it will just "click" and you won't have any problems/anxiety about building a mobile application. It will, in fact, become fun and extremely rewarding as you see your app in the App Store or on people's devices. It's worth the learning curve!

See also

- The *Creating a complete app with Iron Router* recipe in this chapter

Adding social sharing

With the ever-increasing demand to integrate social media into your apps, you'll want to gain a basic understanding of how to send/post/share directly from within your app. This recipe will show you how to add Twitter posting (tweets) to your application.

Getting ready

We will be using the Quotes application, from the *Creating a complete app with Iron Router* recipe found earlier in this in this chapter. Please complete that recipe before proceeding.

We will also be using the `npm twit` module to complete this recipe. For a step-by-step recipe with a full explanation of each step, please see the first part of the *Handling asynchronous events* recipe in *Chapter 11, Leveraging Advanced Features*.

Quickly, here are the steps you'll need to install and configure the `twit` module:

1. Execute the following terminal commands:

    ```
    $ meteor add meteorhacks:npm
    $ meteor
    ```

2. Open `packages.json` and add the following code:

    ```
    {
      "twit" : "1.1.20"
    }
    ```

3. Run the following terminal command:

    ```
    $ meteor
    ```

4. Create `[project root]/server/config-twit.js` and add the following configuration:

    ```
    Twitter = Meteor.npmRequire('twit');

    Twit = new Twitter({
      consumer_key: '…',
      consumer_secret:'…',
      access_token: '…',
      access_token_secret: '…'
    });
    ```

With our Twitter keys, tokens, and secrets all in place, and with `twit` initialized, we are ready to start tweeting!

How to do it...

We need to create a server method, update our UI, and give an indication that a quote has been shared. Thanks to twit, the actual call to the Twitter API is fairly easy. Let's get started.

1. First, let's create the `twuote` server method.

    Create a file named `[project root]/server/tweets.js` and add the following `Meteor.methods` declaration:

    ```
    Meteor.methods({
      twuote : function(id){
      }
    });
    ```

    We will first do our checking to make sure that a user is logged in and that we were passed the `id` argument of a valid `quote` variable. In the `twuote` function call, add the following lines:

    ```
    if (!id || !this.userId) return;
    var quote = Quotes.findOne({_id:id});
    if (!quote || !quote.quote || !quote.author) return;
    ```

    We now need to manipulate the `quote` and `author` strings, making sure it's only `140` maximum in length. Just below the previously inserted lines, add the following string manipulation logic:

    ```
    var tweet = '"';
    if (quote.quote.length>138){
      tweet += quote.quote.slice(0,135);
      tweet += '..."';
    } else {
      tweet += quote.quote + '" --' + quote.author;
    }
    if (tweet.length>140){
      tweet = tweet.slice(0,137) + '...';
    }
    ```

    After combing the quote, we are ready to send the tweet! Just below the string manipulation logic, add the following `Twit.post()` function and wrapped callback function:

    ```
    Twit.post('statuses/update', { status: tweet },
      Meteor.bindEnvironment(function(err, data, response) {
      Quotes.update({_id:id},{$set:{tweeted:true}});
    })
    );
    return tweet;
    ```

    Our method is complete. Let's modify our UI.

2. We'll start modifying our UI by adding the share button.

   Open the `[project root]/client/detail.html` file and add the following button just below the `toggle-edit` button, inside the parent container element:

```
<div class="container">
  <div class="btn btn-danger toggle-edit pull-right">
    . . .
  </div>
  <div class="btn pull-left {{tweetColor}}"
   id="btn-tweet">{{tweetText}}
  </div>
</div>
```

   We want to give our button just a slight downward nudge, so add the following CSS directive at the bottom of the `[project root]/client/styles.css` file:

```
#btn-tweet{margin-top: 2.4rem;}
```

   We need to add a couple of additional helpers for our button, as well. Open `[project root]/client/detail.js`, and add the following two helper functions to the bottom of the `Template.detail.helpers` code block (don't forget the comma on the line before, as usual!):

```
editing: function () {
    . . .
  },
  tweetText: function (){
    return (this.tweeted)?'shared':'share...';
  },
  tweetColor: function (){
    return (this.tweeted)?'btn-success':'btn-info';
  }
});
```

   All that's left is hooking up the click event. Open the `[project root]/client/detail.js` file, locate the `Template.detail.events` declaration, and add the following click `event` handler just inside the closing bracket (don't forget the comma on the line just before the handler!):

```
  },
  'click #btn-tweet' : function (e) {
    if (this.tweeted) return;
    Meteor.call('twuote',this._id);
  }
});
```

Save all of your changes, navigate to your app in a browser (usually `http://localhost:3000`), click on a quote to pull up the details page, and click on the button labeled **share...** shown in the following screenshot:

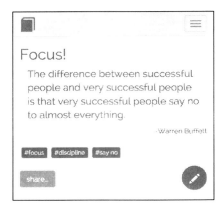

Give your server a moment or two to send the tweet. The **share...** button will turn green and the text will change to **shared**. Your tweet will be live on Twitter, as shown in the following screenshot:

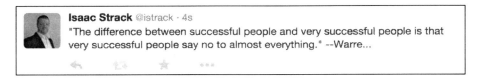

How it works...

The important code is all found in the `[project root]/server/tweets.js` file, in the `Meteor.methods({})` declaration.

We are calling `Twit.post()`, which takes a callback for its last argument. That callback is asynchronous because `twit` is a Node module. Because it is asynchronous, we need a way of preserving the current state of the environment while the call is out and we need a way of putting the process back into the `event` loop when the callback is executed (see the *Handling asynchronous events* recipe in *Chapter 11, Leveraging Advanced Features*, for a full explanation).

We accomplish both of these items by wrapping the callback with `Meteor.bindEnvironment()`. When the callback does fire, we update the `Quotes` collection, adding a `{tweeted : true}` property to the corresponding quote.

This property, in turn, causes our UI to update with the green button and disallows additional tweets (checked in the `click event` handler, in `[project root]/client/detail.js`).

So, just like that, we've added social sharing. From here, you can take and expand this recipe to other social platforms to be even more seamlessly integrated in to your applications.

There's more...

It is very, very important that we caution against using the preceding code in production! We stripped out all the security and error handling. There is no validation, and the example is hard-wired for a single server-side user. If you use this code as it is in a production app, something not so pleasant will happen, and it won't be our fault (no blamezies allowed!).

Instead, we recommend that you flesh these elements out, particularly around allowing the use of the logged-in user's access token rather than that of a hard-wired user.

With just a little bit of spit and polish, you can easily use this code to complement your Meteor apps and extend the functionality to Facebook, Instagram, LinkedIn, Pinterest, and so on.

For a full write-up on what you can do with the `twit` module, please visit `https://github.com/ttezel/twit`.

See also

► The *Adding Meteor packages* recipe in *Chapter 2, Customizing with Packages*
► The *Handling asynchronous events* recipe in *Chapter 11, Leveraging Advanced Features*
► The *Creating a complete app with Iron Router* recipe in this chapter

Index

Symbols

Thank you for buying
Meteor Cookbook

About Packt Publishing

Packt, pronounced 'packed', published its first book, *Mastering phpMyAdmin for Effective MySQL Management*, in April 2004, and subsequently continued to specialize in publishing highly focused books on specific technologies and solutions.

Our books and publications share the experiences of your fellow IT professionals in adapting and customizing today's systems, applications, and frameworks. Our solution-based books give you the knowledge and power to customize the software and technologies you're using to get the job done. Packt books are more specific and less general than the IT books you have seen in the past. Our unique business model allows us to bring you more focused information, giving you more of what you need to know, and less of what you don't.

Packt is a modern yet unique publishing company that focuses on producing quality, cutting-edge books for communities of developers, administrators, and newbies alike. For more information, please visit our website at www.packtpub.com.

About Packt Open Source

In 2010, Packt launched two new brands, Packt Open Source and Packt Enterprise, in order to continue its focus on specialization. This book is part of the Packt open source brand, home to books published on software built around open source licenses, and offering information to anybody from advanced developers to budding web designers. The Open Source brand also runs Packt's open source Royalty Scheme, by which Packt gives a royalty to each open source project about whose software a book is sold.

Writing for Packt

We welcome all inquiries from people who are interested in authoring. Book proposals should be sent to author@packtpub.com. If your book idea is still at an early stage and you would like to discuss it first before writing a formal book proposal, then please contact us; one of our commissioning editors will get in touch with you.

We're not just looking for published authors; if you have strong technical skills but no writing experience, our experienced editors can help you develop a writing career, or simply get some additional reward for your expertise.

open source
community experience distilled

PUBLISHING

Getting Started with Meteor.js
JavaScript Framework

Develop modern web applications in Meteor, one of the hottest
new JavaScript platforms

Isaac Strack   [PACKT] open source *

Getting Started with Meteor.js JavaScript Framework

ISBN: 978-1-78216-082-3   Paperback: 130 pages

Develop modern web applications in Meteor, one of the
hottest new JavaScript platforms

1. Create dynamic, multi-user web applications
   completely in JavaScript.

2. Use best practice design patterns including MVC,
   templates, and data synchronization.

3. Create simple, effective user authentication
   including Facebook and Twitter integration.

4. Learn the time-saving techniques of Meteor to
   code powerful, lightning-fast web apps in minutes.

INSTANT
Short | Fast | Focused

Meteor JavaScript
Framework Starter

Enjoy creating a multi-page site, using the exciting new
Meteor framework!

Gabriel Manricks   [PACKT]

Instant Meteor JavaScript Framework Starter

ISBN: 978-1-78216-342-8   Paperback: 78 pages

Enjoy creating a multi-page site, using the exciting new
Meteor framework!

1. Learn something new in an Instant! A short, fast,
   focused guide delivering immediate results.

2. Create multi-page Meteor sites.

3. Learn best practices for structuring your app for
   maximum efficiency.

4. Use and configure a NoSQL database.

5. Publish your finished apps to the Web.

Please check **www.PacktPub.com** for information on our titles

PUBLISHING

Building Single-page Web Apps with Meteor

ISBN: 978-1-78398-812-9   Paperback: 198 pages

Build real-time apps at lightning speed using the most powerful full-stack JavaScript framework

1. Create a complete web blog from frontend to backend that uses only JavaScript.

2. Understand how Web 2.0 is made by powerful browser-based applications.

3. Step-by-step tutorial that will show you how fast, complex web applications can be built.

Learning Meteor Application Development [Video]

ISBN: 978-1-78439-358-8   Duration: 01:52 hours

An informative walkthrough for creating a complete, multi-tier Meteor application from the ground up

1. Master the fundamentals for delivering clean, concise Meteor applications with this friendly, informative guide.

2. Implement repeatable, effective setup and configuration processes and maximize your development efficiency on every project.

3. Utilize cutting-edge techniques and templates to reduce the complexity of your applications and create concise, reusable components.

Please check **www.PacktPub.com** for information on our titles

CPSIA information can be obtained
at www.ICGtesting.com
Printed in the USA
FSOW02n1900090817
37402FS